Out of
Control

Volume 189 Sage Library of Social Research

RECENT VOLUMES IN . . .
SAGE LIBRARY OF SOCIAL RESEARCH

Out of Control

Family Therapy
and Domestic Disorder

Jaber F. Gubrium

Sage Library of Social Research 189

SAGE Publications
International Educational and Professional Publisher
Newbury Park   London   New Delhi

For information address:

SAGE Publications, Inc.
2455 Teller Road
Newbury Park, California 91320

SAGE Publications Ltd.
6 Bonhill Street
London EC2A 4PU
United Kingdom

SAGE Publications India Pvt. Ltd.
M-32 Market
Greater Kailash I
New Delhi 110 048 India

Printed in the United States of America

Library of Congress Cataloging-in-Publication Data

Gubrium, Jaber F.
   Out of control : family therapy and domestic disorder / Jaber F. Gubrium.
          p.   cm. —(Sage library of social research; 189)
   Includes bibliographical references (p.   ) and index.
   ISBN 0-8039-4632-5 (cl).   — ISBN 0-8039-4633-3 (pb)
   1. Family psychotherapy—Social aspects.   2. Family psychotherapy—Political aspects.   3. Problem families.   4. Problem families—Counseling of.   I. Title.   II. Series: Sage library of social research; v. 189.
   RC488.5.G83   1992
   616.89'156—dc20   92-4213
                                                         CIP

92 93 94 95   1   2   3   4   5   6   7   8   9   10   11

Sage Production Editor: Judith L. Hunter

Contents

Preface

Personal troubles, from juvenile delinquency to drug abuse and codependency, implicate the family in many ways. Some claim that the "broken home" goes a long way in explaining delinquency. Others charge that poorly structured family life is the root of abuses. Still others believe that domestic sentiments uncommunicated among family members result in the inability to share and understand others, producing a destructive egocentricity. Focal is the home, the texture and tone of which need fixing in order to repair lives out of control. It is a simple enough view: Heal the home and cure the person.

Yet, this view screens a rather opaque object—domestic disorder. We can readily imagine a set of marbles in disarray, scattered about without any discernible pattern. But how does the imagery apply to the household? What is the social counterpart of marbles? Minds? Attitudes? Feelings? Authority? Roles? Emotional ties? And what parallels disarray? A refusal to follow rules laid down by the head of the household? Who is to be understood as in charge? Or is the parallel found in an inability to rationally display emotions? How is rational display to be interpreted? Is one person's rationality the same as another's? The view also fails to take account of the practical circumstances in which repair is undertaken. It is one thing to implicate the home and family life; it is quite another to address the many questions that arise in the process.

In this book, I focus on a common venue of domestic repair—the treatment facility—to argue that, in their application, institutional images of home life construct the very disarray taken, in turn, to be the source or context of troubles. I will compare two facilities as different from each other in their understandings of the home as night and day. In analyzing the ordinary business of discerning disorder and mounting repair in ethnographic detail in family therapy—from touching expressions of emotion communicated by distressed spouses in self-disclosure to the stern responses of parents in aftercare who "won't take it anymore"—I will pay particular attention to the way disorder is concretely recognized in the densely complicated family lives presented.

Institutional images come alive in their application. By themselves, the images are potential designs for recognizing the social logic of everyday life and its troubles. It is the associated "reality work" of staff, family members, clients, and significant others that articulates the images to assign meaning to lives in distress by understanding the homes that figure in. These reality workers are presented in the following chapters—giving voice to domestic experience through images and related vocabularies, yet competently attuned to the enduring contingencies of descriptive practice.

My aim is to show how much and in what ways the privacies of personal and interpersonal domestic life are defined and altered in public context. The examination is part of a long-standing cultural debate about the decline of privacy in modern times. Diverse intimacies of the home, after all, are shown in the process of interpretation by institutional agents conveying particular images and formulas for change. The examination also is part of a related debate about the rationalization of experience that many, from Max Weber to Michel Foucault, have made the centerpiece of modern living. But it is not a nostalgic lament for a return to domestic independence from the organizational enmeshments that entangle persons and families in enterprises far removed from households. Rather, it points to the ways in which troubles and domesticity might be construed, presenting an appraisal of what public contexts fashion for families in distress: not a single solution, but options for resolving the problem of what domestic disorder is and how order can be restored.

Acknowledgments

This book has less of a conceptual origin than it has a place within a continuing concern for the problem of how experience is given voice in everyday life. Several friends and colleagues have shared the concern and taught me from their own ideas and work: Jon Bernardes, David Buckholdt, Robert Dingwall, James Holstein, Gale Miller, Andrea Sankar, and David Silverman. I thank them all. The presentation itself has benefited from the suggestions of Bruce Bellingham, Robert Emerson, Barry Glassner, Donileen Loseke, Warren Peterson, and R. Satyanarayana, who read it in manuscript or otherwise commented on it, for which I am grateful. Stephanie T. Hoppe provided excellent copyediting. I owe a special debt of gratitude to Maude Rittman, my doctoral student and fellow fieldworker on the project. The field can be an intellectually lonely place; Maude offered welcome companionship. Finally, I wish to acknowledge the support of the many clients, the staffs, and family members who participated in the study.

For Aline, Erika, and Suzanne
who bring order to my domestic life

PART ONE

Themes and Settings

ONE

The Troubled Home

It is a common enough phrase—"out of control"—found in the advertising copy of magazines and newspapers for therapeutic programs for wayward adolescents and troubled adults. An ad for a wilderness school in *Southern Living* magazine begins in bold type: "DEFIANT TEENAGER?" The ad continues: "Is your teenager irresponsible, rebellious, or out of control? Running with the wrong crowd? Headed down a path with no future? Help your son or daughter before it's too late. [The program] stops self-destructive behavior and places parents back in control!" In the same magazine, an ad for a different school queries, "TEENAGER OUT OF CONTROL?" and goes on to ask, "Is your son or daughter going down the wrong track because of rebellion, ingratitude, manipulative behavior, and/or drugs?" Similar copy in the *New York Times Magazine* promises that through its program "adolescents regain self-esteem, families are reunited, and hope for the future is reborn."

In a local newspaper, a half-page advertisement for a hospital-based program portrays a mother and her son next to a quotation from the mother stating: "No one understood my secret . . . my son was out of control. . . . " Her narrative continues:

For a long time I hid my son's angry and destructive behavior. He saw nothing but conflicts in his life and felt sad and worthless. His grades dropped, he had trouble sleeping, and he saw no meaning to life. When he simply got more and more violent and out of control, I couldn't hide my secret any longer.

The ad pledges, "If your child is experiencing behavioral, emotional, alcohol or drug-related problems, you can be assured of help."

A widely distributed mail brochure announces, "Families are torn apart by substance abuse." Referring to adults out of control, the brochure explains: "Addiction is a family disease. Whether it's Dad's drinking or Mom's prescription drugs, the impact on the family can be devastating. Unless someone intervenes. . . . There's too much at stake to wait. . . . We put families back together again."

THE PROBLEM AND THE THEMES

The vocabulary is familiar, with a recognizable subtext of cultural and behavioral linkages communicating domestic disorder. Words play on the image of family life conveyed by an opposite vocabulary—the language of order, control, and domestic tranquility. This opposite signals an idyllic domain where the common rules of the home guide everyday life and the conduct of individual members is contained for the benefit of all. The household is a refuge, untouched by the disorderly influences of the outside world: the wrong crowd and track, the path with no future, ingratitude, rebellion, drink, and drugs. The opposition is aptly captured by Christopher Lasch's (1977) depiction of the home as a "haven in a heartless world."

The advertisements tell of personal despair and domestic travail. The turmoil of life vividly spills over to spoil what is only partly individual. Portrayed are family members, especially parents, who are unprepared to deal with the onslaught of lives out of control. A domestic world shared with children and other family members is disintegrating. The individual behavior of the boy or girl, man or woman, who is out of control threatens a larger order—home life. It is not just the teenager or young adult who is out of control, not just the mother or father whose distress can no longer contain the momentary havoc of a son's or daughter's behavior, but domestic order, something all of them experience over and above their individuality. Does failed family life produce personal troubles or do problems such as self-destructiveness, drug, and alcohol abuse infringe on domestic order? Cause and effect are unclear, but one thing seems certain: Domestic disorder is the featured background of the drama.

This book is about domestic disorder, the larger entity that both sets the tone of daily life in troubled households and provides a meaningful context for understanding adolescent rebelliousness, drug abuse, alcohol addiction, and other troubles that plague the family. It is only indirectly about the troubles themselves. It examines how human service professionals, clients, kin, and significant others in two treatment programs with different images of the home construe domestic disorder in family therapy and thereby come to understand troubles.

There are two themes. One is that family troubles take on their meaning in relation to interpretations of domestic disorder. Individual behavior such as poor grades, getting drunk, smoking marijuana or crack, and truancy are not meaningful in their own right, but only in relation to the larger order they are perceived to infringe upon or form a part of. It is the perception of the infringement of domestic order, as elusive and arguable as that might be to family members and others, that presents turmoil and despair. Those who voluntarily bring their troubles to professional attention or are required to do so by employers, courts, or welfare agents, contend as much with domestic order as they do with the individual behaviors that challenge it. Service professionals, in turn, are presented with troubled homes, not just individual behaviors, as personally destructive as the latter might be. The challenge to all is not only to treat, cure, and recover, but to define the character of the troubled household in order to mount programs of rehabilitation.

The second theme is that the abstract entity that is the disordered home is interpreted through very concrete, localized signs and conditions. The abstract is assigned meaning and constructed through the mundane (Pollner, 1987). The larger entity is distinct from the physical household, its individual members, and their conduct. The home is what members are, were, or could be writ large. Still, the home is real enough. All concerned repeatedly refer to, and act upon, it as they speak of matters such as the impact of home life (domestic order) on adolescent development, a mother's sanity, and siblings' attitudes, among other individual characteristics. What they concretely pinpoint are immediate, ordinary signs of domestic order, such as the tidiness of a front yard, taken to represent a well-run and socially integrated home (Gubrium & Holstein, 1990). What is more, those concerned denote in relation to descriptive contingencies of their observation, such as taking acknowledged signs as exceptional in particular circumstances. In the process, they reference the larger entity in its own right.

THE CONSTRUCTED HOME IN
SOCIOLOGICAL PERSPECTIVE

There are many larger entities in everyday life, abstractions seen as distinct and separate from personal and physical being: society, the state, community, family, the home. We commonly convey our sense of the abstractions by location. For example, we refer to justice as what an official of a government bureau stands for. Or an official announces that he or she represents the people or a sovereign jurisdiction, say, Canada. One might speak of him- or herself as "the law" and hailing from the juvenile court or the county welfare department. A child, parent, or other family member may claim to represent a particular home, but is not taken to be the home in its own right.

Abstract as these entities are, they are nonetheless the stuff of social reality. Émile Durkheim (1893/1964a) was a pioneer in formally conceptualizing society as a larger entity, which he saw as a moral order separate from individuals. He did not write extensively about the home as such, but referred to various social forms as *collective representations,* by which he meant that social objects such as a religion, community, and the home abstractly represented the organization of their members' lives together (Durkheim, 1961 [1912]). The entities name the collectivity writ large people are, as, say, citizens or family members. They are something over and above their lives as individuals and, in that sense, collectively represent the lives.

In a seminal methodological essay, Durkheim (1895/1964b) urges the scientific study of what he called *social facts*. Especially in the United States, this approach informed decades of positivistic research targeted on measurement, explanation, and prediction. Yet it is possible to read Durkheim from a different viewpoint, as laying the groundwork for the study of collective representations (Silverman, 1985, chap. 2). From this perspective, the Durkheimian project can be seen as an attempt to discern the ways in which larger entities such as community, home, or domestic disorder fit into the reality of everyday life.

Durkheim was particularly keen on examining the moral effect of the larger social order on individual self-worth (Durkheim, 1893/1964a, 1897/1951). He did not directly research everyday life, only its more distant social facts. In contrast, the study of the everyday experience of social forms aims to understand how its spokespersons construe who and what they are as homes, communities, and the like. This ultimately requires the analysis of ordinary language and communication.

With the concept *family worlds*, Robert Hess and Gerald Handel (1959) take us directly to family and home as larger entities. They write of the family as being a reality separate and distinct from personality and other social forms: "However its life spreads into the wider community, there is a sense in which a family is a bounded universe" (p. 1). A family is a world of its own, a separate reality. Although this reality encapsulates individual family members' lives, it arises out of the members' interpersonal experiences.

Family worlds have *themes*. Hess and Handel explain that a "family theme is a pattern of feelings, motives, fantasies, and conventionalized understandings grouped about some locus of concern which has a particular form in the personalities of the individual members" (p. 11). The larger entity and its themes give meaning to individual members' lives by acting as sources of collective identity: "In the family themes are to be found the family's implicit direction, its notion of 'who we are' and 'what we do about it'" (p. 11).

Peter Berger and Hansfried Kellner (1970) do not explicitly consider the family or the home as an object, but they do focus on a related social form—marriage. Referring to marriage as a *nomos*, they underscore its status as a regulating moral order, like society, which surrounds the marital partners. Substituting the term marriage where the authors write of society yields a description of the larger marital entity: "Every [marriage] has its specific way of defining and perceiving reality—its world, its universe, its overarching organization of symbols" (p. 51).

Berger and Kellner's nomos or marital order is conceived as a social construction in which the larger entity that is the marriage, although experientially distinct from the individual partners, is built up out of an ongoing marital conversation. This view is more explicitly narrative than Hess and Handel's. As Berger and Kellner write:

> The reconstruction of the world in marriage occurs principally in the course of conversation, as we have suggested. The implicit problem of this conversation is how to match two individual definitions of reality. By the very logic of the relationship, a common overall definition must be arrived at—otherwise the conversation will become impossible and, *ipso facto*, the relationship will be endangered. (p. 61)

What is communicatively realized, in turn, acts back upon its subjects to give their common life meaning and solidity, making a marriage. In the course of being together, the marital partners virtually talk themselves into what they are as a whole and, for better or worse, respond to what they have produced.

The vision of communication and social construction in Berger and Kellner's analysis is highly consensual, as it also appears to be in Hess and Handel's. The nomos—the marriage—that the marital partners create is uniform and orderly. What is more, the order is cognitive, a configuration of consistent ideas or symbols about the joint reality represented. There is little or no sense that the order is a by-product of actors with particular agendas, located in a particular domestic circumstance (Wiley, 1985). We are not apprised of the possibility that one partner concedes to another a certain understanding of their relationship "for the sake of the marriage," or that outsiders, such as parents, friends, or marriage counselors, with different views of what a marriage should be, articulate contrasting nuptial orders. Quite apart from what ostensibly gets constructed in the marital conversation are any number of circumstances, from the households of in-laws to support groups, in which partners pursue the definition of marriage in general and interpretations of their own marriages in particular. Separate and distinct as the marriage is from the individual partners that compose it, it does not exist in a social vacuum, but is interpreted, shaped, and given form in many places.

More recently, David Reiss (1981) presents a model of the abstract family entity based on laboratory experience. Borrowing from Thomas Kuhn (1962), Reiss applies the term *family paradigm* to families' distinct ways of dealing with the world—separate from their social environments and different from each other. Reiss writes:

> We now speak of the *family paradigm* as a central organizer of its shared constructs, sets, expectations, and fantasies about its social world. Further, each family's transactions with its social world are guided by its own paradigm, and families can be distinguished—one from another—by the differences in their paradigms. (p. 1)

Again uniformity is highlighted: *The* family paradigm is a central organizer. *It*, not competing understandings, guide the family's transactions with the outside world. The source of this uniformity or central organizer is internal to family living. Over time, living together, family members come to share definitions of their environment based on their collective existence. Reiss explains:

> Through the course of its own development, [the family] fashions fundamental and enduring assumptions about the world in which it lives. The assumptions are shared by all family members, despite the disagreements, conflicts, and differences that exist in the family. Indeed, the core of an individual's membership in his own family is his acceptance

of, belief in, and creative elaboration of these abiding assumptions. (p. 1)

Taken as a whole, this work on constructed domestic forms
presents two analytic problems. First, although the forms are
envisioned as emerging from social interaction, the by-products,
once formed, are conceived as relatively homogeneous. Family
members form *a* world with particular themes. Husband and
wife talk themselves into *a* particular marriage. The family develops *a* characteristic paradigm. We have no way of evaluating competing perspectives and alternate senses of order. We are granted
no possibility of multiple narratives for marriage, family, or home,
with separate assumptions about their respective realities. We
have no way of dealing with a question such as what the relation
is of a mother's image of the family to the father's view of the whole,
or how their respective conceptions relate to outsiders' perceptions.

Second, although family members or marital partners are said
to construct or fashion these larger entities through social interaction, the actual social mechanics of the construction process is
missing. We are given very little sense of how agents or organizations outside the household figure in the creation of images,
which becomes critical as definitions of home increasingly are
embedded in other social forms. Berger and Kellner's marital conversation, in particular, seems to simply develop. The narrative
organization of exchanges is absent, that is, the ordinary communicative processes by which the larger entity is constituted.

Still, these authors do offer a basis for considering the home or
domestic order as a social construction. Berger and Kellner's
analysis is particularly suggestive, with entities in the large narratively envisioned and knowledge of home life taken as inter-
actionally derived.

KNOWING THE HOME

Available ethnographic evidence of family discourse shows the
narrative of the home includes a range of voices (see Emerson,

1969; Dingwall, Eekelaar, & Murray, 1983; Gubrium & Holstein, 1987). Formal membership in families, marriages, or households does not delimit the talk and interaction constituting the respective social forms. If we ask broadly, who speaks for the family, who communicates the marriage, or who makes claims about households, voice includes any and all who narratively give shape and meaning to the larger entities referenced. The range extends to voices cognitively opposed to the forms, as suggested in Edward Said's (1978) argument that the Western idea of the Orient was created by what Western writers imagined the Occident was not and in Marianna Torgovnick's (1990) persuasive case for the invention of primitive innocence in mirror opposition to anthropologists' civilized sophistication. More to the point, David Silverman (1970) uses home and family as metaphors for what bureaucracies are not.

Elsewhere I have considered the issue of who speaks for the family as a matter of "privileged knowledge," the question being whose knowledge of family life is taken to represent the home (Gubrium & Holstein, 1990). Data gathered in settings where family comes under consideration as a social form show that there are many answers, not necessarily privileging the knowledge of family members, marital partners, or household occupants.

Take the support groups for family care givers of Alzheimer's disease victims that I studied in two different cities (Gubrium, 1986). Some groups are facilitated by service providers, usually a social worker or a nurse, and are affiliated with sponsoring organizations such as a hospital or the Alzheimer's Disease and Related Disorders Association (ADRDA). Other groups are coordinated by seasoned care givers. Participation in most groups is open to anyone with a direct interest in the home care of the Alzheimer's disease victim, although a few groups limit membership to particular family members such as spouses or adult children.

An enduring question in all groups is whether the benefits of home care for the increasingly demented victim outweigh the risks of the stresses of care giving destroying the family. And whose advice is taken in formulating answers? The questions ultimately

center on the issue of privileged knowledge, that is, who best
knows the home.

There is no guarantee that members of the household hold privileged knowledge of home life. Long-standing residents, such as
care-giving wives who have lived with their now demented
husbands for 40 years or more, frequently present distressed
pleas for answers, openly wondering what is happening to their
families. "What has been happening to us?" they ask. "What kind
of family are we that it should come to this?" In their search for
answers, they encounter diverse interpretations of their domestic
lives, including compelling conceptualizations of the type of
family they are in the large as opposed to the types of families they
contrast with, along with different views of what they always
have been.

A care-giving wife learns from others that she is fortunate to
have "the kind of family" (caring kin) that one can depend on
and thus feels that she might never have to consider placing her
deteriorating husband in a nursing home. Another care-giving wife
admits that she is only now discovering, with the group's help,
what a weak and selfish family her kindred have been "all along."
They learn the meaning of family responsibility from the type of
family they are in the large. The different typifications have concrete
implications for assessments of how realistic continued home care
is. Like others, these wives learn about the larger realities of domestic life from voices outside the home.

Although particular typifications may be rejected, it is evident
that typifications of some kind are needed to sort and define who
care givers and their kin are as family, and what courses of action
are warranted as a result. It is not uncommon for care givers to
admit being at a complete loss as to how to figure out what their
families "are all about," referring not to other members' inten-
tions but to the entity they collectively form. Disclaiming privileged knowledge, the care giver characteristically notes that no
one in the thick of things can see matters clearly. Likewise, group
participants frequently assert that care givers are too close to the
scene of care giving to perceive the shape and substance of domestic
life. It is said to take an outsider, someone more distant from events,
to discern things for what they actually are. Still other family

members base claims precisely on long-standing acquaintance with, or presence in, households and insist on being heard as the privileged voices of the home. Those who typify the family are a diverse lot, comprising any and all who convincingly claim to speak for the home, including outsiders.

ORGANIZATIONAL EMBEDDEDNESS

Ethnographic data also suggest that the social construction of the home is affected by organizationally contingent understandings or images of domesticity. Those who speak for the family or the home do so in connection with distinguishable roles or under the auspices of particular organizations. For example, the facilitator of a support group for care givers of Alzheimer's disease victims not only lends her individual voice to the interpretation of domestic order, but does so as a facilitator. Her function is to facilitate conversation and the sharing of care-giving experiences. She urges all participants to voice their views, encouraging the open consideration and typification of the home as a social form. Should the support group be sponsored by an organization such as the ADRDA, the facilitator not only incites the voicing of domestic order, but locally articulates the organization's formal understanding of the care-giving process and its ostensible effect on family and household.

I have referred to these organizational features of the talk and interaction that constitute the home as *organizational embeddedness* (Gubrium, 1987). Increasingly, the voices that aim to heal the home are heard in formal therapeutic settings: wilderness camps, boarding schools, board-and-care homes, residential treatment centers, hospital-based programs, divorce mediation, outpatient counseling centers, substance abuse rehabilitation programs, and support groups. Their agents include family doctors, nurses, psychiatrists, psychologists, social workers, lawyers, marriage counselors, family therapists, special education teachers, pastoral counselors, child care workers, and support group facilitators. The organizations not only offer settings for therapeutic practice, but also provide discernible frameworks for interpreting household events.

A residential treatment center for emotionally disturbed children studied in the seventies based its treatment philosophy on behavioral principles (Buckholdt & Gubrium, 1979). Officially, domestic disorder was interpreted as a calculus of inappropriate activities or exchanges, not as a configuration of deep meanings. The facts of home life, as they entered into children's emotional disturbances, were described likewise in organizational assessments and reports, and read accordingly. Not all staff members were firmly committed to the official treatment philosophy, however, some being decidedly Freudian, Rogerian, or eclectic in their orientations. One of the center's three rotating psychiatric consultants was Freudian and, as he routinely put it, searched the "deep meaning" of domestic attachments as a way of understanding children's conduct. He voiced the language of emotional life in assigning meaning to the home as a context for understanding troubled youth. The center's behavioral programming, with its point system for monitoring appropriate and out-of-control actions and its token economy, made it necessary to translate the consultant's "deep" narrative and recommendations into behavioral terms to assure the outside acceptance of program documentation. Another rotating consultant was assiduously behavioral in his orientation. His case reviews and recommendations provided fewer narrative difficulties. Although the insights of both consultants were appreciated by the staff, the contrasting domestic realities they voiced in a context officially accepting of one only, locally complicated the social construction of disorder.

The emotional disturbance and related troubled homes of the patients treated by this facility were organizationally embedded in the sense that the social construction of domestic disorder got done in narratives located in the organization. The question of what went on in the home was worked out in semiannual psychiatric conferences, parent effectiveness training, multidisciplinary team meetings, and point assignment sessions, among other organizational contexts. A broad range of organizational factors conditioned what was made of the troubled home, from officially sanctioned readings to narrative complications. Related local understandings of home life became a meaningful part of something the organization was not, namely, the disturbance and domesticity themselves.

What happens to the troubled home as an entity when the purview is extended to other organizations, with different philosophies and additional voices? Following the argument that family troubles take on their meaning in relation to interpretations of domestic order (or disorder, as the case may be), we would expect the narrative constructions of the home to expand dramatically. The overall sense of a particular troubled home for one organization could contrast with its sense in another organization. To borrow Hess and Handel's terms, the "family themes" and "worlds" assigned to a troubled home by the organizations actually could differ in kind. In Berger and Kellner's usage, the meaning of the "marital conversation" in one context could narratively deny that of another context. Modifying Reiss's view, local organizational images of troubles might construct substantially different family paradigms for the same homes, pertinent to their particular organizational understandings.

In arguing for the organizational embeddedness of the troubled home, a word of caution is in order. It is important to distinguish between the reality of household events on the one hand and domestic order or disorder on the other. In making the distinction and focusing on the organizational construction of domestic disorder, I do not mean to trivialize the concrete facts of home life. Often troubling and distressing, they are real enough for those concerned. What I claim to be socially constructed is not individual household events and conditions in their own right, but what is made of them as a whole by those who attempt to understand the home in the process of seeking and giving help, including family members. Although the actual drama of domestic life and its troubles is played out in the home, it is increasingly scripted elsewhere.

PRODUCING THE TROUBLED HOME

I present the social construction of the troubled home by documenting how speakers narratively produce domestic life through family therapy. This centers on talk and interaction. The working question, "Who speaks for the home, and how?" turns our attention to the particular persons who account for, depict, visibly display, or otherwise explain the disorder of the household.

The process of narratively giving shape and substance to the troubled home is not automatic. It entails the practical interpretive work of linking an abstract, experiential entity—the home— with immediately available, concrete signs (Garfinkel, 1967). The work resembles what Claude Levi-Strauss (1962) calls *bricolage*, which can be likened to a cognitive salvage operation in which clients, family members, significant others, and professionals use bits and pieces of their lives, such as the pitch of a father's voice or children's posture in the presence of their mother, to describe a home's abstract disarray. When a family counselor informs co-workers that the way all of them heard an adolescent talk to her or his parents obviously shows what kind of home it is, the counselor presents the home in the abstract through the familiar. By mundanely specifying the domestic meaning of signs such as a manner of address, the abstract and unseen is made evident. As Jon Bernardes (1987) emphasizes, those concerned virtually "do things with words."

Strictly speaking, concrete particulars are not the troubled home in its own right, only signs of it. It is as if, in hearing the pitch of a voice or viewing posture, listeners or observers witness, but do not actually perceive, domestic order. The distinction is important because considerable discretion enters into the working process of concretizing the abstract. When someone specifies domestic disorder in, say, the obstreperous behavior of a stepchild, and another disputes the representation by responding "That doesn't convince me of what the home is like," the abstract not only is unsettled, but its particular experiential reality is negotiated. Although domestic disorder is socially constructed, it is always subject to reconstruction.

It has been said that the sign has an arbitrary character (Saussure, 1966). Something can stand for any number of other things. The pitch of a family member's voice can be claimed to represent domestic disarray and, in a different context, said actually to show that "the home is intact despite all the yelling" because "a really weak home would fall apart under the circumstances." The practical and contextual quality of interpretation tells of the arbitrariness. But the arbitrariness is not random; it is socially organized. The bricoleur of everyday life routinely does his or her interpretive work at a particular time and in a specific place. I refer especially to the organizational embeddedness of the many voices who speak for and construe the home. The official or preferred signs for disorder of an organization dealing with troubled homes confines the arbitrariness of their representation. Our bricoleur is very circumspect, being a veritable practitioner of everyday life, well attuned to situations.

In presenting the social construction of domestic disorder, I take each voice of the home as attendant to both articulation and circumstance (Gubrium, 1988a). Voices articulate domestic disorder by selecting and communicating from an array of concrete particulars that can stand for the troubled home. At the same time, organizational auspices specify locally pertinent patterns of meaning for domesticity.

We do not actually enter the household to present its disorder. If we did, we would of course see concrete particulars, such as voices pitched this way or that and children's demeanor around the dinner table, which we might not otherwise observe. But domestic disorder or order would still have to be assigned to what was heard and seen. The overall meaning of particulars would be no more evident than what might be secured in a different venue. The quandary and questions of those who have spent lifetimes in troubled homes tell as much.

TWO

The Settings

Westside House and Fairview Hospital are pseudonyms for two family-oriented treatment settings. They are located in different cities approximately 50 miles apart. Westside is an outpatient facility; Fairview is inpatient. Some staff have been employed in both facilities, just as some patients and families have, on different occasions, been clients in each program. By and large, Westside House treats a poorer, less educated clientele likely to be referred by courts or the state department of human services; Fairview's admissions commonly are self-referred or mandated by employers.

For both wayward teens and troubled adults, the problems treated are similar, ranging over the variety highlighted in advertisements and the media. Given the family orientation, clients' next of kin or significant others are required to participate in counseling and ancillary therapeutic activities at both institutions. Regardless of diagnosis, identified troubles, or patients' demographic characteristics, the common assumption is that domestic disorder is the key ingredient to understanding what ails individual family members. Home life is the crux of treatment and recovery. The collective disorder of the household is focal and provides the broad framework for taking stock of individual differences and similarities.

The overriding contrast between the institutions lies in their images of domestic disorder. Westside House defines the social order of the home in terms of authority; Fairview Hospital conceives of it as a configuration of sentiments. Whatever background differences or similarities patients and families bring to the organizations, and regardless of the administrative differences or similarities encountered in the settings, these images sort the particulars.

THE FACILITIES

The contrast in institutional understandings of domestic disorder differentially highlights the facilities. As simple a physical characteristic of setting as the seating arrangement of family members in a counseling session speaks tellingly of the domestic disorder of the home in one facility but signals little in the other. In staff members', patients', and families' encounters with each other and their environs on the two premises, different things are witnessed regarding the question of what goes on in the home.

On first entering Westside House and Fairview Hospital, I found the physical trappings one would expect: public spaces and areas set aside for treatment, furnishings, promotional literature and clinical publications, audio and video recording equipment, ashtrays, and tissue boxes. I soon distinguished the institutions by their contrasting definitional uses of spaces and amenities, but only when I learned that the settings' social and physical environs were concretely linked with differential understandings of the home did the mundane features of their public and private spaces come alive with meaning.

Westside House

Westside House is supported by federal and state social service funds, the United Way, and fees for services; fees represent only a small portion of total revenue, because the sliding fee structure based on the patient's or family's ability to pay often is adjusted to relatively low incomes.

Westside's affiliations with a large network of community human service organizations make the institution highly visible locally as a source of help for troubled low-income families. At the same time, Westside's general dedication to the domestic challenges of substance abuse brings families of various backgrounds to its attention, from the families of service professionals themselves to the impoverished black homes located in the midst of virtual drug cultures.

According to a promotional brochure, Westside House is "dedicated to excellence in youth and family service." In cooperation with other human service organizations, Westside provides diverse offerings: family counseling; 24-hour residential care on other premises for teens in crisis; training for teachers in behavioral management and drug education; parenting skills classes; drug abuse counseling; support groups for parents, spouses, and friends of drug abusers; and a variety of educational and work improvement skills.

Westside's programs are expressly family oriented. The treatment philosophy assumes that problems of youth and young adults are related to the condition of the home. Problems not only are rooted in home life, but also, in turn, have a profound effect on family functioning. The two are intertwined.

Westsiders maintain that the broader context of contemporary living makes it inevitable that many young people and families will be troubled. They speak of the tremendous pressures on today's youth—from peers, the widespread availability of abusive substances, and the desire for independence. Times also are changing faster than ever: This year's fashions and desires are next year's discards and trivia. These conditions combine with the natural problems of growing up to place considerable strain on families. The brochure notes: "Families must absorb the shocks of social change and the storms of adolescent development. Often the stress is too much and the family's structure becomes fractured. With prompt, professional assistance most fractures heal. Last year, [one of Westside's affiliated programs] helped 150 families resolve their problems and stay together."

Westsiders say that the troubled youth, adults, and families they serve represent only a fraction of the overall problem. In these troubled times, all families are at risk. Even the seemingly healthy and well-functioning home is likely to be only just bearing up under the stress of it all. Regardless of the particular family trouble presented for treatment, cursory probing is likely to reveal a host of other domestic problems. In this regard, Westsiders face the times just as much as they treat troubled homes, providing Westsiders a bottomless pit of ailments to service and counsel. A family trouble that suddenly disappears or is quickly ameliorated in treatment is easily replaced by the family's other treatable problems.

In appearance, Westside is not particularly distinguished. It is housed in two small buildings facing a major street. Immediately upon entering the main building, one finds a waiting area with several chairs at one side and a counter at the other. Behind the counter sits the facility's receptionist-secretary, who serves several functions. She greets visitors, families, and patients, and bids them to take a seat if they are due for counseling. She keeps records, makes appointments for continuing counseling sessions, schedules urine tests screening for drugs and other clinical services, and collects fees. There are stacks of promotional and informational literature in the waiting area and several bulletin boards with flyers and announcements, all dealing with family problems and institutional programming.

Leading away from the reception counter and waiting area is a long hallway, along which can be found the counselors' offices. Most are small, outfitted with a desk and chair for the counselor and client seating typically comprising a comfortable couch and several armchairs. For large families, extra chairs may be brought in or one of the larger offices borrowed for the counseling session. At the end of the hallway, opposite the waiting area, is the associate director's office, which is the largest office on the floor. Also leading off the long hallway are toilet facilities for staff and clients, where urine samples for drug screening are collected. Located nearby are a staff lounge, small kitchen, and administrative offices. The second floor of the building houses other administrative offices. The top floor of an adjacent small building has offices for several part-time counselors. It also contains one big room, useful for counseling large families or for case reviews.

As I spent time observing at Westside House, my growing awareness of institutional images of the nature of domestic disorder cast a distinguishing light on the setting. The manner in which families enter the waiting area and seat themselves gives counselors and the receptionist initial evidence of a home's authority structure, often used to assign domestic meaning to particular problems. A counselor who walks the hall from his or her office toward the reception counter to greet for the first time a patient, family members, or others who reside in the household, not only stands to make an initial acquaintance, but is about to witness concrete evidence of who commands the home and who follows commands, among other features of domestic authority. For example, a father who is found seated adjacent to his wife, with the children seated on either side of them, signals greater parental command than an arrangement in which the parents are separated by the children. The strategic location of the receptionist's desk is significant in this regard, especially as the receptionist usually is taken by the counselors to be a disinterested party to counseling. Her presumed disinterest means that what she conveniently observes in seating arrangements and related features of family positioning in the room serves as a relatively objective check on the counselors' initial observations. Counselors routinely chat with the receptionist about her observations in the waiting area as well as informally compare their own observations with what the receptionist reports.

Complications arise regarding such signs' interpretation. What a receptionist notices in the waiting area may not corroborate a counselor's independent observations of the family's seating arrangement during therapy. Another counselor or a consultant may witness a particular counselor's spatial encounter with families and express a different opinion about domestic structure. Family members' reports of the social order of their homes may not coincide with what staff members read from members' spatial arrangement on Westside premises. But these are taken to be interpretive complications and do not spoil what is understood to be the essential reality of the home and how to discern it.

Fairview Hospital

Fairview is a private, accredited psychiatric facility. The hospital is supported by fees for services, a good share of which are paid by insurance companies. Fees cover inpatient psychiatric, educational, recreational, and social services as well as continuing counseling and support groups for former patients and their families.

The facility is divided into three units. A 28-bed, adult psychiatric unit (APU) serves general psychiatric and geriatric patients. A 20-bed, adult, addictive diseases unit (ADU) originally served patients with drug and alcohol abuse problems and was called the chemical dependency unit, or CDU. During my study, its therapeutic mission was broadened to include a variety of treatable addictive diseases, from the depressions accompanying eating disorders and compulsive gambling to drug and alcohol addiction, resulting in the renaming. A 20-bed adolescent services unit (ASU) treats boys and girls with alcohol- and drug-related disorders and other emotional problems. Paralleling the focus on wayward adolescents and younger adults at Westside House, I limited my observations at Fairview to the adolescent services and the addictive diseases units.

The usual length of stay in the ASU is 45 to 60 days. Incoming adolescents enter the 5-week treatment cycle of programs at whatever point they are admitted. The average length of stay in the ADU is 4 weeks. The treatment cycle is 4 weeks, with patients admitted to join the cycle on Mondays. There are four groups of patients, each group participating in a particular week of the treatment cycle.

Like Westside House, Fairview offers a family-oriented treatment program. The clinical staff and the administration firmly believe that substance abuse and emotional problems have strong links with home life and that therapeutic intervention must include the home and the family. A promotional brochure states that although "people with emotional or substance abuse difficulties suffer a great deal of unhappiness . . . their families suffer, too." The brochure explains, "Family involvement is a vital element in successful patient rehabilitation. The dynamics of the family unit must be analyzed and possibly changed." Another brochure, aimed at the families of troubled adolescents, stresses the benefits of family involvement:

> This is a difficult time. For the patient . . . for the family. Because family life is so much a part of an adolescent's world,

we believe in supporting and integrating family members
into the treatment process rather than isolating them. It has
been found that when family members become involved in
treatment, participation has a positive effect on the adolescent's progress toward recovery.

As at Westside House, the staff at Fairview believe that being
an adolescent or young adult in today's world presents great pressures and hurdles. Because it is so very easy to have problems, all
young persons are at risk, even without the natural stresses and
strains of coming of age, a time, according to a Fairview brochure
of "tremendous change and adjustment." The brochure adds, "Unfortunately many young people experience complex emotional
problems during this period of growth." The result is that Fairview,
too, is a facility with an unlimited population of potential patients.
As one staff member habitually points out in addressing family
members, "We're not only treating your troubled sons and daughters, we're treating a generation." The implication is that however normal the contemporary family appears to be on the surface, it is likely to be underlain by a medical cornucopia of problems.

Fairview's physical setting contrasts with Westside's. Promotional literature describes the facility as placed "amidst gently
rolling hills" in a country-like setting. Its three units are located
in two single-story wings converging on common recreational,
dining, and administrative areas. The ASU is housed in one of the
wings; the ADU and APU, separated by a large nursing station,
share the other.

At Fairview, it is not so much spacing and physical arrangements that distinguish the facility as a mundane context for
interpreting domestic disorder, as it is the sights and sounds of
participants, especially family members, in treatment. How family members enter treatment areas or how they arrange themselves in counseling sessions tells little about the local understanding of home life. Odd as it may seem at first, voices and
tissue boxes tell more. Soon after I began observation at Fairview,
I was struck by the extent to which all concerned, from staff members to patients and their families, dwelled on voice and affective
demeanor in talking and sharing ideas about troubles and family

life. Some staff members took special care in how they verbally addressed family members, and staff were particularly alert to the oral delivery style of patients and family members. A parent's raised voice told something significantly different about domestic affairs than a voice organized in carefully modulated tones. Weeping was particularly telling, as it signaled the emotional bonds understood locally to be at the core of domestic life.

On one occasion, while observing on the ADU, I saw tissue boxes poignantly tie together the mundane and the abstract, that is, the physical sights and sounds of patient participation with the local image of domestic disorder. I was about to accompany Tim Benson, a family therapist, to a midweek evening discussion session for patients and family members. He planned as usual to begin the session with a short videotape dealing with the domestic dynamics of alcohol addiction. The families had arrived and were waiting for us, seated in a circle in a small room located across the hall from Benson's office. As Benson collected the material he planned to use in the session, he noticed the time, turned to me, and quickly stated:

> It's getting late. I can't seem to locate that tape. See if you can find three or four boxes of Kleenex over there somewhere, will ya? I have a feeling we're going to really need them tonight.

At the time, I was only dimly aware of the significance of the request. I guessed that tissues might be used in the role-playing that Benson had planned for the evening. I found one full box of tissues. Curiously, it read "family-size." I called to Benson that I could find only one box. He sighed and asked me to search in a nearby storage area. I found two more boxes and brought them along. As we walked across the hall to the room where the patients and their families were waiting, I asked Benson why he needed all the tissue. He tellingly remarked:

> I can see you haven't been around very long. Something gives me the feeling that this is going to be a pretty tough session. I mean there's going to be a lot of gut spilling. Those are pretty uptight wives and parents in there. Wait and see.

As soon as they get into it, there's going to be all kinds of bawling and hard feelings and then you'll really see the nitty-gritty of their lives. They'll lay it all out, straight from the hip, right there in front of you. [Describes diverse emotional expressions] You better be ready to hand those [tissues] around. They're gonna need it. I hope you're ready. It can be pretty emotionally draining on you, too, to see the family dynamics in full color right in front of you. [Jokingly] I think sometimes that the more they use those [tissues] up, the truer picture I'm getting of what's going on at home.

As in the interpretation of a family's seating arrangement at Westside, I soon realized that tissues were about more than weeping and overall emotional composure during therapy. Tissues mundanely signaled the fundamental reality of the home as locally understood: a configuration of emotional bonds. For Benson, their usage virtually put the domestic disorder of the home on display, locating the home's social order in the minutiae of emotional expression.

STAFF

Westside and Fairview staff members have a variety of educational backgrounds and personal sentiments about institutional orientations to domestic life. Their differences do not as much counter local understandings of what the home is "all about" as the differences are used to articulate contrasting institutional images and commitments.

Westside House

The regular treatment staff at Westside House comprises five family counselors, or therapists (the terms are used interchangeably). The head counselor has a graduate degree in social work, three other counselors have had graduate training in counselor education, and the fifth has a master's degree in psychiatric nursing. Most are openly committed to Westside's preference for group or family, as opposed to individual, therapy. The counselors attempt to limit cases to those in which families agree to participate.

The educational background of the counselors is informally used to sort the assignment of cases. It is also taken to account for the typical focus on domestic authority blurring in individual cases. For example, Tammy Horton, the counselor with the master's degree in psychiatric nursing, is known as one who takes on the so-called crazies, that is, cases that seem on the surface to be inscrutable or especially bizarre. When she occasionally dwells on a family's emotional life or, as she is sometimes accused of doing, attempts to "get into the heads" of the members rather than focusing on family structure and dynamics, the common explanation for this picks up on Horton's educational background and ostensibly related personality. As one of the counselors jokingly explains in a case review after Horton has just gotten into the "deep, nasty feelings" of a client's mother:

> There she [Horton] goes again. Wouldn't you just know that it would be our own sweet little nurse Miss Horton who wants to get right in there and get at all those deep, nasty feelings and see what deep, dark secrets lurk in their hearts. It really takes a nurse, doesn't it? That's our Tammy.

Horton responds in kind:

> Look guys. I can't help it. It's the nurse in me. You know nurses—they want to care and get into it all. [Pause] It's just me. It's a personality thing. [Others chuckle sarcastically] Come on, you guys.

It is a good-humored joke that a staff member has veered from the institutional understanding that the fundamental reality of family life is domestic authority. Horton is a quirky exception to the rule. The other counselors can be exceptions too. Kelly Seever is routinely assigned, or is supposed to take an unusual interest in, the sex cases, sometimes excessively exploring their emotional side. This is similarly explained as due to a "certain personal professional interest." When Donna Reddick, the head counselor, goes straight to the heart of the family's problem without spending much time discerning its informal dynamics, the others say it is the social worker in her. As exceptions, the idiosyncratic actions prove the general rule of authority for interpreting domestic disorder.

Year-round, counseling interns, also of diverse educational backgrounds, spend time practicing at Westside, handling cases under the supervision of regular staff members. Their differences, too, are overshadowed by the common view toward domestic authority. Their status as interns sometimes makes alternate orientations less than a joking matter, however, more a sign of their need to learn and put into effect what it means to do family therapy.

In a case review centering on how to take account of individual and group differences in counseling sessions, Keith Borelli, an intern temporarily taking on a full caseload, has a disagreement with regular staff member Kelly Seever. Borelli describes the differences in personality in a particular family and suggests that it might be useful to see two family members alone in individual counseling sessions because the differences get "washed out" when family members are seen together.

> What I thought I'd do is to get Bill [an alcoholic son] in here alone and try to get to all the hidden hostility. I think it's really there but he just withdraws and it gets washed out when Mom and Dad are around.

Seever responds that she would prefer that Borelli stick to group counseling, explaining that she feels an individual approach hides the most important ingredient, namely, the family dynamics, especially the way broken lines of authority figure in the presenting problem. Borelli respectfully comments that he prefers to be eclectic in the selection of counseling techniques, adding that he finds any number of approaches useful. Seever then reminds Borelli that he's at Westside to learn family, not individual therapy, and that he'll undoubtedly discover that the group approach is more effective.

I don't think you want to get into that [individual counseling]. Here, we're committed to the group approach. That's where it's at . . . what's real. People live in groups, not as individuals. If you see each of them alone, you're just going to get burned. Each of them is going to set you up to see things his way and you're going to miss the bigger picture. [Borelli mildly objects] Look, how're you going to know what they're like together in real life at home if all you do is talk to them individually?

Borelli describes what he might learn from seeing individual family members alone, but Seever curtly remarks that individual therapy works at cross-purposes with group therapy, reminding Borelli of what she said earlier about the reality of group life. Borelli reacts sharply to the perceived orthodoxy. Tension increases in the room as Seever insists on the advantages of family and system, over individual, therapy. She emphasizes, "Because we work on the family here; it's the system that we're interested in." Other counselors jump in, lending support. Donna Reddick, the head counselor, repeats didactically, "A lot of times, it gets to be at odds, working at cross-purposes." The disagreement ends as Borelli quietly concludes, "I guess I'm reacting to taking a hard line on anything."

Westside counselors' work with families is aided by consultants who, weekly, individually participate in and advise the counselors in case reviews called "group supervisions" or simply "group soups." The consultants also pursue private family therapy practices in the community. Their backgrounds, like the counselors', vary. Two are licensed clinical psychologists with doctorates. The third is a former head counselor at Westside with a background in counselor education, who has since "gone out on his own," as is frequently noted. It is commonly understood among the counselors as well as by the administrative staff that Westside provides valuable experience for family counseling and is a stepping-stone to private practice. The counselors integrate the consultants' advice into their ongoing work with families at Westside, aiming to view and deal with troubled family homes as the consultants do.

Fairview Hospital

The treatment staff for Fairview's adolescent services and addictive disease units comprises program directors, attending and consulting psychiatrists, nurses, family therapists, and mental health technicians or aides. Family therapists on the adolescent unit have the most extensive contact with families in treatment, both conducting formal family therapy and facilitating the various support and discussion groups held on weekday evenings and on weekends. Psychiatrists figure significantly in the ASU's weekend family program. The nurses and mental health technicians are in daily and nightly contact with patients of both units.

The family therapists have varied educational and professional backgrounds, ranging from master's degrees in social work and rehabilitation counseling to bachelor's and master's degrees in psychology. Each therapist has had extensive experience in mental health. On occasion, such as when there is a patient crisis that keeps a therapist from a scheduled session with families, other experienced staff members, such as a nurse or mental health technician, may temporarily substitute.

At Fairview, staff members' personal backgrounds are an important ingredient in the treatment process, used by staff to exemplify "what it's like" to be, say, the "codependent" of an alcoholic parent, child, or close relative, that is, inadvertently supportive of the latter's bad habits. It frequently is pointed out that those who work in the human service professions do so because their own personal and family troubles cause them to make careers out of helping and healing others; they turn family troubles into jobs. An ADU therapist puts it this way one evening in a family group:

> When parents are unavailable and the family is operating in a real dysfunctional way, we send out a role model. It's real typical for someone who grows up in a dysfunctional family to marry an alcoholic. Most people who work in helping professions are from dysfunctional families. I'm typical. My dad was an alcoholic and I just got right out there, went to college, and tried to make up for it by helping alco-

holic families. One of the statistics I've heard is that about 85% of the families out there are dysfunctional. I know that sounds high, but I really don't know what a so-called normal family is.

This therapist is fond of pointing out that the statistic for the families of human service professionals is even higher, upwards of 90%. Indeed, the numbers are said to be so high overall that most families should be seeking some type of formal help, although only a small fraction actually do.

Therapists on the adolescent services unit similarly make use of their personal experiences as troubled adolescents or with wayward children of their own. One therapist, for example, routinely describes to the family groups he facilitates how he grew up in a family with a very autocratic father, explaining that his father had no interest in other family members' opinions or feelings, least of all the children's. The therapist usually relates that he knows what it is like when family members do not bother to effectively listen to one another; he dwells on the dysfunctional consequences, especially the feelings they engender. Another therapist on the same unit, who has young children of his own, exemplifies the conditions that can lead to dysfunctionality by describing how he manages his children's constant bickering and scuffling. He, too, reports what it feels like as he compares his own experiences with what parents of adolescents in treatment either went through or currently are undergoing.

The I've-been-there character of these accounts does not mean that the families of Fairview staff are actually dysfunctional or that individual family members currently suffer from alcohol or drug addictions. The accounts are about staff members' experiences in an earlier period of their lives. They may be about other members who have been plagued by such problems. They might suggest how current and still normal domestic experiences can lead to dysfunctionality. The accounts imply that, but for the knowledge and skill that effectively manage those out of control, anyone can suffer from addictions and family troubles. More important in the context of Fairview's institutional understanding of

domestic order, the I've-been-there character of staff accounts is
a basis for displaying and sharing feelings.

The contrast with Westside House in this regard is striking. In
communicating with troubled families, Westside staff members
rarely discuss their own personal experiences. Staff's attention,
centered as it is on families' authority structure, suggests that structure and authority are not for "sharing," only for rationally deline-
ating. There is nothing internal or deep to communicate in the
treatment process at Westside. Those who engage in even limited
communications of this kind are humorously indulged as exceptional, roundly reminded that family structure and dynamics, not
sentiments, are the key to domestic troubles, or told that the resulting information is ancillary, not central, to what domestic disorder is "all about." At Westside House, "joining" (a technical term)
is not a sharing of feelings with clients and families but a political
alignment with a particular family member, usually a parent.

In some ways, Fairview staff are warmer in their relations with
families than their Westside counterparts. This is not a characteristic of individual staff members, but an institutional imperative
tied to the organizations' contrasting images of domestic disorder. Staff members in both facilities work diligently to establish
rapport with patients or clients and their families, empathize
with their situations and troubles, and mostly show a deep commitment to resolving problems; Fairview staffers articulate their
concern in distinctly emotional terms, but their Westside counterparts do so as interpersonal strategists. Staff members' backgrounds are also accorded a different relevance in treatment. As
Mary Douglas (1986) might put it, we virtually see how the two
facilities "think" about domestic disorder in their respective staff's
expressive demeanors in therapeutic encounters.

TREATMENT PROGRAMS

Treatment programs and therapeutic apparatus also draw significance from institutional understandings. Although Fairview's
treatment schedule is more extensive than Westside's, reflecting
the fact that the hospital is an inpatient program, the common

task of discerning domestic disorder prompts all concerned to use the programs and apparatus that exist in each organization with similar interpretive aims, namely, to display their respective images of disorder.

Westside House

The primary mode of treatment at Westside is family counseling. The treatment philosophy is based on the model of brief family therapy, in which particular domestic problems are focal, rather than personality or other global structures. The idea is that problems like truancy, delinquency, and drug abuse can be dealt with effectively through direct, short-term intervention into family dynamics. According to a family therapy sourcebook used at Westside (Simon, Stierlin, & Wynne, 1985, p. 29), brief therapy as a rule consists of a limited number of sessions, usually 6 to 15, spaced over a period of several weeks.

As a treatment philosophy, brief therapy recently has been inclined to target epistemological problems, that is, the family's basis for knowing itself and the way communication figures in its dynamics (deShazer, 1980; Weakland, Fisch, Watzlawick, & Bodin, 1974; Watzlawick, 1984). The philosophical turn centers on questions of knowledge applied to therapeutic principles themselves in an approach called "constructivism" (deShazer & Berg, 1988; Efran, Lukens, & Lukens, 1988; Hoffman, 1988). The root argument is that the family not only comprises a system of knowledge underpinning and sustaining its dynamics, but the therapeutic project is itself a moral system with principles, preferences, and polemics. As such, therapeutic encounters are engagements between epistemological systems.

The commitment to brief therapy at Westside has less grandiose philosophical claims. Although the program is nonetheless problem oriented and an attempt is made to limit the number of therapeutic encounters, it is the objective family system, particularly its authority structure, that is emphasized. A signal text, which I will discuss at greater length in part 2 as it relates to the social construction process at Westside, is Jay Haley's (1976) book

Problem-Solving Therapy. Well-thumbed copies of the paperback edition are frequently referenced and shared by the five counselors. The book is recommended reading for counseling interns. In a word, it is the local bible for resolving fundamental questions of therapeutic philosophy and procedure.

Westsiders are drawn to Haley's language of authority. Although the family is admitted to be a system of communication, what is critical for the staff is who controls what is said to whom and how that control is manifested. The interpersonal structure of expression commands the counselors' attention. It makes a difference, for example, whether the parents or the children communicate the rules of the home. Hierarchies of communication can make or break families, as it were. The consultants reinforce the view, embellishing it with wide-ranging advice and myriad examples of both dysfunctional structures and successful realignments from their private practices.

It is customary in brief therapy to videotape counseling sessions or otherwise monitor them from a remote location. The mechanics are informed by the idea that, as a real-life group, the family and other significant members of the household actually present their dynamics and structure as they interact with each other and outsiders, something that easily can be hidden, remain unarticulated, or become confused in individual reports. Domestic order, especially the family hierarchy, does not belong to anyone in particular. It has a social logic of its own, coming forth, separately and independently, in members' interactions. The distinct reality of the home's domestic order appears in the process. This is what is expected to be captured on tape and camera and what those who view or review cases attempt to discern, catalog, and realign.

Family members are apprised of the therapeutic format in the intake process, including the rationale for the videotaping or camera monitoring, and are asked for their written consent to participate. But they sometimes forget what they were initially told or later may not recall having consented to be taped or monitored. This leads to questioning and repeated explanation in the therapeutic process. By and large, on the assumption that the taping and monitoring will enhance intervention or that refusal to participate will further damage their reputations with referral agents, families usually agree to the format.

The counselors regularly review tapes of previous sessions in their continuing work with families. Group soups routinely make use of videotapings. But sometimes, the videotaping equipment cannot be located or is not properly set up. A tape may be lost or an old tape of unexpected current interest is found to have been recycled and taped over. Less frequently, it is judged to be inappropriate or not very useful to videotape a session. On such occasions, case reviews in group soup are based on written reports and eyewitness accounts. The problem this presents is that counselors, consultants, and others cannot themselves witness what they take to be the actual domestic disorder of the home, but must verbally constitute it. This makes the working reality of home life in group soup less vibrantly evident and more subjective in appearance.

The therapeutic format and mission of live supervision or "live soup" is similar to group soup, except that as the counseling session actually takes place, its proceedings are monitored and discussed elsewhere by counselors, interns, and consultants. Other facilities have provision for conducting live soup from an adjacent room with a one-way mirror looking into the counseling chamber; Westside House makes use of nearby rooms connected by video equipment.

Live soup is a particularly poignant treatment and consultation format. Although family members are more or less alert to the fact that the camera may be activated at any time, and they have been informed that all proceedings are confidential and used strictly for professional therapeutic purposes, they do not always know who is watching. The explanation by a counselor that video equipment must be set up for simultaneous monitoring by a consultant who will be of great help to the counselor has its way of raising concern. It temporarily places family members and the working counselor on a more immediately visible plane than they otherwise might be. Yet, open concern and wariness typically subside as the proceedings unfold.

The therapy process in the counseling room is interrupted in live soup when the consultant decides to intervene in the counseling process. It is customary in brief family therapy for the treatment process to include direct and immediate outside intervention, with the working counselor advised, usually by telephone, how to proceed in the counseling process. At Westside, the consultant calls the counselor on the interoffice telephone and offers suggestions or gives directives. The results are visible on the monitor located in the viewing room.

Interruptions may or may not be treated as routine telephone calls. Some working counselors are disconcerted by them, especially when they occur in rapid succession, even though the counselors know the practice is normal and generally accepted. Family members may openly wonder what is going on, even after they have been generally told about and formally accepted the procedure. Yet, mainly, live soup runs its course without many hitches, with participants adjusting to its periodically intrusive ups and downs.

Fairview Hospital

Fairview Hospital provides individual and family therapy along with diverse educational and recreational activities (without systematic videotaping). The programs in the adolescent services and addictive diseases units combine highly varied therapeutic orientations, from behavioral point systems on the ASU to the twelve-step philosophy of Alcoholics Anonymous on both units. A Westside counselor who has been on Fairview's staff compares the two facilities in this regard:

Here [Westside] we use the brief [family therapy] philosophy. There's a consistent therapeutic approach that's clear. Over there [Fairview], they mix up all kinds of things. You've got all that hard behavioral stuff going on with the kids [ASU] and that sits alongside the effective parenting stuff. On top of that, you've got the As thrown in . . . you know like AA [Alcoholics Anonymous], NA [Narcotics Anonymous], GA [Gamblers Anonymous], and what have you. They're all [the As] basically coming from the same place. They even do toughlove [a popular hard-nosed child management philosophy for dealing with incorrigible adolescents].

Acceptance for treatment on the units requires written consent to a contract highlighting cooperation and abstention from alcohol and mind-altering chemicals. Upon admission, patients must surrender any drugs to the staff and agree to complete all phases of the treatment program. They are reminded that failure to comply with these conditions may be grounds for discharge.

The addictive diseases unit has separate inpatient programs for the addicted and for codependents. The addictions treated are mainly to alcohol and drugs, especially cocaine, less often gambling or relatively exotic intoxicants such as "loving too much" for women and uncontrollable sexual desire for men, with their concomitant psychiatric problems, typically depression. A hospital brochure defines codependency as "an unconscious addiction to another person's dysfunctional behavior" and notes that the condition most frequently is caused by "growing up in a family where there is a dysfunctional person and/or dysfunctional ways of communicating." Traditionally, the dysfunctionality has been associated with alcoholism, with family members uncontrollably "enabling" the alcoholic's behavior. Increasingly, the brochure explains, codependency is "also identified with drug addiction, abuse, neglect, physical disability, mental illness, or simply someone with an oversized ego and a high level need for attention." Codependency now characterizes any person who directly or inadvertently supports so-called dysfunctional behavior—which also is broadly defined.

The treatment program for the addicted is a daily regimen of learning, counseling, and therapeutic recreation, rotating every 4 weeks. Weekdays begin with 15 minutes' meditation, from 8:00 to 8:15 a.m. Patients then participate in therapeutic recreation under the supervision of an activity therapist until 10:00 a.m. Activities include body conditioning, occupational therapy, and horseback riding.

The first week, from 10:30 a.m. until noon, patients attend classes in alcohol and drug education, which include films and videotapes, group counseling, lectures, and discussions. In the second week, the period is devoted to assertiveness training, in which patients learn to effectively communicate feelings and needs rather than hide or aggressively express them. In the third week, attention in the same period concentrates on materials provided by the As, especially Alcoholics Anonymous's "Big Book," a classic text that presents the organization's popular, twelve step recovery program (see Alcoholics Anonymous World Services, 1939/1976, 1952; Kurtz, 1979). In the fourth or final week, the time slot is set aside for the analysis and discussion of the antecedents of addiction and the conditions for relapse.

For the afternoons, informal discussion and support groups are emphasized. In a discussion group called Disclosure, patients learn how, and are encouraged, to share intimate thoughts and feelings. Following dinner and visiting hours, family members and patients attend discussion groups together, in which individual problems are related to the home and family living. These groups were an important site of my observations on the ADU. Afterward, AA, NA, and related meetings are available. The day ends with a recreation period in the gymnasium.

Weekends are less formal with more extensive visiting hours, activity therapy, and lengthy periods of free time. After the first week in treatment, at the staff's discretion, patients may secure passes for home visits.

The ADU program for codependents is shorter but similar in organization. Over a 9-day period, inpatients are apprised of the causes, conditions, and domestic consequences of addictions, in particular how they, as codependent family members, fit into the picture. An extensive offering of films, videotapes, and other educational materials details both the psychological and social dynamics of dependency. Again, the twelve-step philosophy and its language are evident throughout.

The weekday rhythms of treatment, learning, and recreation are reversed in the adolescent services unit, so as not to clash with the ADU program. For example, adolescents are scheduled for recreation in the afternoon, when the gym is not being used by ADU patients. Following breakfast and free time, the teens attend school in special classrooms located on their unit, staffed and coordinated by the local school district. School hours are from 8:30 to 12:30 a.m., with a break for group therapy. Afternoons are devoted to therapeutic recreation, discussion groups focused on life management issues, and communication skills. Evenings are set aside for homework, visiting, and additional recreation. Patients' individual and group psychotherapy with their attending psychiatrist and family counseling occur throughout the day, Monday to Friday.

Weekends are different. Saturdays are relatively unstructured, but Sundays are devoted to family therapy. Family members are scheduled to arrive at noon, after the adolescents have met with staff members to decide the question or issues related to their problems that they would like family members and significant others to discuss with them. During the hour from 1 to 2 p.m., called "multi-family group" but usually referred to simply as "group," discussion and counseling, with both children and family members in attendance, is facilitated by a consulting psychiatrist or one of the family therapists. Occasionally, a nurse or experienced mental health technician presides. Parents arrive on the premises before group and, from noon to 1 p.m., participate in parent education classes taught by the family therapists, which the teens are not allowed to attend. Following group, from 2 to 3 p.m., the teens return to their rooms while the parents meet for an hour of what formally is called "toughlove," after the child management philosophy of that name (York, York, & Wachtel, 1983). Although toughlove materials and concerns are indeed part of the hour's proceedings, the meeting routinely becomes a general discussion and support group.

Cutting across the therapies, schooling, recreation, and general activities of daily living on the unit is an elaborate point levels system, described in an ASU family handbook as "defining the privileges and responsibilities earned by each patient each week," indicating his or her progress. Staff and patients meet weekly to decide the levels, which distinguish individual teens by "demonstrated ability to handle responsibility and on willingness to deal with personal problems." Upon admission, patients are placed on Level 1, indicating close supervision by the staff and few outside contacts. Patients are expected to progress toward Level 4 as they move toward discharge, gaining latitude in self-monitoring and opportunities for outside contact, such as overnight passes and daily permission to use the telephone.

The logic and language of behavioral programming is evident throughout the ASU. The idea is that the highly rationalized environment offered by a point levels system replaces the typically unsupervised, confusing, or chaotic life the adolescent is used to at home. This provides the opportunity to learn self-control and the etiquettes of interpersonal relations. The family handbook explains that this form of behavior modification enhances "productive behavior for individual patients as well as the entire adolescent group." The terms *time-out* and *out of control* are commonplace. "Time-out" refers to a period separate from regular behavioral programming in which the adolescent is isolated from others to take stock of misconduct or regain self-control. "Out of control" pertains to negative, unmanaged conduct, including emotional outbursts, hostility, verbal threats, physical violence, and suicidal gestures.

One or two evenings per week, for an hour and a half, ASU therapists conduct three types of discussion and support group meetings at the hospital for family members and adolescents. One is the adolescent transition group, which meets two weeks before and two weeks after the patient's discharge. The aim here is to share thoughts and feelings with parents or significant others about the patient's forthcoming discharge. The effect on domestic order of the adolescent's reintegration into the household is a prime concern, together with the possibilities for continuing personal adjustment. The other two types of group meeting, called "aftercare," are limited to former patients and their families. Aftercare is billed for before the patient is discharged and provides six months of follow-up weekly contact with the therapists. Aftercare meetings are designed for discussion of issues and problems that occur in the former patient's and the family's daily life after discharge, largely centered on the patient's continuing relations with members of the household, especially parents. One of the two aftercare groups is meant for former patients whose primary problem was substance abuse; the family issues group is for former patients whose problem was primarily behavioral, such as chronic hostility toward parents or being a repeat run-away. Along with the weekend program, the weekday evening transition and aftercare meetings were venues of my observations in the ASU.

Effective parenting is a special concern in the ASU, particularly in weekend classes for parents. The primary text is Don Dinkmeyer and Gary D. McKay's (1983) guide to parenting entitled *STEP/Teen* (for Systematic Training for Effective Parenting of teens). This guide targets intrafamilial communication, illustrating techniques for properly conveying individual attitudes, especially feelings. The emphasis is on controlled communication, not just expression. Other important texts on the ASU are *Toughlove* (York, York, & Wachtel, 1983), the original version for parents, and the self-help manual for children (York & York, 1983). Parents and their children are shown the so-called harsh facts of rule breaking and how to accept and manage the consequences. Fairview family therapists turn to the toughlove philosophy as a last resort; the therapists are fond of saying, "When the communication of feelings doesn't work, toughlove kicks in." (Part 3 will discuss these texts at greater length as they relate to the social construction process at Fairview.)

As the Westside counselor with Fairview experience suggested, the combination of behavioral principles, the disclosure and explication of deep feelings, communication strategies, assertiveness training, individual and group psychotherapy, the twelve-step approach, and toughlove seem to add up to a contradictory therapeutic mix. The highly rationalized calculus of the point levels system, for example, seems at odds with the ideals of the effective communication of feelings. Yet, Fairview staff members appear untroubled by any inconsistencies. Although they sometimes point out differences in the approaches, particularly how each relates to solving family problems—as do family members discussing on their own how best to deal with domestic troubles—the differences are not taken to be philosophical inconsistencies, but considered technical alternatives. The point levels system is a tool for managing emotions, just as the approaches laid out in *STEP/Teen* and *Toughlove* are, respectively, means of dealing with the unexpressed feelings and the stresses of growing up and taking responsibility for one's life. The twelve-step approach is not taken as gospel, but seen as one path among many to self-control. All told, Fairview offers a panorama of treatment modalities, linked together in a well-planned therapeutic format and brought to bear on what is believed to be the fundamental reality of domestic living, namely, the interpersonal sentiments of family members.

PART TWO

Westside House

THREE

Discerning Domestic Authority

A good deal of Westside counselors' and consultants' work with clients and families centers on discerning domestic authority. Who has the power at home? Is there a clear and distinct line of authority? Are there signs of overdomination such as child battery or sexual abuse? The answers figure significantly in understandings of, and explanations for, family members' troubles. A vague or confusing structure of command among the adults of a household is considered to be an important source of the children's delinquency, warranting action to restore a well-defined hierarchy of decision making.

THE REALITY BEHIND THE SIGNS

Like other abstractions, domestic authority is not self-evident, but must be distinguished by interpreting concrete signs, through the mundane minutiae of family members' presence in treatment. The discernment takes time and effort, but it is the domestic authority, not the signs as such, that is the primary reality.

Take the seating arrangement of family members in the waiting area near the reception counter. On one occasion, typical of others, I observed Donna Reddick, one of the counselors, walk down the hall toward the area and, along the way, engage both the family and, a short while later, the receptionist, in talk quite telling of the distinction between signs and reality. As Reddick approaches, she smiles, greets everyone, and asks the mother, who is seated farthest to the right in a row of five chairs, whether she expects her husband to show up for the session. A teenaged son and a younger daughter sit together, one chair removed from the mother. The daughter holds her sister, a toddler, on her lap. The toddler had been seated between the mother and daughter until she became restless.

There is no immediate indication of the father's whereabouts. The mother says they got a flat tire, her husband is in the parking lot taking care of it and should be in shortly. Reddick peeks outdoors but finds no one about. She turns to the receptionist and asks for the log book, which contains the schedule of appointments. Reddick remarks for all to hear that she is particularly concerned that they start on time this evening because she has an appointment with another family in about an hour. As Reddick tends to other business at the reception counter, family members wait patiently for about 5 minutes, chatting and fussing with the youngest child. The father then enters, sits down, and talks quietly with his son. He is seated farthest left in the row of five chairs.

Moments pass. Reddick looks up from what she is doing and asks the family to come into her office and make themselves comfortable, pointing down the hall to the first door on the right. This is to be the family's second counseling session. The son has been "popped" (arrested) for cocaine possession and, following other brushes with the law for fighting, has been referred to Westside for drug counseling.

Before Reddick joins the family, the receptionist asks her:

> The old man [father] doesn't seem to be too interested. I didn't think he was going to show. Do you believe that flat tire story? [Pause] The last time, he was a half hour late. Did you get much on him? I'd bet he's not around very much.

Reddick answers that she still does not know much about the father, but that Mom seems to run the show, which, she guesses, is why the son is out of control. In an exchange of views about how the father fits into the picture, the receptionist remarks:

You know, he could have sat down next to his wife. But he's always kinda in the background. To me . . . that says something. I mean . . . why should he always be in the background?

Reddick picks up on the remark, initially discounting the suggested significance of seating arrangement:

Well, . . . I wouldn't read too much into it this time, Paula [the receptionist]. After all, he did come in late because of the flat and all. [Chuckles sarcastically about the father's attempted deception] It's only natural to sit down over there [next to the door]. Just because he sat over there [nodding to the left] doesn't mean anything, I don't think. [Pause] Then again, you never know. Didn't he just stand there the last time they were in here and he let the kids sit? Maybe you're right, Paula. [Pause] Who knows? Right? Maybe he just likes to stand? [Both laugh]

As Reddick and Paula banter, they continue to chuckle over what they believe is the father's not-too-subtle attempt at deception, making repeated references to seating and domestic marginality. The discussion never dwells on seating alone, but only in connection with what, as it is sometimes put, "it's [seating and related matters of personal spacing] telling us." Seating is more or less important only as it is a sign conveying something of greater local interest. Indeed, the idea that seating on this particular occasion might be the result of walking into the room late and taking the nearest available chair, makes seating a temporarily inconsequential matter. It is only when Reddick rethinks its possible importance, because it might be part of a pattern and not coincidental, that the significance of seating is briefly entertained. When Reddick finally asks, "Maybe he just likes to stand?" seating is again trivialized.

Mundane as this commonplace exchange and its concrete concern with chairs, standing, and seating seem to be, the exchange and concern are doing important interpretive work. Chairs, standing, and seating are serving as possible clues to the reality lying behind them—domestic authority—a matter of fundamental interest in dealing with family troubles in this facility. In their own right, chairs, standing, seating, and the like are signs of nothing. Their significance arises only in relation to what it is believed, imagined, guessed, or debated they stand for. As a rule, at Westside, seating arrangement, posture, verbalization, and related conditions of the immediate environs and bodily demeanor routinely concretize authority and, thereby, effect the social construction of domestic disorder.

THE PRESENTING VERSUS THE UNDERLYING PROBLEM

In accordance with the philosophy of brief therapy, Westside counsels families for particular problems, from a teenage daughter's repeated fighting in school to a son's crack habit and truancy. The problems are considered to be the working surface of a more basic, underlying dysfunction. It is sometimes said that any presenting problem is only "the tip of the iceberg." As counselors encounter presenting problems, which are usually focused on individual family members, they orient to the broader social context of the home that locates the underlying problem. A presenting problem that disappears after one session of counseling is no obstacle to continued treatment, since any one problem of a "sick" home can readily be replaced by another.

The distinction between presenting and underlying problems shows up in the difficulty the counselors sometimes have with the designations "patient" and, to a lesser extent, "client" (which the counselors prefer, echoing as "client" does its counterpart in private practice). Counselors believe they are treating group life —families—not particular patients or, in the final analysis, even individual clients. The use of the term "identified patient," or IP, is telling in this regard. IP refers to the patient of record, the one member of the family who, for administrative purposes, is the case on file, whose record contains both patient and family information. The term suggests that what is named in documents is a partial (individual) and therefore artificial designation, not the whole (family group) "patient."

In a group supervision, a brief discussion of the term IP underscores the commitment to family as opposed to individual counseling as well as the reality taken ultimately to be undergoing treatment. Sara Brighton, a counseling intern, reviews the bed-wetting problem of a young black girl who is frequently truant from school. Brighton reports that the girl, Latisha, is very shy and hardly speaks when Brighton has the family in for counseling. Brighton feels that the family dynamics are such that Latisha remains silent when her mother and siblings are present. Brighton suggests that it might be helpful to see Latisha alone, to "get her side of the story and maybe get to the bottom of the bed-wetting," before the family is seen again as a group.

It is a familiar counseling problem. Staff members sympathize with the situation. Unlike counseling intern Keith Borelli's perceived philosophical challenge to Westside's family-focused therapy, Brighton presents the option of individual counseling only as a means of circumventing a significant social obstruction to further treatment.

As is typical in group soup, the suggestion is discussed. Counselors are of two opinions, one supporting Brighton's contention that an individual session with Latisha might help to clarify matters. Another opinion, argued by counselor Gary Nelson, maintains the artificiality of individual counseling. At one point in the discussion, Nelson prompts comments on the concept of the identified patient as he recommends against individual counseling:

> Hold on a minute. We're not individuals. We don't believe that, do we? No one lives alone in this world. We're social beings. [Elaborates] At least that's what we keep telling ourselves. I don't see this case as that much different from the others. So Latisha won't open her mouth. Big deal. I'd figure a way to reframe the family dynamics in there [the counseling session] so that she does. [Offers a few suggestions] Like, get Mom or one of the others to get their sister to talk. In real life, there are no individuals, only members of groups like the family.

Counselor Donna Reddick immediately turns to Brighton and adds, "It's kinda artificial that Latisha is the IP," to which Nelson responds:

> Like Donna mentioned, that label IP is unreal. The term "patient" is really not what we're about. I tend to prefer "client" myself. IP artificially labels one member of the family the patient and it can suck you into focusing on that person's presenting problem. That gets you into this sorta trap where you labeled someone the patient . . . you know, the IP . . . and so you want to just cure *that* patient. The family's the main thing; it's the real underlying problem in all this mess. [Pause] It's a conceptual thing. The more we all get into it, the more we want to focus on that individual. I think the reason we use IP is that we all know it's just a convenient label, but we sometimes seem to fall into that trap. It's a bad habit.

Emphasizing the distinction, Reddick turns to Brighton:

> You may find out that as you work with the family that there's a clearer presenting problem. You might want to look into lying as presenting because they [Latisha's family] all lie and then you can look for underlying causes of that.

Responding to Nelson's suggestion that Brighton work on each member of the family rather than focus on Latisha, counselor Nancy Cantor jokes about the artificiality of the IP designation, "That way, she'll [Sara] have three IPs in one family. Right, Gary?" The mood lightens as several other counselors joke about the designation. Finally, as if to say that the structure of the counseling relationship goes a long way in sustaining the reality of the entity believed to be undergoing treatment, Brighton jests:

> I think I'll get back to individual counseling after this [internship] because, with these families, they're such a group and it adds to everything. It complicates who the IP is. When you have one-on-one in counseling, the IP is just there and that's it.

Although signs such as a child's silence in the presence of family members, the place a father seats himself, or his posture while

seated are seemingly individual characteristics, they are understood at Westside to be distinctly social. They are not about the
father or child as such, but about his or her relations with others in
the home—the real patient, not the IP. They are signs of domestic
order or disorder. Signs are, in effect, about the underlying problem. They reference the abstraction that is only signified by individual characteristics, the IP's among other individual family members' characteristics.

THE LANGUAGE OF AUTHORITY

At Westside, a language of authority represents domestic order.
Home life is comprised of roles and relationships, put together into
a hierarchical system of decision making and command. Roles
are comprised of rights, duties, and obligations. Although sentiments are thought to be an integral part of daily life in the home,
Westsiders believe that sentiments take second place to authority
in the functional operation of family systems. According to the
counselors, dysfunctional families tend to have systemic priorities confused, so that, among other domestic pathologies, emotions displace properly functioning structures of command.

As a rule, a functional structure of command has a decidedly
traditional flavor. Not only does the functional family system
have a well-defined authority structure, with no cross-cutting lines
of command, but the hierarchy of control distributes members in
a particular way. In homes with the full complement of parents
and children, the father is preferably in charge, with mother fully
supportive. Although there is a division of authority between the
parents, the division is considered to be most functional when it
operates in concert in relation to the children. A father who deni-
grates his wife undermines the contribution her loyalty makes to
his ability to "run the family." A mother who "puts down" her
husband, especially in front of the children, risks disturbing the
vertical equilibrium of a well-run home.

Children, too, have their proper place in the scheme of things,
reflecting the adage that children should be seen and not heard.
What this means in theory is not necessarily that children should

be silent, but that they should not be principal figures of command in the home. A functional family is one in which parents make the central decisions on behalf of the family as a whole, and the children faithfully fulfill their responsibilities for the well-being of all.

The preferred hierarchy of the family system is elaborated in the therapeutic context. Successful counseling is based not only on a particular understanding of the functional home, but also works most efficiently when the counselor "joins" the family in treatment, especially parents, so as to firmly and effectively support its preferred domestic order. Although the term *join* is used in a number of ways in therapeutic practice—ranging from references to the initial establishment of a working relationship with family members in treatment to alignments with particular members, notably parents—it also references the overall preferred association between the counselor and the family system as a whole. The counselor joins the family system to alter its ineffective chain of command, temporarily taking control over its members. The hierarchy of authority in therapy ideally has the counselor on top, the parents second in command, and the children below them.

A related term is *elevate*. Counselors work to elevate parents in relation to their children. As will be shown in greater detail in chapter 5, this is done in a number of ways. For example, to compliment Mom and Dad on their recent success in working together to make a runaway daughter feel wanted is to elevate the parents in relation to the child. The term, of course, generally resonates with hierarchy: Parents are elevated, rarely children.

In everyday practice, the language of authority repeatedly displaces the language of sentiments. Counselors reviewing family dynamics in particular cases zero in on signs of authority. The counselors may be annoyed, even angered, when emotions come to the fore, because these are believed to take the counselors away from the fundamental reality behind the signs. Weeping, verbal expressiveness, and other emotional displays are smoke screens that hide the actual, underlying problems of the home. It is not that Westsiders are uncaring; rather they understand their therapeutic target to be a fundamentally different category of experience.

The consultants, too, advocate the language of authority. Like the counselors, consultants not only eschew displays of sentiments, but also steer away from therapeutic strategies that focus on emotional experience, particularly at the individual level. For example, they show a decided impatience with the twelve-step approach of Alcoholics Anonymous. Clients presenting as alcoholic or drug abusive are likely to have come into contact with one of the As, but the consultants resent the individualistic bias of the twelve-step approach, in which personal values such as faith, commitment, and serenity are taken to be the basis for restoring family members to (emotional) health.

During live soup, a consultant highlights this view with disparaging remarks about the admiration of a drug-abusing son and his former therapist for AA. Observed in progress on the monitor located in an adjoining room, the son has just described, at considerable length, how good AA is, how useful Alanon (a family-focused offshoot of AA) is for the family, and how he learned that the family is part of the problem and are "codependents." Responding to the son's comments while watching the proceedings on the monitor, the consultant angrily remarks to the other counselors in the room:

> She [the working counselor] needs to tell him [the son] that those psychologists who are into AA are full of shit. They're always inventing new words and trying to get people sucked in by them. Now they want us all to be patients. Codependency is such nonsense.

When the therapy session ends and the working counselor comes into the monitoring room, the consultant advises the counselor, again denigrating AA's individualistic focus on sentiments. The consultant displaces the language of codependency with a preferred orientation to authority.

> Tell Dad [IP's father] that all this jargon his son is into is just so much nonsense. [Elaborates] This [the family] is a real enmeshed and powerful system. When you talked to them, they sucked you right into them. So you've got to confront

them with . . . take over . . . with "What would it take for
Dwayne [the IP] to be gay without him using drugs?" These
[family members] are experts at triangulation. The son is into
feelings and wallowing all over himself and wants to get the
whole family wallowing into codependency. It's a real line.
The difficulty of this case is to make interventions and pull
out before you get caught in the triangle. Part of the problem,
Donna [the working counselor], is that you're too gentle with
them. Don't let him [the IP] get away with that AA bull. You
need to be more directive and make firm, conclusive statements. You might want to take a look at Haley's book [*Problem-Solving Therapy*] . . . the stuff about giving directives and
triangulation.

Haley's book is frequently referenced by Westsiders as they
discuss the general framework and assumptions that guide their
work. They also use it as a moral authority, to suggest how to
think about particular presenting problems and their underlying
sources, or to warn those who deviate from local understandings
that "Haley doesn't see it that way." The suggestions and cautions may refer to precise passages, or even particular arguments
outlined in the book, but mainly convey an overall sense that the
book lays down local therapeutic law. The staff has made *Problem-Solving Therapy* a legitimizing voice of their institution, conjured up time and again to designate authority as the fundamental reality of domestic life.

SIGNS OF AUTHORITY

The most common signs of authority observed in counseling
include the seating arrangement of family members, individual
members' postures, and members' relative verbalization. Signs
may be combined with more unusual indicators, such as the interpretation of overdomination through the posture and bodily size
of a member of the household or the reading of authority in the
age differences of those in particular seating arrangements. Indeed, a sign may be considered exceptional in a certain case, warranting that which it is an exception to as a normal rule for discerning authority.

Seating Arrangement

The seating arrangement of family members observed in videotaped counseling sessions is a regular point of discussion in
group soups. Consultants attempt to decipher the social relations
of the home as a basis for providing counselors with strategies
for effective intervention.

Before a tape is run, Keith Borelli, the counseling intern, introduces a case for which Tammy Horton, a regular counselor, did
the intake. Dick Billings, a former Westside counselor, is the consultant. All regular counselors are present. Borelli begins:

> Tammy did the intake on this guy [the IP]. She said that he
> paced all the time and got all excited. Well, he *was* very angry.
> [Borelli describes his own experience with the IP] He's 25
> and she's [wife] 38.

Loud groans are heard around the room. The counselors comment disparagingly on the spouses' reversed age order. One of
the counselors, Gary Nelson, remarks loudly, "He's a full 13 years
younger than she is!" to which Kelly Seever, another counselor,
adds, "He's just a baby!" Prior to a discussion of seating, an animated conversation develops, dwelling on the mother-and-child
metaphor. The IP is the helpless young boy whose every move is
guided, even dominated, by an overbearing mother. The wife, in
turn, is a maternal figure of authority who accepts no insolence
from any of her children, demanding respect and firm allegiance.
One counselor surmises that the wife is a strong, even hard, woman.
The metaphor suggests a dysfunctional relationship, a situation
that Nancy Cantor, another counselor, summarily guesses "must
be real bad."

Borelli continues with a brief description of the presenting
problem:

> They're court-ordered for spouse battery. He's [the husband]
> on drugs. He says the drugs are not the problem; it's the
> marriage. She [the wife] says drugs *are* the problem. From
> what I can figure, they both beat each other up. He's got into
> hitting her a couple of times. Says it's accidental. She gets

him riled up and one thing leads to another. She's laid into him too, but he's the only one who gets charged with battery. She's never been arrested for battery. [Elaborates] He called me a half hour before the [counseling] session and asked me not to bring up the older daughter because he said he'd get angry and walk out. He's got a real power thing with the older daughter. There are a bunch of her kids in the house. The older daughter is 21.

Lengthy discussion follows about the small age difference between the older daughter and her stepfather, especially as it relates to what Borelli has called the "power thing." The wife and older daughter's ages, in comparison to the IP's, suggests to all that being an effective father under the circumstances is difficult at best, which begins to explain the IP's explosiveness and his attempt to manage it through drugs. As Cantor remarks, "You can see why he explodes and escapes; none of them listens to him."

Dick Billings, the consultant, asks Borelli to play the tape of a counseling session with the family, so that, "We can see the dynamics and power thing," picking up on Borelli's usage. The tape starts with the IP and other family members walking into the counseling room. As family members begin to take their seats, Billings points to the monitor and tells the counselors to watch where everyone sits:

Now let's see where they decide to sit themselves down. Maybe we can pick up some of the relations there. [Asks Borelli to repeat the spouses' age difference] Let's see if Mom takes the power seat. [Asks Borelli to stop the tape momentarily] Where do you think she'll sit?

A lengthy exchange takes place about the relation between domestic authority and the position of the chairs in the counseling room. Various opinions are offered, with little consensus. Some see the so-called power seat in the middle; others guess that Mom's authority will lead her to take the seat closest to the counselor, which is the end chair at the left on the screen. Despite the lack of consensus, the rule that domestic authority can be read from seating arrangement encourages all to form hypotheses about who will seat themselves where in the next few moments.

The tape runs on. The IP takes the seat at the left on the screen, closest to the counselor. His wife sits in the middle chair, with the oldest daughter seated between the wife and the IP. Another, younger daughter is seated at the right with an unidentified young boy, whom the counselors later learn is the oldest daughter's son. Hypotheses are forgotten for the time being, as those gathered for group soup watch and listen to the proceedings. Billings leans over, lowers the sound, and asks if anyone notices the oldest daughter's position. Borelli blurts, "Yeah, she's sitting between Chuck [the IP] and Rosie [the IP's wife]!" Billings responds didactically:

> That's right. Good. That's what we'd expect if the daughter is joining Mom against Chuck. It's a classic arrangement. Mom's at the center. The henpecked husband is at the end and the daughter who is old enough to be his wife, but isn't even his daughter, makes sure that she takes her place in the power structure.

The hypothesis that Mom will take the "power seat" closest to the counselor is forgotten. The focus of attention now is on the daughter and what her particular seating location tells about the IP's relation with his wife. As the staff continue to observe and point to the monitor, their references elaborate the domestic structure seemingly apparent immediately in front of them. Indeed, when Gary Nelson suggests that both the IP and his wife are sitting in power seats and thereby vying for authority, hinting that the daughter might not really have that much to do with what is going on at home, Nancy Cantor, also pointing to the screen, objects:

> Oh, come on, Gary. Look at them. Just look. [Pointing] We all know what's going on. You can see what's happening. The guy [IP] is caught in a vise. It's written all over the daughter's face. Look how she's sitting there. She's just right in there next to Mom and doesn't want Chuck to get any closer. She's protecting Mom and Mom knows that she can get the daughter

to keep him at bay, right? You can see, too, how the age thing
is coming into play. Mom's the oldest and she's got the floor.

The last comment ties age discrepancy to seating arrangement,
further warranting Borelli and Cantor's reading.

The significance of these comments and judgments is not who
is right or wrong, nor whether the ordinary reasoning of the
proceedings is formally logical. What is important in the context
of the practical discernment of domestic authority is that a rule
of mundane assignment is being followed, one characteristic of
Westside House. Namely, seating arrangement is used as a sign
for something too abstract to be directly perceived. In this case,
it is combined with age discrepancy to further warrant the meaning assigned to the social order of the home, which in turn serves
as a basis for understanding the battery and substance abuse, the
presenting problems.

At this point, another sign comes into play—verbosity—but in
this case is interpreted as exceptional because of what verbosity
is "covering up." Borelli complains that the session was very
tough on him because the IP was so talkative, ordinarily a sign
of authority:

> The IP—Chuck—says he's off crack but that he needs his
> reefer to handle the situation or he'd blow up, or so he says.
> [The drug problem is discussed] This was a tough session
> because it wasn't without some intimidation. I couldn't for
> the life of me see them [married] as a couple. It was very hard
> for me. He gets all riled up and stands up and starts talking
> a mile a minute. You can't get a word in edgewise. I often feel
> like he's completely in control of the interview. He's a motor
> mouth. I want to show a portion of the tape, not for the
> content, but I'd like you to see the process here. This is at the
> end of the tape.

The tape is played and all watch. Reddick asks, "Does she [the
wife] talk at all?" Borelli answers:

> No. The session was all like that. He talks all the time and he
> even cut me off and keeps making the same point over and
> over. You feel like you're losing control sometimes. It's hard

because all that talking is his way of letting off steam. It's covering up what's really going on at home. She [wife] rules the roost, not him [IP]. She's, like, letting him shoot his mouth off because it doesn't matter and she knows, I think, that he's just making a fool of himself. She just lets him go on and on.

Borelli casually theorizes about the place of signs such as verbosity and seating arrangement in the interpretation of the case. This prompts Tammy Horton, who did the intake on the family, to recall the seating arrangement at the initial interview, together with other evidence of domestic authority:

When I think back to the intake, I could swear those two [husband and wife] sat next to each other. I'm awfully sure of that. I remember thinking that they might be pretty close, but that they fought all the time. But, now, I agree with Keith . . . it doesn't really show the conflict and distance in the family. I remember when they walked out of the building, they really walked far apart when they went to the parking lot . . . like she was way ahead of him . . . like she was leaving him behind or something.

Here, the seating arrangement of the couple at intake is treated as exceptional to its own rule. Horton reports that, in retrospect, she was seeing the family's actual domestic authority in the way the couple departed from the building.

At the consultant's request, Horton goes into telling detail about the couple's relations during intake. The consultant wants to compare the sessions. Horton's remarks about alternate signs of authority again show the importance of exceptions, in this case a near exception, for the rule-like quality of signs.

Dick [consultant], I wouldn't say that they were all that close when they were in the office. Yeah, they were seated right next to each other. But you should have been there. I wish I could show you. I didn't tape it because I didn't get a chance to set it up. Like they just sat there and she was turned away from him most of the time. I mean she really didn't have much to do with him. He just talked a mile a minute, but you

could see that he was kinda just hopping around her like a
little dog. You could just see it. It was written all over her face
and the way she sat: [feigning the wife's thoughts] "He's
nothing and I'm the Queen of Sheba." That's why the guy's
got problems.

Seating arrangement also affects the counselor's own sense of
authority in therapeutic relation to the family. As Borelli complained, because the IP paced so much and talked incessantly,
Borelli felt he was losing control of the treatment process. Counselors not only read domestic authority in clients' seating arrangement, but also interpret their own management skills and sense
of control accordingly. As all staff members advise, it is important
for the counselor to sit in a "power chair," a location that commands attention. Typically, this is the chair placed backward to
the camera, toward which a facing semicircle of chairs is turned.

Posture

The client's posture is another important sign of domestic authority. Tammy Horton's designation of the wife's "looking away"
during Horton's intake interview with Borelli's client is suggestive. The scrutiny of posture can be very detailed.
    Leila Korson, a counseling intern who is a former schoolteacher,
presents the Dean family in a group soup. There is no consultant
present. Korson has been assigned the case, which involves truancy and repeated classroom disruption, on the assumption that
her experience as a schoolteacher will stand her in good stead in
dealing with the presenting problems. Korson begins:

The family situation, I think, is pretty sensitive. Mom has just
been through a divorce. She not only was dealing with Dad's
alcoholism, but she discovers that he's gay. What a blow.
[Discusses the delicacy of the case] There's a 16-year-old
daughter and twin brothers, Johnny and Jonathan, who are 13.
[Counselors are amused by the twins' names] The boys skip
out [from school] all the time and there's suspected involvement in drugs and they raise a lot of hell in school.

The twins' presenting problems are described at length. The counselors ask how a teacher handles such a situation and Korson answers from her own experience.

Korson plays a videotape of a portion of a session with the family.
All watch attentively. The sound soon is lowered and an exchange
between Korson and counselor Kelly Seever quickly follows, pinpointing domestic order.

KORSON: The father lives down the street from the mother and the
kids visit him a lot. As I said, he's an alcoholic—
SEEVER: And he's gay.
KORSON: It's very complicated because they're divorced and living separately, but the kids go over to his house and I
know she [the mother] is in regular contact with him.
She's got to be anyway, because of the kids. But I think
she really gives off mixed messages . . . like there's no
family there, but then she keeps relating to the father.
SEEVER: In other words, there's no family to speak of, but if you
put the two [husband and wife] together, they look like
a family . . . but underneath there's a lot of emptiness and
a lot of times that doesn't add up to much?
KORSON: Well, that could be.

As the discussion unfolds, all agree that Korson is doing satis-
factorily. Questions such as "What's happening in the father's
home?" and "How're the kids dealing with the separation?"
make it evident that the social order of the household or households
is an important ingredient of the problems under consideration.
Several counselors return to Seever's conjecture about what the
family is like "underneath" and consider alternate "hypotheses,"
using that term to refer to the authority structure of the home (or
homes) as it might affect the twins' difficulties at school. Korson
recalls but does not elaborate on another hypothesis, offered by
Craig Kish, a counselor no longer on the staff, who originally had
been assigned the case.

KORSON: Craig's hypothesis I wasn't too sure about. I don't really
know about that. I think my hypothesis is that what's going
on is that Mom needs the kids at home and this [the
separation] is distracting her from facing her own issues.

SEEVER: What's your sense, Leila? Is Mom depressed?
KORSON: I think she is. She sees that she can't control her own life
            . . . in the past she did take control.

More hypotheses are presented. All focus on the problem of control in the face of the competing authority of separate households.

KORSON: You can see why the boys are constantly in trouble. Mom
            doesn't want Dad around but she still talks and thinks
            like he's the Daddy. So she gets all wishy-washy and acts
            like he's supposed to be the twins' role model. But then
            she acts like he doesn't exist. What I think is that those
            boys have just filled in the gap on their own. Like, they're
            only 13 and they're running their own lives. When you're
            still in school, that just don't cut the mustard. There are
            rules and, in this case, the home is not there to tune them
            in consistently.
NELSON: Well, let's see more of it [the tape]. We're all just second-
            guessing this thing right now.

Leila reaches over to the monitor and turns up the volume. The tape had been running silently.

KORSON: [Pointing to the screen] This is just joining. I already had
            talked to the mother and now what I'm doing . . . [Pause]
            I'm talking with the boys here. Like I said, they're twins:
            Johnny and Jonathan.

All listen to Korson on tape as she asks the boys what it's like growing up as twins. Korson reports that some of the earlier taped conversation with the twins had been one-sided, with Korson asking questions, the twins nodding, and Korson filling in for them. Nelson asks Korson to put the videotape on pause and to point to who is who on the screen. As Korson does so, she comments on the seating arrangement, highlighting posture as a sign of the "problem in this home."

KORSON: This one [Johnny] was kinda quiet at first. I couldn't get
            him to say anything. Later in the session, he moved over
            here [points to his current seating position] and then he

started to talk more, like he was the boss around home. I think he's the dominant one [twin]. Look at the way he's sitting. He's like that all the time, even when he was sitting over here [points to a seat to the right, out of camera range].

CANTOR: Now he's in the power seat and he feels more comfortable . . . more like himself.

HORTON: Yeah, like he feels at home.

REDDICK: The mother, to me, is giving mixed messages to the boys about living at home and going to the father. She tells them if they don't behave, they can just get out of the house and go to their father. Then she tells them that they better behave or they'll turn out just like him.

HORTON: [Pointing to the screen] Yeah, . . . and just look at that kid [Johnny]. Look at how he sits at the edge of his chair . . . like he's going to jump all over Mom if she dares to cross him. Just look at him! It's written all over him. That look he's giving her. My God, it's just telling her [mother] that he's in charge. And he knows it. If she crosses him, he'll just march over to Dad and live there.

CANTOR: And would you look at the other one [twin]. He's watching his brother real close-like, waiting to see what to do. And would ya look at Mom! [All watch the screen for a few seconds] Look at how she looks down at the floor all the time, like she's being stepped on when Johnny gets going. You can see what a bad scene it is. That's not a very healthy home. No wonder those boys are delinquent.

As the review winds down, posture becomes focal. Although an altered seating arrangement is seen as indicative of Johnny's real authority in the mother's household, all soon figure that his posture is more significant. Staffers point to the video screen as if they witness domestic order before their very eyes. With comments such as "Look at Mom," "Just look at him," and "That's not a very healthy home," the speakers sound as if they are literally observing the household's social order. Mundane signs tell of much more than bodily positioning. They concretely reference the abstract, in this case, "not a very healthy home," which, in turn, is used to explain the twins' misconduct in school.

It is amazing how detailed attention to posture can be in this regard. For example, in one group soup, as counselors discuss and debate at length the domestic basis of a daughter's school truancy and possible sexual activeness, taking great care to examine the father's appearance on videotape, seated posture, leg position, and hand motion come to represent dominance. We enter the proceedings as counselor Tammy Horton tells those gathered that the father does not take no for an answer. The father is rarely at home, however. The complication in domestic authority is that, although formally the father correctly is in charge, much of the daily decision making in the home occurs in his absence.

HORTON: The mother has a seventh-grade education and works as a maid and she's very insecure. The father's very active. He drives a truck. Neither of them is at home very much because they're both working. He's more verbal than the mother.

Horton continues to describe family members' backgrounds and in the process points out each member on the video screen. A 21-year-old son is not present.

HORTON: [Pointing to the screen] This daughter . . . she's the IP . . . she can't seem to be able to get out of the sixth grade.

SEEVER: How many times did you say she flunked?

HORTON: Three times.

CANTOR: They'll have to give her a social promotion soon.

HORTON: Probably. I just wish Dad would straighten her out. She seems to really take a shine to him. But it's like, well, like he doesn't exist. [Elaborates the father's practical ineffectiveness in daily life at home because of his continued absence]

BORELLI: Will you just look at Dad! I wouldn't say he's ineffective!

NELSON: He looks like a pretty effective guy to me. See the way he's sitting. This is the kind of guy that tells you how to think and feel. I'd bet the kids won't even fart until Dad says it's okay.

BORELLI: I wouldn't say anything if I had someone sitting back like that. He looks pretty intimidating to me. If I was one of his kids, I'd make sure . . . like I'd *ask* if I could stay out later or like even if I could use my sister's bike.

All turn to Borelli as he imitates the father's posture. Borelli leans back slightly in his chair with both feet planted squarely on the floor and puffs out his chest.

BORELLI: Look, guys, if you had Dad sitting around like this . . . and look at the size of him . . . he must weigh 200 pounds. You get a father that size who sits around like this and, if you give him lip, he's ready to get right up out of that chair and clip you. Whack! I wouldn't say a damned thing when he's around, man.

HORTON: [Interrupting] Gary and Keith . . . you guys aren't listening. I can see what you're saying, but . . . [pointing to the monitor] Dad's there . . . I mean he's *really* there. I see him, too, you know. He's a very big and physically dominating man. Just look at the size of that hand and look at the forceful way he waves it around when he's talking. That's not a weak man. I wish more of the Dads we see were like him. The problem is that he's just not around much. At least that's what I seem to be finding. [Turns to Nelson] So what's it matter if he's the rooster?

SEEVER: If he's never around the henhouse . . .

CANTOR: Yeah, the chickies go wild. [All laugh]

There's a momentary, lighthearted battle of wits between the male and female counselors. The males play on the theme of the dominant rooster and elaborate the barnyard benefits of a clear and effective pecking order, especially as it controls the enduring delinquent tendencies of the young. The females fully agree, but play up the theme of intact, but inoperative dominance. The themes and verbal play center on the working, commonplace evidence of the moment: the posture and posturing of the father apparent on the video screen. All agree that he shows clear signs of being a firm decision maker, what with his feet squarely planted on the floor and his imperious, self-assured manner. Still, the counselors' banter, although amused and amusing, is not merely a game, for its language, references, and concrete denotations harken a reality which, except for its claimed complications, might contain a child's poor school performance and premature sexual activity.

Verbalization

Another important sign of domestic authority is verbalization. In general, the rule at Westside is that the sheer amount of talk exhibited by a member of the household is a sign of his or her authority. The more talking, the greater the authority of the speaker. Like other rules for perceiving authority, instances of extensive talking may be treated as exceptional, as seen earlier in Keith's presentation of a court-ordered spouse battery case. In that case, the so-called motor mouth phenomenon signaled the IP's uncontrolled response to domestic repression.

Select qualities of talk further signal domestic authority, such as talkativeness that interrupts others. Consider a consultant and counselors' responses in a group supervision to counseling intern Roger Savage's description of the relative lack of power of the two parents of an adolescent female IP named Kim, who is a repeat runaway and supposed to be disrespectful. Following a lengthy description of the presenting problem, both in relation to the school and the home, Savage points to the video screen as he names each member of the family who participated in the taped counseling session about to be reviewed. The consultant, Al Borba, targets Savage's concern over the IP's disrespectfulness and relates it to the parents' participation in the session.

SAVAGE: [Pointing to Kim] This is the original IP. [Pause] But they're all really IPs. That girl [Kim] really is the most problem because she talks so much and is so disrespectful in the session.

BORBA: I don't know what you mean, Roger. Would you show us what sort of thing Kim does that makes her so disrespectful? I think it's important, at this point, that we actually see what she is doing to affect the family dynamic the way she does.

Savage rewinds the tape a bit until he locates a spot illustrating Kim's disrespect.

SAVAGE: Here it is. Now watch what she [Kim] does when Mom tries to explain how she [Mom] feels when Kim doesn't come home for 2 or 3 days at a time.

The tape shows Mom talking at some length, with considerable emotion, about her worrying when Kim leaves home without notice, giving no clues to her whereabouts.

MOM: [Looking at Kim with tears in her eyes] You wouldn't believe how it makes me feel. I get all panicky in my stomach and my mind races all over the place.... [Turns to Savage] You know how you start imagining the worst, like she was hit by a car or was abducted or something. I see her ... like she's helpless somewhere and I can see her in my mind but I can't help her because I have no idea where she is and ...

KIM: [Interrupting her mother] Oh, come on, Mom. Let's not get dramatic. You're really embarrassing. You're so-o-o-o embarrassing. [Turns to Savage] I just can't look at her when she's like this.

MOM: [Turns to Kim sobbing] Oh, Kim. You don't know how it feels. [Pause] I just can't say anything right now. I'm numb when you say things like that.

Several counselors belittle the mother's emotionality, considering it a poor substitute for firmness. Savage stops the tape.

SAVAGE: Now you see what I mean. That girl made me so mad. She was like that through the whole session. She kept interrupting everyone, even me. It's like she never lets anyone, especially Mom, have a say about anything. Like she'd be real sarcastic-like when I'd tell her to keep quiet for a while and let her parents have a turn and explain how they see the situation.

BORBA: We might want to pick apart what's happening here. What I see is a dynamic ... a power thing ... that's not only affecting the family but is seeping out into the counseling session and even affecting how you're [Savage] dealing with them all. That girl [Kim] clearly has the upper hand in the family. Dad says nothing at all. That's not a good sign. He's probably overwhelmed by the go-rounds between Mom and Kim. The two of them dominate everyone with the power-guilt trips they're pulling on each other and the family. Mom worries and feels guilty because she's embarrassing Kim. Kim's gone to her

> [Mom's] head and Kim acts like she's the head [of the family]. You can see the power she has in that family . . . like jumping in there all the time no matter who's talking . . . even you [Savage]. I know how it feels, believe me. As a counselor, you like to be on top . . . feel like you have things under control. That's what makes for a good session. [Elaborates] But in this case, no one ever gets to talk without Kim snapping her gums, out of control. It's a problem.

SAVAGE: Yeah, and Dad responds just like he'd read Jay Haley's book. The father's kind of slow. He doesn't say much and when he does, it comes out real slow . . . like he knows he's going to be interrupted at any time. I think he's mostly in the background at home.

As group soup continues, the nature of talkativeness as a sign of domestic order is elaborated upon. In the preceding extract, Kim's talkativeness not only is read to represent her domestic authority, but others' relative silence, even hesitance to express themselves, underscores the interpretation. The father is meekly in the background, showing evidence of lacking authority in the home, an interpretation confirmed by his wariness about offering any opinion. Mom responds emotionally to her daughter's accusations of embarrassment, resigning herself to momentarily saying nothing further, her emotionality disparaged as a sign of weakness.

Equally significant are Kim's repeated interruptions. Not only does Kim talk more than she should, but she cuts off those who attempt to enter into the proceedings. This exasperates Savage, who, as if natively informed by conversation analysts' turn-taking rule (Heritage, 1984; Sudnow, 1972), resents the unacceptable power signaled by these interruptions. The turn-taking rule is democratic, with participants in conversation sharing equally in the sequencing of the exchange. Interruptions signal an infringement on equality. In the context of Westside's image of the domestic order, it is parents, not children, who should be doing the interrupting and affirming functional inequality. In Kim's case, an institutionally inappropriate member of the family interrupts and thereby informs the counselors and consultant that things are out of control because something is wrong with the social order of the home. In the hierarchy of the counseling session, the counselor should be most privileged in this regard. Savage is angry because the interruptions suggest that matters may have gotten out of control in the counseling session itself.

The significance of verbalization extends to the form of utterances. There is a difference between making statements and asking questions, with statements signaling strength and questions weakness. In the following extract from a group soup, note how the form of utterance eventually said to typify a mother serves to explain how the home figures in the presenting problem. Counselor Nancy Cantor already has described the IP, a teenaged girl named Nina, who, like Kim, is a runaway. In Nina's case, drug involvement is also suspected. At one point in the review of a taped counseling session with Nina and her mother, consultant Dick Billings advises Cantor to go slower in her intervention because Billings does not believe Cantor yet knows who is in control at home.

> BILLINGS: I think you're moving too quick, Nancy, leading to consequences before you know if Mom has any control. Do we really know what the hierarchy is here? I think we need more data to see what we're working with before you can move on to consequences. I'd do a bit more tracking to explore the background and the structure of this family. We don't really know that much about Mom's control.
>
> CANTOR: What makes you think that, Dick? How do you know it isn't there?
>
> BILLINGS: Because of what she [Mom] says. . . . Listen to the tape.

The tape is played for a few minutes. Billings attempts to illustrate his point.

> BILLINGS: See what I mean. You really get the impression in this case that Mom may not be on top. But we're not sure because . . . is it Nina? . . . doesn't say very much. Like when Mom says, "Well, what do you want to do, Nina?" And later on, remember when you [Cantor] asked the both of them if they would like to get involved in more drug education,

again Mom doesn't answer, but turns to Nina and asks her what she wants to do. Mom doesn't ever seem to have any opinions of her own. She's always asking her daughter for the answers. You don't see daughter doing that.

SEEVER: She hardly says a word! She just has her eyes glued to the floor. Mom's trying her best and that little brat ignores her.

BILLINGS: Let's not jump ahead too fast on this one. We may be seeing a lot of subtle control here. The daughter's not just a brat. She knows how to keep Mom guessing and asking and that, my friends, is power. Did you notice that whenever the daughter does say something, it's a flat statement. Like she's really asserting herself. She's telling her mother the way it is. And guess what? Mom just responds by asking Nina questions like "Is that what you really want, Nina?" and "Do you think we can do that, Nina?"

NELSON: Don't I know the type! I've got one of those. She never can say anything to her old man [husband] or the kids without asking a question. Christ! You'd think that she had to grovel on the ground to say anything to the oldest daughter. They've all got her cowed, especially the oldest daughter.

CANTOR: [Turning back to her own case] I can see how Nina's pulling the same thing on Mom. She's [Mom] a type all right. They can be a little sickening. They go around asking questions and because they never demand anything from anyone, they're not responsible for what happens. You know, kinda like innocent bystanders . . .

SEEVER: And martyrs. Mom puts herself on the defensive all the time and acts like she's been hurt whenever the daughter turns on her. Right?

CANTOR: You got it.

BILLINGS: So maybe what we're seeing here is that Mom really doesn't have that much control. It's like she plans to be out of control and tries to make the daughter pay for it. But the daughter just plays along and gets her way. You can just see how it all works out. That relationship is built for trouble. The daughter knows she can get away with murder and that all Mom will say is, "Is that okay with you, Nina?" So Nina is away and druggin' at a moment's notice.

REDDICK: Hah! At no notice!

Although declarative utterances signal greater domestic power than interrogative ones, again there are exceptions to the rule. Reflecting common beliefs about ethnic and racial differences in family structure, Westsiders' readings of the typical parental interactions of, say, black or traditional Italian homes, can reverse the inferences otherwise drawn from white or nontraditional families. For example, Tammy Horton's presentation in the group soup of an Italian family's difficulties with two sons' persistent use of crack shows evidence of a reverse reading of the parents' relative domestic power. Playing the videotape of a session with family members, Horton asks the counselors, interns, and the consultant to carefully watch the mother and father talk about their children.

HORTON: Now, listen to those two [the parents]. The boys don't say very much until later on. But listen to Mama and Papa. [Pause for watching] See how Papa does all the talking. Mama asks the questions and Papa states the facts. To me, there's something wrong here. In traditional Italian families, Mama deals with the kids and takes care of the home front. She does the talking and Papa sits back. But that doesn't mean he's just listening. He's always listening to make sure whatever is said matches up with what he thinks should be happening. And they all know it! He just lets them all talk, but they know he's keeping an eye on things.

NELSON: So what you're saying is that it just *sounds* like he's [Papa] on top but that in the Italian family it's supposed to show up the other way around, especially when you're dealing with the home and the kids?

HORTON: Sure do. And that tells me that something is basically wrong here. It just doesn't jibe. I'm guessing that Papa is pretty henpecked and is talking and talking to no effect. What he's really telling us is that he's complaining that he has no control over his wife or his sons and that's why the boys are out of control.

Signs of domestic authority in relation to the black family further complicate readings of interaction, presenting other exceptions to the verbalization rule. Rightly or wrongly, it is believed that some black families, especially impoverished ones, effectively run on a principle of matriarchy. They are female headed and female dominated. As such, the father who responds passively in a counseling session, deferring to his more active spouse in presenting home life and its troubles, may be considered typical and normal. In contrast to the image, say, of the effective Italian family, it does not mean that the black father silently rules the household. Rather, the conduct conveys what everyone is supposed to know, namely, that the mother (or grandmother) in black families fully dominates domestic life. A belief about the maternal authority structure of poor black families informs Westsiders that troubles are "normal" for this social grouping, although individual black families are counseled with as much care and concern as others are.

Overdomination

Certain presenting problems are thought to stem from exaggerated forms of otherwise functional domestic hierarchies. Child abuse and wife battery are foremost among them. In such cases, staff members routinely scrutinize the parents', especially the father's, physical bearing in search of underlying domestic sources. Although, in general, the preferred hierarchy of the home has the father and mother at the top and the children lower, with no crosscutting lines of authority, the father who stands too far above the others and forcefully takes advantage of his position, is considered overdominant and, at worst, abusive.

Suspected cases draw on the institutionally customary set of signs —seating arrangement, posture, and verbalization. The understanding is that an authoritative parent rules by general domestic consensus, not force, being respected for carrying out his or her responsibility judiciously. Exceptions aside, the mother who sits confidently in a so-called power chair during a counseling session is read as firmly in authority. It is interesting to note that the father who does the same risks being categorized as overdominant. The assumption is that since the families seen at Westside are troubled, with associated underlying domestic disorder, a father who firmly signals authority in the context of a counseling session must in some way be taking advantage of his position to the detriment of others in the household. Of course, as a rule, the father who does not signal authority of any kind is then evidently part of the underlying problem.

Signs of overdomination can be especially diffuse in cases of abuse, in which attempts are made to trace the pathological subtleties of the authority otherwise visually apparent in bearing. Consider, for example, the discussion of a father's character in the group soup of a suspected case of child sexual abuse. Following a discussion of the father's forceful physical bearing, counselor Kelly Seever remarks that the father is an "odd" man. Interns Sara Brighton, Keith Borelli, and others question this statement, leading to a brief debate and exchange with consultant Al Borba about the difficulty of identifying child abuse.

> SEEVER: He's an odd man. He's not very likeable.
> REDDICK: Yes, he's a very strange man.
> BRIGHTON: What's strange about him?
> REDDICK: Yeah, I hate to say this, but he's so strange that I can see he's the kind of man who could easily be sexually abusive.

Consultant Al Borba walks into the room, sits down, and listens to the proceedings. There's a lengthy discussion of whether Westside House should determine child abuse cases. The father's supposed strangeness is reconsidered.

> BRIGHTON: What's strange about him?
> REDDICK: The way he says things. [Gestures with her hands as if she's talking without expression] He's a sociopath. He could be telling you things straight but underneath there's no sense that you're getting any of the truth.
> BORELLI: Is there a history of violence?
> SEEVER: No, but the way he looks at you and he speaks . . . you know he's capable. But I didn't call the school counselor because she [the supposedly abused daughter] didn't look frightened of him [her father].

Westside's institutional responsibility in identifying child abuse is discussed further. Again, the question of the father's strangeness arises.

CANTOR: Kelly thinks there's something weird about the guy, like the guy could coldly take advantage of his strength.

HORTON: Not all weirdos are child molesters. I mean, we all know that child molesters are weirdos, but maybe this isn't molestation. Do we know that?

SEEVER: Look, . . . he says he's a loner. He doesn't want anyone in his house. He says he doesn't have any close friends . . . although we did talk about some of his friends.

REDDICK: I just know there is something about this man, but I don't know if it's child molestation. [Elaborates] But my question is, is the interview really complete without seeing the daughter by herself? Al, do you have any input on this?

BORBA: I don't think I have enough of a handle on the details of the case to say. I'm inclined to say that we should try to keep as many members of the family involved in counseling. But, then, is the agency [Westside] really set up for this? The only ones who are really trained to assess this are the child well-being monitoring people. They've got doctors and specialists. The problem, I guess, is that we don't really know if it's child abuse, do we? [Pause] I mean, if it is and that's established already, then you're asking the right questions and looking in the right direction. But is it?

The investigation of suspected child abuse is not officially Westside's responsibility. However, staff members do counsel families referred to Westside whose problems have been determined to include the abuse of children or others. The extract is important because it implies that, in such cases, staff understands that overdomination, in effect, turns from sheer power into a character flaw. Although some staff members question the extended personal attributes assigned to this particular father in support of a generalized pathological profile because it is not clear that this is a case of child abuse, it is evident that there would be little or no objection to such interpretations in a clear-cut case. Horton's comments at one point are telling in this regard. She questions

whether all so-called weirdos are molesters, but she takes for granted that all molesters are weirdos, that, indeed, all staff members
also do, implying that the diffuse character traits of overdomination would be an important concern in cases of molestation. The
consultant's comment, at the very end of the extract, confirms
this view. He remarks that if this were a clearcut case, the counselors are asking the right questions and properly considering
how the father's character enters into the problem. The questions
and brief debate inform us of the rule commonly expected to apply,
as if to say that in cases clearly presenting domestic abuse, look
beyond bearing to the "weird" abuse of power for an explanation.

FOUR

Constructing the System

At Westside House, disorder refers to domestic authority gone
awry, but it is a broader system of control in the home that counselors and consultants engage in their work with clients, family members, and significant others. The system is more or less effectively
overned by parents or substitute bearers of authority such as grandparents or other relatives. Yet, the system is more than just governance: It is the related domestic effects of governance or malgovern-
ance. In a word, it is the nation, not just the king or queen or the
royal house that staffers behold as they manage a counseling
session, review a videotape in group soup, or watch sessions in
progress from an adjacent room. The actual household, of course,
is not brought into counselors' offices. Videotapes do not show
the physical environs of houses or other living arrangements.
Live soups do not immediately reveal the daily domestic schedules and related rhythms of the home. But the therapeutic encounters and reviews are believed to reveal the home's system of
social relations, including the contributing actions of those who
conduct daily life within the home, blood kin, in-laws, or live-ins.

THE LANGUAGE OF THE SYSTEM

Westsiders use the language of the system to reference the collective conduct of those they see and hear in treatment. This language

does not reference individuals, but participants in home life. When a consultant asks a counselor "What's going on at home?" the question refers to a distinct order of social relations; not particular family members or other individual occupants of households, but the interpersonal domestic connections and networks and their larger dynamic.

Consultant Al Borba's response in a group soup to counselor Nancy Cantor's report of difficulty in therapy with a teenaged boy's drug abuse shows how words distinguish the larger reality understood to be paramount. Cantor has presented background information on the Moynihan family. For the last 5 years, the father has been unemployed. Repeated bouts of heavy drinking and emergency hospitalizations have made it difficult for him to hold a job. The father apparently hallucinates and also accuses his wife of being unfaithful, even of sleeping with their teenaged son. Before Cantor details her problem with the son, an exchange tellingly distinguishes the system.

> BORBA: Wait a minute. We're getting a lot on Dad here. So the old man's a boozer and . . . did you say he's been trying to dry out?
>
> CANTOR: Well, I'm not sure about that, Al. I think his wife mentioned that he'd been hospitalized several times because he went into an alcoholic coma or something like that. I'm pretty sure about that. He [husband] came in the last time [to a counseling session] and he sounded pretty sober. [Describes the husband's demeanor and conduct] The guy's real rational-like and he's really got a vocabulary. Does he have a vocabulary! I mean, he uses words like I never heard before.
>
> BORBA: Well, okay. So who else are we talking about here?
>
> CANTOR: Mom comes regularly. And there's a 22-year-old daughter that lives at home. There's a younger daughter, too. They [parents] bring her along. She's 10. The IP is 17 and is heavily into crack and other drugs. [Elaborates] I think he's selling, too, but I'm not sure. He's been busted for having drugs in his possession . . . they [the police] found the stuff under the seat of his car when he was popped for speeding. Dad doesn't say too much most of the time. But when he does . . . well, it's like he sorta wakes up all

of a sudden and . . . like he's reciting from a book. It's real bizarre.

BORBA: I thought you said you were having trouble with the boy. What's his name?

CANTOR: David. Dad's David too. They usually call the son Buddy. Don't ask me why. The kid's anything but a buddy to his father, the way the two go after each other. Dad's something else. I don't know what motivates that man. I just wish I could go into their heads sometimes and see what makes them tick, so I could get to the bottom of things. Dad's really got them all going. . . .

BORBA: Nancy, Nancy. Let's talk a minute. [Pause] Let's keep one thing up front here. What you're getting [in counseling] is not some deep emotional stuff or the dad's innermost thoughts working themselves out. What you're seeing is a system. [Elaborates] Do you really think that all that "going after each other," as you say, is the old man just being himself? [Pause] No ma'am! The son's got as much to do with this as Dad does. It's Dave-on-Dave! [All laugh] The family system's working itself out, with all its spiraling subsystems adding fuel to the fire. You're *not* seeing just Dad here. I really wouldn't know what it would mean, anyway, to see "just Dad." You can't place blame like that.

Several counselors discuss the incomprehensibility of the idea of the isolated individual. Donna Reddick attempts to summarize.

REDDICK: I think what we're all saying is that, like Al said, what we're seeing in therapy is the home. Like it's not just Dad or just Buddy. [Whispering] Even if we think that Dad or Buddy is really an SOB deep down inside.

BORBA: Well, we all have our personal opinions. That's natural. You can't help what you feel. I don't know of any counselor who doesn't. Hey, look, . . . take a good look some time at what you've done in a session. I mean, when you review a tape, what are you seeing? [Turns to Cantor] When we review the tape of the last session you did with this family, what are we going to see?

CANTOR: We're going to see what's going on in that family, of course. Like the whole ball of wax. I know, I know. [Pause] You

know, it's just really neat how, even when you think that
one of them's trying to hide something or trying to fake
it, that when they're together, they just can't help themselves. If you can get them going, you can see it all right
there. It gets scary sometimes, because they just start up
and get going and get going and . . .

Two senses of the reality at hand have emerged. One is that there
are distinct personalities: Dad, Mom, younger Dave, and the daughters. At one point, Cantor dwells on the bizarreness of Dad's behavior, especially on his eloquent use of words and sporadic intelli-
gibility. She wants to "get into their heads" to see what makes
each family member tick. In another sense, there is something separate and distinct, the system of which these personalities are a part.
Just as the counselors themselves frequently caution each other,
Borba persuades Cantor to keep the system at the forefront, emphasizing, as the appropriate focus of attention in counseling, the
cause of what happens in the home. Although none of the counselors denies either version of reality, it is evident they give the
system working priority.

Particular personalities do not, in their separate rights, make
home life what it is. When Borba asks rhetorically, "Do you really
think that all that 'going after each other,' as you say, is the old
man just being himself?" he himself answers that the son contrib-
utes equally to what is a family problem. The implication is that
even Mom and the daughters contribute. No one is innocent. Yet,
by the same token, no one in particular is to blame either. If blame
is to be considered at all, it must be assigned in the context of the
family system as a whole, aimed at something extra-individual,
targeting the insidious workings of a larger entity—the home.

Separating the household's functional composition into two categories—system and personalities—provides a discursive basis
for considering their relationship. Being distinct from the individual members of the household, the system can be spoken of
as causing the presenting problems of particular members. Thus,
no one in particular causes Dad's drinking or is especially to blame
for young Dave's drug habit. Cantor's penultimate comment in
the extract, "If you can get them going, you can see it all right

there," is methodological. Accepting the categorical distinction of system and personalities, she refers to the practical problem of evidencing the respective realities. As long as family members in counseling behave as individuals, silently ignoring each other or relating separately to the counselor, the system remains dormant. But as Cantor states, if you can "get them going," interacting with each other in the session, you can "see it all right there."

For this, counselors rely on a range of techniques, from named strategies available in the brief therapy literature to ad hoc procedures. *Reframing*, for example, is a strategy of presenting clients with an alternate or provocative sense of what they are like as a family, on the assumption that this will lead members to react openly, "correcting" or otherwise dealing with the alternative (see Simon, Stierlin, & Wynne, 1985, pp. 286-287). This strategy is one means, as Cantor puts it, of "getting them going." Needless to say, the techniques also serve in intervention, in which systems are variously shaped and formed to alter the underlying problem clients present.

As the discussion continues, the connotation of system becomes an issue in its own right. Counseling intern Leila Korson recalls Al Borba's earlier remarks about subsystems. Borba had stated that "spiraling subsystems [add] fuel to the fire," but had not elaborated.

> KORSON: Al, you spoke earlier . . . I believe you said that [Pause] . . . something like subsystems adding fuel to the fire? I'm not really sure how you phrased it, but I was wondering if you're saying what I think you're saying. What I have in mind is something I've been seeing in counseling and I'd like to know if that's what you mean by subsystem.

Korson describes at length a family in which the older children are separated from the younger children by several years in age, and how the difference seems to make the two age groups subsystems because, as Korson then puts it, "The two seem to work at cross-purposes all the time."

> BORBA: Yes, I'd say you're right on the mark . . . especially if you're seeing a separate dynamics. Like if one of the

older kids decides to side with the younger ones, does he get pulled back into the older group by the older kids?

KORSON: I'm not sure I've seen that happen, but I get the drift.

HORTON: Leila, it can really, really spiral! I know most of us have had to deal with that sort of thing. You've got one group working against the other. And they all get sucked in. It's not unusual, really. The subsystems are all over the place . . . and the overall system gets bent all out of shape in the process. You can imagine what a place that kind of home is. Like Mom and Dad can be a real doozy of a subsystem. . . .

KORSON: I have a family I'm working with right now. It's a single-parent home. I was wondering . . . if there is a single parent, how would you do anything to deal with the couple system? Wouldn't you be dealing with an individual?

BORBA: If it were that easy, the family wouldn't need any help. All you'd have to do is deal with that one person. But there's a [system] function for why they're doing what they're doing. Like someone else in the family is probably taking one of the parent's roles. There's still an executive sub-system.

NELSON: [Addressing Korson] I think what you have to do is think in terms of the system and what it has to do. Like some part has to do what the mom normally does and some part does what the dad does. Sometimes, Mom has to do it all and that can be a real mess, especially when Mom can't make decisions.

REDDICK: You often can't see it right away. You've got to work with the family for a while before you start to see the various parts and the different functions.

NELSON: It's the same for all of us. At first, you've got a bunch of people with problems in that office. You've got to sort things out so that you start to see the dynamics, if you can, and all the subsystems and stuff.

REDDICK: Group soup really helps. I've seen myself come in here and not be able to figure what the heck is going on at home. I just don't see a pattern. Does Dad work with Mom? Are the kids working against Dad? Do Mom and Dad have it together as parents?

BORBA: Until you can get a handle on the system, you're just comin' and goin'. In no way are you going to be able to join in

and move things around. You've got to know what you're
dealing with.

The connotation of the system does not just puzzle counseling
interns. Although intern Leila Korson's concern was the source
of discussion in the preceding extract, all staffers deal with related categorical and methodological issues as a regular part of
their work with clients. For example, in a live soup overseen by
consultant Dick Billings, working counselor Nancy Cantor's response to a family friend's remarks about the control of a sexually
promiscuous teenaged daughter prompts counselor Kelly Seever
in the adjacent monitoring room to ask about the place of persons
who are not family members in the scheme of things. In the
following extract from the resulting discussion, we see that system is a concept that only partially overlaps formal kinship.
Because system refers to the dynamics of the home, it includes
anyone, kin or others, who participates in home life. To borrow
a phrase, it is the "broken home" more than the broken family
that conjures the system as a central operating entity in clients'
troubled lives.

SEEVER: [Lowering the sound on the monitor and turning to
         Billings] What Nancy just said to Jim [the family friend]
         . . . something about being part of the family. I know we
         talk about family subsystems and systems and all that,
         but he [Jim] seems to be fitting in some way. Isn't he
         Mom's live-in partner? I don't know . . .
HORTON: He [Jim] seems real dependent on her, if you ask me. He's
         more like her kid than her lover.
SEEVER: Well, maybe, . . . but what I was wondering was . . . well,
         we see a lot of cases where there are all kinds of people
         living in . . . like runaway friends of the kids and sexual
         partners and . . . you've got some really sick combina-
         tions. Remember that case of mine where Mom's boy-
         friend was living in and screwing around with the oldest
         daughter? And Mom knew about it! I think she felt that she
         could keep a man around the house if she let him have
         access to her [the daughter]. [Elaborates] I'm not saying he
         wasn't good to the kids. That girl was really out of control,

too, and you can see why. It's just, . . . well, . . . how does it all fit in . . . to the system, I mean?

BILLINGS: Why shouldn't it? I don't see that it makes any difference. We're talking about the home here. That includes everyone who's around. You've got to remember that there's a function here that needs doing . . . and Nancy has to figure out if this guy Jim is doing it. Of course, if his sexual contact with the daughter is true, we can't put up with any of that either.

SEEVER: No, that was my case, Dick. We don't know if that's what's happening in this case [the one in the counseling session in progress].

BILLINGS: Whatever. We'll soon find out, won't we? The point is, is Jim functioning as the head of the household? Does he make the system work or is he dragging Mom under with him so that the kids have no direction and are going off in every direction? Maybe he's trying, but the kids don't accept him as the daddy, in which case there's no executive system to speak of. But there's always a system, no matter who's involved. Of course, that doesn't mean it's working right.

BEHOLDING THE SYSTEM

The system that "always is" is not confined to the household, although the physical bounds of the household commonly locate home life. The system is potentially apparent wherever and whenever members are together. A dynamic organized around an inappropriate line of authority, such as might occur when a teenaged son commands daily life at home in place of his derelict father, can display itself in counseling. The challenge, as Nancy Cantor notes, is to "get them going." Once that happens, one can virtually behold the system. Just as Westsiders point to the state of authority they witness in seating arrangement, posture, and verbalization, they also take for granted that the system is detectable in therapy.

There is something intriguing, exciting, and yet frightening and frustrating about the system as it presents itself in counselors' offices. The system is intriguing because its energetic quality confers on it the characteristics of a living and breathing dynamo that can be unpredictable. It is not just a system of record, whose background and current status can be perused at a distance in professional dossiers and institutional files. It is not a system merely represented by an individual member, who provides secondhand reports of the flowing details of home life. Treated at Westside is the system in its own right, in all its bluster, deceptive dormancy, fits, and starts.

A living and breathing dynamo can be exciting. Once it gets going, as it were, it seems to take on a life of its own, its interactions feeding on themselves. It is both a self-consuming and expanding entity. An ostensibly irresponsible, rebellious, and self-destructive teenaged son who insolently and unaccountably "gives Mom lip" during a counseling session, sparks a vicious confirmation by an older sister. The sister "jumps on Mom," fuming about the mother's weakness in the face of her "old man's" drinking and drugging habits, repeated in her timid reaction to the son's insolence. The mother whimpers at the daughter's accusation, feeling that she, the mother, is now the victim. The tirade quickly expands as the son and daughter zero in on Mom's "wimpy" reaction and bemoan their inadvertent incitement of it as part of the problem. The son's rebelliousness emerges to consume his relation with the mother, growing full-blown with the recognition of what he seems to be uncontrollably doing to her.

Once such a system gets going, the counselors, consultants, and interns take its dynamic as unfolding before their very eyes. They behold the system consuming itself in interpersonal outbursts, hostility, accusations of irresponsibility, sullenness, and weeping, among other displays. This emotionality is the surface manifestation of problematic authority. Westsiders behold the system in both the heated and indifferent responses of family members—indifference that often sparks greater anger than reactions in kind. At the same time, Westsiders' orientation is colder, focused as it is on the home's system of authority. What they observe and aim to eventually alter is the rule of command they believe to be the source of all presenting problems, not its ancillary sentiments. Still, the seemingly ineluctable combination charges the structure of authority.

Intriguing, too, is the way otherwise separate and independent members of the household, not just kin, can be encapsulated by the system. It is portrayed as a kind of vacuuming, which draws in all members of the household, perhaps slowly at first if one is at the system's margins, but increasingly quickly as one approaches the inner flux and turmoil. Al Borba put it this way in a live soup:

> You're seeing the strength of the system. It [system] just sucks them in—relatives, friends, whoever's around—and it wants to work itself out. It's like none of them can help themselves, but follow along. The dynamics of the home can be really powerful, over and above each of them. That's what you're seeing, we're all seeing here. That's why they need counseling.

Later, in the same live soup, Borba reemphasizes:

> You see it constantly. The family system is so powerful that the mother gets sucked into the system and she's getting nowhere fast. [Extended discussion about the power of systems] The family comes to have a whole life and force of its own and no matter how anyone tries, each time they try to break out, it all comes at each of them in full force. It's like each of them against the family.

At one point in a group soup, counselor Gary Nelson echoes this depiction. Confirming consultant Dick Billings comments on the power of the system, Nelson remarks:

> You bet they [family members] do. I've seen it time after time. They can't break out of it. It's a vicious circle. It really is. And, man, what it can do to them. Like this kid [called a budding incendiary because he sets fires] . . . it's more than one-on-one [between the kid and his father]. That kind of home's got 'em all screwed up. Dad's a loudmouth and doesn't give a shit about the kids. All he cares about is how much he can sell. He's weak. Mom's worried about everyone and can't get her act together. It's like [pause] like no

one can break out of it. It's even got Mom's live-in girlfriend involved. It's just sucking them in and crushing them
and they don't know what to do. All they know is how to
feed into the system. It's a whirlpool, man; it's like it's got
a mind of its own.

Separate and distinct though it is from household occupants'
individual personalities, the system can take on personality characteristics of its own. Like any person, the system can blow up and
let off steam. Like a sullen teenager, the system can just sit there and
seem nonexistent, oblivious to everything. Or it can drift along
as if nothing were wrong, and suddenly get heated when it is pulled
in one direction or another. It even has a kind of memory in that
it rebounds to a former state of equilibrium, healthy or not. Sounding like pioneer family scholar Ernest Burgess's (1926) reluctant
description of the separate properties of family living, Westsiders
at times speak as if the system were a superpersonality. Indeed,
as reviewed, assessed, and treated, the descriptive features of the
system can refract the full range of ways Westsiders and others
communicate individual lives. Applied to the system, Westsiders
and their clients collectively represent themselves as something
they individually are not.

As exciting as the system can be when it comes alive, it also can
be inscrutably inactive. On such occasions, the system needs to
be provoked, picked at and shoved, to reveal its dynamic. Quies-
cent as the system can be, its potential for coming alive with all
the humanlike characteristics it can manifest sustains the intrigue
for Westsiders, an enduring, curious wariness for what can happen at any moment in group counseling. As intern Roger Savage
once remarked, "Even when it's boring, it's nerve wracking because
you never know for sure how they're going to react." To which
veteran counselor Gary Nelson added, "It's like that for all of us;
that system's just around the corner waiting to jump out at you,
but when, you don't know." And consultant Dick Billings confirmed, "That's the system, all right."

Billings likens the witnessed excitement of the system to counselor voyeurism. In a group soup, Donna Reddick describes a
swirling family dynamic. The IP is a 23-year-old schoolteacher

whose parents have brought her to Westside for drug counseling. Before the tape of the fifth counseling session with the family is played, Reddick reports that she has been considering terminating the case because, "All I seem to be getting now is a lot of excitement without any progress on the drug front." Those gathered for the review eagerly express interest in having a "look see."

REDDICK: I've seen the family now . . . I believe about five times. First it was Karen [IP] and her mother and . . . [pause] at first I thought it would work out to keep seeing Karen and Mom. But that didn't seem to click. I mean, I didn't see very much [during the session]. [Elaborates] They mostly reported the problem and how they were working on it. Things like that . . . not much dynamics there.

BILLINGS: What made you decide to bring Dad in?

REDDICK: I think it was the second time I saw them when I mentioned to Mom that it might be a good idea to have Dad come in . . . like he was available and it would be a good idea to see him at the same time. Well! Did that cause a stir! She [Karen] really didn't want that, but she wouldn't say no either. You could see that she was resisting. So I invited Mom to bring him next time.

CANTOR: It sure made a difference. I watched one of the tapes. Wow! Did they have it out!

SEEVER: Let's have a look see.

REDDICK: I don't think I saved that one. That was quite a while ago. [Audibly disappointed groans] I'm sorry, you guys. But I did bring the one I did last week. It's not quite as exciting, but you can see what I mean. The coke's [Karen's cocaine habit] been taken care of. She's not on coke anymore. She only has marijuana once in a while. I'm pretty sure she's just a weekend user.

BILLINGS: Well, let's have a look then.

Reddick starts the tape and soon grows impatient, noting, "It's not a very exciting part." She fast-forwards the tape.

REDDICK: You'll see the family in motion in just a second here. [Plays tape] Here it is, I think.

As the tape plays, all eagerly lean forward to watch.

HORTON: I don't see anything. Dad's just telling Karen to watch her step, like she might lose her job or something. . . . Sounds like she's got a real power thing with her father. Where's the action?

BILLINGS: [Laughing] You know, I was just thinking. Look at all of us. Just look at us. Did you ever see such a bunch of Peeping Toms?

SEEVER: Excu-u-u-se me . . . most of us here are Peeping Tomasinas. [All laugh]

BILLINGS: My apologies to the ladies in the house. [Pause] But take a look at us. It's counselor voyeurism, is what it is. It's like that system is going to spring out of there and just blow up . . . and each of us has our noses pressed against the tube [monitor]. Boy, are we bad or aren't we?

HORTON: [Chuckling] Oh, Dick, you're the worst. You know you just love it. When that system gets heated up, you can't help it. It's raw energy.

NELSON: Christ, you'd think we were looking at a triple X [hardcore pornographic film] or something. [All laugh]

According to the counselors, beholding the system has its risks. As staffers put it, referring to members of the household, the system "sucks them in" whether or not they choose to participate or have a personal stake in the system's hierarchy of control. In its immediacy, the action can spread to engulf the counselor also. Thus, the very aspects that make the system exciting can be frightening. Nancy Cantor tellingly depicts the "unnatural feeling that you can get, sometimes, that you've stirred things up so much or forced things out that you probably should have let be." The counselors admit to anxiety about their own vulnerability to the social enticements of a dynamic that can overwhelm any individual's attempt at control.

At other times, the system can be frustratingly inert. In a group soup, Cantor comments on the unexciting inertia of a family she's been counseling and the feeling that she has been sucked in so far that all she can do is go along with the customary pattern of relations presenting themselves in treatment. Cantor compares this to the interactional economy of family membership:

One thing about the system is . . . that the problem with family therapy is the system is so powerful that you [the counselor] become a family member yourself. It's so tight that you can't shape it because it's there and you're there in it. You know what I'm saying? Like, so you haven't been doing urines [screenings for drugs] because she [the IP] says she's on drugs, but you just keep not doing it because that's the way things have been for so long . . . when you think maybe you should be doing it. Like you don't have the energy . . . or don't know if you should exert the energy to get things doing. It's easier to let sleeping dogs lie, like you're actually one of them.

Beholding the system, then, is a two-way street. It is an encounter with that thing, categorically larger than individual members of the household, that stands over and above each of them, an entity that can present itself vividly and, it is to be hoped, tellingly, during counseling. At the same time, as the system grows full-blown, apparently available for treatment, it threatens to engulf the counseling enterprise itself.

MECHANICS OF CONSTRUCTION

Although the system of authority is beheld in various ways, it is not something simply there, evident to anyone who just gave a "look see." The system spoken of so poignantly at times is as much revealed through Westside staffers' practical efforts to show its effects as it is an entity separate and distinct in its own right.

Mundane interpretive work constitutes the system. Its mechanics are evident in the presentation of videotapes in group soup, the monitoring of live soup, and the consideration of verbal reports of counseling proceedings. The ordinariness literally extends to machines, namely, videotaping and monitoring equipment. Simple and seemingly straightforward operations such as "fast forward," "pause," "rewind," "play," "stop," and "volume" serve to peruse, scrutinize, categorize, isolate, secure, hypothesize about, highlight, and otherwise discursively edit proceedings to locate and reveal the system. This, in turn, offers varyingly convincing and coherent evidence of domestic disorder.

Keeping in mind that what appears on videotape, on monitors, or is reported are voices and activities—people saying things and moving about—consider how the shape and substance of the larger system gets mechanically drawn out. Consultant Al Borba walks into the group soup room just as case reviews are scheduled to begin. There are greetings all around, Borba sits down, and asks, "Who has a problem?"

NELSON: I've got one and I've got a tape if you want to see them at intake. This is a family I saw yesterday. They were re- ferred by [an agency] for excessive truancy.
SEEVER: Yeah, but Gary, it's summer. So what's it matter now?
NELSON: And there's suspected drug use.

There is an extended discussion about the difficulty of counsel- ing truancy cases when school is not in session, followed by con- sideration of whether this particular family will cooperate if its members see the problem mainly as the truant daughter's, not the family's.

BORBA: Well, okay, we've heard this sort of thing before and have had to deal with it. [Elaborates] I think that under the circumstances, we'll just have to live with it. There are suspected drugs. Right? [Gary nods] So that's the pre- senting problem you can work on.
NELSON: It's only suspected.
BORBA: I always say it's just the tip of the iceberg with these families. [Pause] Let's see what we're talking about.

Nelson plays the intake tape. Approximately 30 seconds pass be- fore Nelson interrupts. The tape continues to play at the same volume.

NELSON: I saw more than truancy here. There appear to be no rules in this family. [Nelson lowers the sound but keeps the tape playing] The mother says that on any given morn- ing, "We can see two or three kids [her children's friends] sleeping on the floor." One of her kids [one of the mother's children] just up and left for 3 or 4 days and no one knew where she was. There's a 14-year-old live-in friend. She's a friend of one of the daughters and I believe she's the older son's girlfriend.

BORBA: I'm not sure I see what you're saying. So they have kids in overnight. It's summer vacation, isn't it? A lot of families do that. Of course, we can't excuse the daughter for taking off without Mom knowing. But that's a far cry from no rules. Turn up the sound a bit.

Nelson raises the sound.

BORBA: What are we seeing here? Mom's talking about her problems at home, isn't she? Is that the daughter? [Nelson nods and there's further watching and listening] Sounds like she's got her head on straight. Look at Dad. He doesn't seem to be saying very much. [Nelson reports that the father hardly spoke in the session] So Mom's running the show and the kids are frisky because it's summer. [More watching and listening] Okay, why don't we turn down the volume. From this minute or so, what are your hunches?

NELSON: You mean from what I know after the whole intake or from what we've just seen?

BORBA: No, just from what we've seen here. Any of you.

NELSON: Well, uh, from what we've seen so far, I'd guess that the daughter was real withdrawn. You saw the way she was always looking at Mom and it was going to be tough [to get her to express her own opinion].

BORBA: Sort of like there's a coalition between Mom and the daughter.

HORTON: Where are you getting that, Al? I didn't see any of that. Are we watching the same tape?

BORELLI: Maybe the daughter's afraid of something.

BORBA: Gary. Fast-forward a bit, will ya. [Tape is fast-forwarded] Okay, now, stop.

All look and listen to the tape for approximately 15 seconds. The daughter and mother are talking to the counselor about a younger daughter, who is present.

BORBA: Can you hear them sorta in cahoots and working on the younger girl. What's her name?

NELSON: Faye.

BORBA: Faye looks to me like she's the butt of this system. [Borba then points to the older daughter on the video screen] Look at the way she [the older daughter] looks at Mom. The way she's sitting between the parents raises the question of whether she's mediating their fighting. [Turns to Nelson] Do they fight? [Nelson shrugs] Again, these are just hunches, hypotheses, but they allow you to interpret what is going on.

BORELLI: I think Dad is depressed. Gary, . . . rewind the tape a bit. I think I remember a spot. I'll tell you when to stop. [Tape is rewound] Okay, I think there. [Tape is stopped and played] See how he [Dad] keeps looking away whenever the subject of drugs comes up and how he's always looking down at the floor.

REDDICK: I don't think you can read that into it, Keith. I agree with Al . . . the system is getting to him. He's feeling it . . . the coalition between Mom and Sharon [older daughter] is just too strong for him and Mom's probably too weak . . . and just too dumb . . . to do anything about what's going on right in front of her face. . . .

NELSON: [Interrupting] Why don't we just fast-forward to more interesting stuff? There really is better stuff later on.

As group soup progresses, participants continue to theorize about the system, arguing for different interpretations of domestic authority while fast-forwarding, rewinding, or stopping the tape to listen and watch for evidence. What is proven for some is considered to be unfounded by others, just as particular hunches or ostensible hypotheses seem convincing or uncompelling. Whether the purported evidence is supportive of one theory, hypothesis, or another, it is assumed, nonetheless, that the real system that stands over and above individual members of the home is "there" on tape, to be distinguished in the various voices and activities being heard and seen. A lack of evidence does not as much raise questions about the distinct reality of systems as it suggests that the system in this instance remains hidden or unactivated. A seemingly plausible theory makes it altogether reasonable to fast-forward from a portion of the tape taken to be vacuous. An alternate theory justifies a careful review of the same, but now telling portion. Interpretive momentum is sustained by what is taken for granted, realizing the object of interest by and through the equipment at hand.

There is little or no sense among staffers that the concrete mechanical options—play, pause, fast forward, stop, rewind, volume—are part of the reality of focal therapeutic concern at Westside. The options are merely convenient operations for finding and locating domestic reality. An attitude of empirical discovery and treatment guides the perception of a larger reality in what otherwise are mere voices, movements, and video equipment. In that sense, the consultants, counselors, and interns together construe the abstract in the mundane. Fast forward efficiently, yet momentarily, leads them to the system, just as play serves to vividly present it. A turn in theory reverses the significance of the operations' intended by-products. Theory informs or detracts from what mechanics variously reveals, the system of domestic authority nonetheless being somewhere "there." A careful and systematic review of an entire tape would not as much eliminate the discursive editing of this interpretive activity as it would expand a case's empirical horizons.

Searching for "more interesting stuff," group soup continues as Al Borba reaches from his seat to fast-forward the tape. Meanwhile, Gary Nelson remarks that he wishes the tapes were metered so that one could keep track of where the so-called interesting stuff is. All turn to the monitor as Nelson is heard on tape asking family members if there's something about the family they would like to keep the same. The father responds, "They're all getting big." At that point, the family is silent. The sound is lowered, the tape still running, and the counselors discuss the children and friends' unrestricted comings and goings. Borba soon interrupts.

BORBA: Did they ever say what they wanted to keep the same?
NELSON: The only thing they said is that sometimes they sit down and eat together.

Extended discussion follows about the importance of family rituals for maintaining the strength of the system. Meanwhile, Nelson raises the sound on the recorder and puts the tape on pause.

BORBA: That's a very, very, very important thing for the family to
do [eating together]. That maintains the family's strength.
I'd say this is a very workable family. The only question
is are they here just for the truancy or do they want to
work on the family?

An elaborate discussion centers on the concept of the "workable family." The question of whether this particular family is
workable is considered. Suddenly, the preset timer on the pause
function of the videotape recorder expires and the tape automatically plays audibly. The particular portion of the tape playing
catches everyone's attention and becomes material for determin-
ing the workableness of the family.

BORBA: Let's just see if this is a workable family. [Pointing to the
video screen] You're [Nelson] doing a nice job of joining
there. [This refers to Nelson's facilitation of the session] I
think that the truancy is just a symptom of the underlying
problem. [Pause] It does sound like a lack of discipline in
the executive subsystem. What Keith said about the father
being depressed is because he has no control. [Pause for
watching] Now, look there! See how Mom is smiling at the
daughter and how Dad is smiling at her, too. They really
care for each other. To me, that's workable. There really is
something there that you can work with, Gary. It's just
that . . .
NELSON: [Interrupting] According to the father, he says that there
is no family. In so many words, there's just a bunch of
people living in the house. Actually, I kind of paraphrased
it for him [during the counseling session]. I wish we could
find the place [on tape] that he talked about it. I remember
saying that there's no family and he said something like,
"That's right, just a bunch of kids going in and out." So
there is no structure in this family I can see.
BORBA: Gary, if this family decided not to come in anymore, who
do you think would initiate that?

Long pause.

NELSON: I think the kids, . . . who'd say . . . they'd think, "That guy
[Gary] is crazy!"

BORBA: If it weren't the kids but the parents, who do you think
        would say that?

Long pause.

NELSON: I think, . . . well, uh, I'd guess Mom, because she's a bit
         more comfortable about what's going on at home.

Borba speaks at length about the need to work on "elevating"
Mom because she seems to be the current strength of the family.
In the long run, Borba emphasizes, this will serve to strengthen the
whole family hierarchy, even raise Dad's esteem to its proper level.

BORBA: Even if you think there is no hierarchy, you [Nelson]
        should act as if there is one and get the parents to take over.

The mechanics of construction is not determined by equipment. The social construction process is a multilayered engagement with the system. Each layer—the counseling session, case
reviews, and the equipment—has separate and distinct communicative features that mundanely add to the flow of interpretation.

The voices and activities on tape are not the ultimate grounds
for what is construed by staffers, even though staffers routinely
turn to tape recordings for a "look see." This empirical attitude is
handily eclipsed by various delegitimizing accounts and claims.
For example, taped counseling sessions might be said to be "really"
hiding the underlying problem. It may be claimed that family
members are not talking enough to provide a detectable reading
of the system. The lack of usefulness of a particular session might
be accounted for by it being "too early [or too late] in the game,"
implying that intake, for example, is too soon to see the system
for what it really is or a much later session so routinized into a particular pattern of interaction as to limit full system dynamics.

Case reviews themselves, although intelligent, deliberate, and
sometimes highly analytic, are nonetheless suffused with rhetoric. The working counselor whose session is being reviewed may
claim to know the family better than most because he or she has had
closer contact with members. The consultant may override the

claim on the grounds that he has had more experience working with troubled families in general, especially with families of the type under consideration. At Westside, the consultant has no formal authority over counselors. Counselors have limited authority over interns. Interns might be said to be relatively inexperienced in reading the system underlying presenting problems, or regular staff might assert that individual interns do not fully understand the philosophy of group therapy. But the interns themselves may proffer claims of greater experience or specialized knowledge in select cases, such as the former schoolteacher who now counsels truants and their families.

Video recording equipment adds its own layer of mundane constructive intrusions. The play function evidences the ostensible empirical grounds for case reviews. Yet the questions of what to show, where to start, and when to stop are not fixed by any set of formal rules. The only provision is practical. Taping is valued as a means of replaying what happened in a session. The exception is the tape that does not show what really happened, evidenced by remarks such as that one "had to be there" to know what actually was taking place. The fast forward and rewind functions, while working to efficiently locate telling facts, simultaneously skip over others. Even the timing feature for the pause function can thrust arbitrary empirical grounds into case reviews, making an opportunistic sampling of a taped counseling session the basis for taking a "look see."

On methodological grounds, it might be said that each layer leaves something to be desired in revealing the system. There is limited knowledge, limited ability, and limited technical facility. The limitations are not unique to Westside; all investigation is better or worse in these regards. More important is that no matter the methodological soundness, the rhetoric of legitimation is always present. Are system facts "really" real? Is observation "really" competent or efficient? Are the tools "really" accurate or unobtrusive? In this broader context, the social construction of domestic disorder at Westside, as multilayered as it is, is natural and ineluctable, the abstract being bound in practice to the mundane.

The layering is highlighted in live supervision. While consultants, counselors, and interns watch and listen, a working coun-

selor engages family members and significant others in therapy
in an adjacent room, the two settings linked by telephone. The mechanics of construction is a confabulation of several conversations:
working counselor with consultant in the monitoring area while
family members wait in the counseling room; family members
with working counselor; working counselor with consultant by
telephone; consultant with observing counselors and interns;
observing counselors and interns with each other while the consultant speaks by telephone to the working counselor; and, throughout, family members and significant others speaking with each
other. The unity that is the system is articulated from bits and pieces
of experience in each, producing abstract coherence out of simultaneous and sundry considerations. The system, in turn, more or
less provides the context of meaning for understanding and treating
troubles in the respective conversations, the abstract being constructed out of, and repairing back in vivo to, the mundane.

Consider one of working counselor Kelly Seever's live soups.
Before the supervision begins, as Seever is about to leave for her session, she telegraphically describes the family to consultant Al Borba.

> This is the woman. . . . I've seen her three times with the
> daughter, Sue Ann. Sue Ann is 15 and was popped for driv-
> ing underage. Drunken driving. There are six kids: three
> boys and three girls. Sue Ann is the youngest. The father is
> an alcoholic and has problems with drugs or something else.
> Mom's name is Sue. She's the one who has the whole fam-
> ily working at [a fast food restaurant]. The manager's been
> living with Mom. Sue Ann is the IP and was court-referred.
> She's the only kid who lives at home. The rest of them are
> in town, out on their own. The oldest daughter, Rita, has
> got real psychological problems. Last week, when Mom was
> out of town, Rita got drunk and attempted suicide.

As the other counselors listen to Seever, they discuss how they
expect the family to present itself. Meanwhile, the family walks
into the counseling room and appears on the monitor. Pointing
to the monitor, Seever introduces each member. Borba asks several clarifying questions and the counselors discuss among themselves how individual family members "must think" of the home

situation, what members' respective roles in the family seem to be, and the relative influence of the mother in the system, among other hypotheticals concerning the domestic order presumed readable from seating arrangement, posture, and verbalization.

Seever leaves for the counseling room. Following the usual greetings and small talk, Seever reminds the family that this is a live supervision with Al Borba, the other counselors, and the interns watching and listening in the adjacent room. Staff members comment about the flow of Seever's introduction, the seeming rapport between the working counselor and individual family members, and the approach apparently being taken to the presenting problem.

Approximately 5 minutes pass. Counselor Nancy Cantor suddenly blurts that something the mother just stated reminds her of a problem she is having with one of her own families, a home that "really leaves something to be desired." As Borba responds to Cantor, the others turn away from the monitor, focusing their attention on Cantor's problem. Audible and visible on the monitor, the proceedings in the counseling room continue unabated.

Considering Cantor's problem, Borba refers to cases of his own in which domestic life, he echoes, "leaves something to be desired." Borba picks up on remarks he and others overhear on the monitor from the adjacent room's live counseling session. As Borba describes how, in one of his cases, a drunken father backing out of his driveway almost killed one of his children, Seever is overheard saying to the mother in the adjacent room, "The death of a child is probably the hardest thing. . . . " Borba integrates the statement, word for word, into his comments, explaining how the system responds to a child's death: "Like Kelly [Seever] said, the death of a child is the hardest thing on the family system—the executive subsystem sometimes goes haywire." Several counselors in the monitoring room briefly turn to the live counseling session shown on the monitor. As Borba proceeds to address Cantor's problem, with the live counseling session in the background, parts of the talk and concerns of the counseling room continue to be appropriated into the matters under discussion in the monitoring room.

Eventually, those in the monitoring room turn their full attention to the adjacent room's proceedings. Borba asks rhetorically, "I wonder if we should get Kelly [working counselor Seever] to probe for Mom's place in the home a bit more." He explains that Seever seems to be dwelling on peripheral matters and not getting to the underlying problem. He telephones Seever and asks her to get Mom to focus on the rules laid down when the children are home. Simultaneously, Mom and Sue Ann, the daughter, have the following, barely audible conversation about the telephone call:

> MOM: I think she's [Seever] talking to those supervisors.
> SUE ANN: Something about . . . what did she [Seever] say?
> MOM: Sounds like something about rules or . . .I don't know. I don't know about this.
> SUE ANN: Shit, Mom, that's none of their business.
> MOM: Be quiet. They're trying to help.

As Borba speaks with Seever by telephone, the counselors in the monitoring area strain to hear the exchange between Mom and Sue Ann. The counselors quietly discuss the "hidden hierarchy" that the mother and daughter comprise within the home. Sue Ann's apparently strategic place in the scheme of things is underscored. Tammy Horton hypothesizes that the arrangement, "throws the other children off." Referring to what he hears Sue Ann say, Nelson interrupts:

> Do you hear that? Sue Ann thinks she's a big deal. [Snidely mimicking Sue Ann] "It's none of our business." That little snot. Boy, does she hold Mom by the nose.

Focusing on Sue Ann's posture, Horton adds, "And look at how she's [Sue Ann] sitting, like she's on top of the world."

Live soup continues with the separate conversations converging, overlapping, and combining with amazing inventiveness. Bits and pieces of one conversation are integrated into another and yet another, fleshing out their respective concerns and logics. Each conversation references the system, from parts that are claimed to be none of Westside's business to the hidden hierarchy of the home. Whether or not any of the participants in the rooms

are correct or justified in what is said, the complex layering nonetheless articulates recurrently unified senses of domestic disorder, a pastiche drawn from and through the ordinary communicative conditions and resources surrounding speakers.

F I V E

Restoring Hierarchy

The counseling process and its supervision are full of talk: counselors talking to family members; family members and significant others conversing with each other; counselors, interns, and consultants deliberating over domestic disorder and the treatment process. There is talk about talk, such as whether a counselor's depiction of home life "tells it like it is." The term *counsel* itself connotes a process of deliberative instruction intended to affect another's judgment or behavior.

Yet, there is something decidedly nondiscursive about staff members' sense of what confronts them in the counseling process. Although they "process" or sort through information of various kinds, from talk to behavior, demeanor, and interpersonal environs, the activity is all about what they behold in the counseling situation. Staff members also "process" in the sense of keeping mindful of the ongoing shape and substance of counseling activity, managing it as it unfolds. But, again, this is more than therapeutic self-consciousness; it is the awareness of an immediate engagement with the system. The commonly used term *tracking* suggests that counselors metaphorically prowl the system to discern how it works and then enter its domain to affect its order. It is an engagement with domestic disorder as disorder is immediately witnessed. As Simon, Stierlin, and Wynne (1985, p. 339) explain in their book *The Language of Family Therapy*, "The therapist may 'track' the family interaction by allowing, or even encouraging family patterns to unfold naturally before intervening overtly."

Intervention, though communicative, is not considered to be a form of talk therapy. Talk therapies such as psychoanalysis and other forms of personal counseling affect the home and family life through individuals, not directly through the system. Intervention at Westside, in contrast, is taken to be an encounter with the system itself; the engagement is expected to result in a new operating order—a proper hierarchy and structure of command—without encapsulating the counselor and counseling process in the underlying system of disorder that brought the family to Westside in the first place.

TAKING CONTROL

Engagement with the system informs counselors that intervening places them in a precarious position. An alleged therapeutic slip, such as a slip of the tongue, is not simply correctable by rewording or otherwise sharing an insight into communication. A slip carries the risk of inadvertently and undesirably altering the system in its own right. This is one of the advantages of live supervision, in which the precarious position of the working counselor in relation to the system is monitored by his or her consulting supervisor and other counselors. Although live supervision lays bare to institutional scrutiny the therapeutic skills of the working counselor, it also provides a layer of defense against the system's potentially overwhelming presence in the counseling process.

Emphasis is placed on control in intervention. Like the lion tamer who enters a cage of seemingly domesticated but resiliently wild animals, the counselor needs protection from, and tools of direct manipulation for, the system's potential. These tools, such as the threat to report unresponsive IPs to community control agents, are thought to therapeutically shape the system, not just keep clients in therapy. The preceding threat, for example, might be said to demonstrate to family members that each of them not only has more or less rights, but also has related duties and obligations to the family.

Above all, a counselor must seize the high ground, never letting on to the possibility of losing control. The signs that reveal domestic authority—seating, posture, and verbalization—signal counselor control. High ground is represented by the counselor's placement in the room and his or her presence and posture during counseling. The strategy is to display the counselor as in charge, "on top" of whatever family hierarchy presents itself, as domestically unworkable as that hierarchy might be. Once control is established and apparent to all, the counselor can start to realign the system.

The control issue is evident throughout the group soup of counseling intern Keith Borelli's session with a drug-abusing mother and her daughter. Dick Billings is the consultant. Note how the mother's wavering authority eventually casts supervisory doubt on Borelli's own show of control in the session. We enter the proceedings as the group watches the videotape recording and Borelli presents background information, ending with a hypothesis.

BORELLI: So this is a drug problem . . . mainly coke, I believe. There's some pot, too. It's mostly Mom and her boyfriend, but the daughter is the IP. She's [the IP] having a lot of trouble in school and is suspected of shoplifting, but I don't think she really did anything. Mom and daughter have a pretty close relationship, but it's weird. One of my hypotheses is that the daughter . . .

BILLINGS: What's her [the daughter's] name?

BORELLI: Carrie.

BILLINGS: So what's weird about Carrie?

BORELLI: One of my hypotheses is that Carrie is afraid for Mom. [Detailed description of Mom's drugging relationship with the boyfriend] Mom had to bail him [the boyfriend] out of jail in [State]. He was popped for coke.

Billings turns off the recorder.

BILLINGS: [To Borelli] I was interested in what you think is the process that was going on between Mom and the daughter.

Long pause.

BORELLI: I saw it as Mom has to have control. Mom has this great
need for control. Like . . . you saw . . . remember when
the two of them [Mom and Carrie] were going at it a
minute ago, like we saw the system at work there. Mom
was in a very weak position and I think she knows it. You
can really see it, like when Mom . . . like there's hardly
anything Carrie can say that Mom doesn't discredit it.
She [Mom] needs to put Carrie down all the time.

HORTON: Needs!?

BORELLI: I mean, . . . Mom's just not on top of the game, that's all,
and she more or less knows it, and that's why she needs
to pick on Carrie, like to show she's in control. That kind
of need.

SEEVER: What do you see, Dick?

BILLINGS: The primary thing I was seeing is that Mother "needs"
[turns to Horton and signals quotation marks in mock
deference to Horton's earlier objection, at which all laugh]
to devalue the daughter and Daughter fights to put the
mother down. And they're both fighting back and forth
to control you [Borelli] and who's right. They're drawing
you into the system. [Details the process] It would appear
that this daughter has too much power in some areas. So
I would explore which areas she has too much power in.

Several counselors focus on Borelli's place in the matter. An
analogy is drawn between Carrie and Mom on the one hand, and
the two family members and Borelli on the other. The group suggests that Borelli may not be in control in the session because he
appears defensive. Counselor Gary Nelson notes that whenever
Borelli acts as if Mom is in full control, attempting thereby to
"elevate" her, Carrie turns on Borelli to alter the relationship. Nelson cites a brief extract of recorded conversation in which Carrie
bluntly tells Borelli, "Mom really wants to take charge of her life,
but she just can't get it together; I worry about her sometimes."
The counselors refer to other recorded comments, in which Borelli
seems to "back off" when Mom or Carrie are confrontational.

The counselors discuss similar situations of their own, as if to
inform Borelli that even veteran therapists must work at main-

taining control. Nancy Cantor recalls not ever being able to get "on top" of a family in which the father was suspected of child sexual abuse. Cantor reports that whenever she attempted to "elevate" Mom, "Dad would just come right back at me and tell me to stay out of their business." Counselor Kelly Seever is reminded of a sexual abuse case of her own in which an infant was alleged to have been diagnosed with gonorrhea of the mouth, the suspected source being the father. At first, the father refused to attend counseling sessions. The mother attended with two older teenaged daughters and a 12-year-old son. Regarding the difficulty of taking control in the case, Seever explains:

> I just had to make up my mind that I was going to be assertive, to show them that I meant business. When I finally got him [the father] in here, I made sure that I was on top of things. You know how you can set things up so that . . . like he's [father] in the corner and I sit right there in the middle of the room . . . and you never let down your guard, either. Like I didn't take any shit from him. Whenever he tried to jump in, I just got louder and kept going. He wasn't going to interrupt. I gave him a dirty look every time he tried.

Before the discussion returns to Borelli's case, counselors share other anecdotes about sessions in which they lost control and families with whom they never seemed able to take charge in the first place.

Interrupting, consultant Billings plays the tape and remarks:

> We'll watch a little more. [Turns to Borelli] In general, I think that was a good process, but I think, like we said, we better make sure that you have a bit more control here, okay?

As the tape plays, Borelli points to the monitor and explains that he is attempting to get Mom to list the rules of the house, something with which he had some success earlier. But Mom and Carrie ignore him as they argue over the family cat's shedding and the mess it makes of the furniture and their clothing, causing Mom to state that she cannot trust her daughter to be responsible for anything. On tape, Borelli then refers to a family rule noted earlier, "According to this, there's a lot of trust and you gave her [Carrie] responsibility," to which Mom dissents, "How do you get that out of that?"

When Mom and Carrie abruptly resume their earlier argument about household responsibility, Billings stops the tape. Following a recitation of Mom's control problem, Billings asks Borelli about his aims in the case and returns the discussion to the problem of counselor control.

BILLINGS: Okay. What do you [Borelli] want to work on?

Long pause.

BORELLI: One is how to shift it, to get Mom to have more control. My thoughts are that Mom is starting to lose control more and more. The way she's going about it, it's just escalating her daughter to be more and more unreasonable. [Elaborates] So to get Mom to put in a little more thought on what she's doing. The other thing is to bring the boyfriend back into the picture. He lives with Mom off and on. According to Mom, he got busted for possession, but she says it was planted. Mom occasionally does pot now. [Elaborates] I kinda want to get the daughter out of the picture. I've always had the two together and I think Carrie is too elevated. So I'll try to see Mom and the boyfriend alone. [Details strategy] The problem is that she [Mom] goes from being Mom to being a buddy [to Carrie] and it's not working.

BILLINGS: I like how you've been tracking this. I wonder what you could reframe those problems as?

HORTON: Don't you think it would help, Dick, to work on [counselor] control a bit more here?

The counselors offer suggestions.

BILLINGS: I like those ideas. I like Tammy's thinking on this and Donna's too. I would move your [Borelli] chair closer to Mom. Right now, you're sitting too close to the daughter. It makes it look like you're talking to Mom with the

daughter backing you up. It would compliment Mom
and tell her what a reasonable and intelligent woman she
is. Sit tight-like and don't let Carrie interrupt.

BORELLI: Every time I tried to do that [compliment Mom], she'd
[Mom] negate it.

BILLINGS: [Chuckling sarcastically] I'd tell her [Mom] that she shouldn't
do that because the daughter'll do that enough. [All laugh]

CANTOR: This is going to be real slow, Keith. She [Mom] has a real
investment in keeping her daughter her equal.

In general, taking control means two things: controlling the setup
of the session and running the show. As Billings advised, arranging and rearranging seating is an important part of the setup, mirroring a common sign of domestic authority. The aim is to arrange
the seating to "make sure" that when the system presents itself
and is engaged, things go as planned. Successful counseling depends on it. As consultant Al Borba once succinctly put it:

It's a matter of making sure that things are set up so you're
in control . . . just like the system sets itself up to control
them [family members]. They can't help themselves. Make
sure that you don't put yourself in a position where you can't
help yourself. It's a matter of planning, really, and strategiz-
ing some so the system can't wiggle away on you.

Without doubt, therapists anywhere would consider a modi-
cum of control over clients a prerequisite for treatment. Yet, control
can mean different things in different treatment settings. Westsiders
construe control in signs of therapeutic authority. In contrast, as
we will see later, control for Fairview Hospital staffers leans more
toward rapport; they are decidedly partial to empathetically
guiding the "sharing of feelings" as a means of running the show.

At Westside, counselors "make sure" of their control in several
ways besides arranging a commanding environment. Threats play
a part: The threat of discontinuing therapy or increasing the fee
for counseling can figure in behavior contracts between the agency
and the family. Formal contracts routinely are used to reshape the
structure of domestic authority, such as an agreement by parents
not to overdelegate authority to children. These agreements are

considered to be particularly urgent when members of the household are thought to be involved in grossly unacceptable behavior. Suspicion or claims of violence of any kind, such as wife beating, are considered urgent. Suspected child neglect and sexual promiscuity in the household are also likely to be objects of formal agreement.

Even when grossly unacceptable behaviors appear limited to one or two family members or isolated incidents, staff believe that the entire system is nonetheless involved. For example, a husband, or even a wife, may assert that the husband's periodic violence against the wife has "nothing to do with the children," but, according to staff's system focus, it "affects everyone in the home, even outsiders." As counselor Donna Reddick once explained in connection with a case she found difficult, involving a live-in lover, "I'm going to get a contract from them on this because you just know they're all suffering, even though Mom says that her sexuality is none of anyone's business, least of all the children's." The idea that a system has parts, that parts are interconnected, subject to mutual influence and internal "ripple effects," works against a claim that an action is isolated. Reddick elaborates:

> Mom keeps saying that things are under control and Jim [live-in lover] just comes in on the weekend and doesn't bother anyone. "The kids don't even know he's around," she [Mom] says. Well I say, "Like hell they don't." They might not say anything, but the system doesn't operate that way. That guy's an authority figure no matter how much Mom denies it, and it's bound to affect the kids' sense of right and wrong. She can't tell me that Justine's [daughter] getting into the wrong crowd because Justine's bullheaded and just feels like it. I know Justine's the IP, but the underlying problem is all this other stuff that's going on at home, all the ripple effects.

Contracts are understood to be ultimately made with the whole system, not individuals. A member who refuses to cease engaging in unacceptable behavior risks the termination of the entire family's treatment. A fee increase might be thought justified in that unacceptable behavior makes the whole family's treatment more difficult.

The quasi-legal language of contracts underscores the requirements they contain. As consultant Dick Billings says, "This way, everything's out in the open, and everyone knows what is expected and that you mean business." Indeed, contracts have a system backing of their own, as agreements made with Westside House, not a particular counselor. Donna Reddick once tellingly informed an intern that this can be a form of protection:

> You don't have to make it sound like it's your own idea. The contract is between Westside and the family—like one system to another. You're just doing what you have to do. It protects you and, at the same time, it shows them that they have, like, a legal obligation to live up to it.

The intersystemic character of contractual obligations is evident in the group soup of a chronically violent IP, the young husband of a thrice-married older woman. Counselor Nancy Cantor, whose case it is, worries about her possible engulfment in the violence.

CANTOR: This guy [the IP] gives me the willies. He's got this violent streak. She [wife] says he's always beating up on her. She's older and has been married . . . I believe about three times before. He gets drunk and comes home mad about something and takes it out on her. But you know how it is. She says that she loves him and doesn't press charges. [Mocking the wife] "No, he's not hurting me." She just wants some help, she says.

HORTON: Why does he [IP] feel he needs to be this powerful?

SEEVER: Let's remember that there's a long, long history that everyone jumps on him. His father dumped on him as a kid. He got beat up a lot by his dad. He had problems at school when he was a kid. I think it's a real long history of power trips and powerlessness. To me, I'd say that the guy is just replaying what he's used to. His dad smacked him around; so he beats up his wife. He's just a violent kind of guy. That's what he knows. You see that sort all the time.

CANTOR: I don't know, Kelly. I think the trouble is in the domestic situation.

This is debated for a time. As Cantor elaborates on the domestic situation in relation to the IP's life history, it becomes increasingly evident that Cantor herself fears an attack.

CANTOR: I hear what you're all saying and, to be honest, I'm getting worried, too, that this guy might act up in the office [during counseling] if his wife gets him going. What if he starts taking it out on me? You all know how it happens, how you can get sucked in. [Pause] Still, you have to feel sorry for the guy too. He said he likes the sessions because he feels I give him a chance to tell his side. You know that there's some love there, too.

BILLINGS: Look, the wife not only needs protection, but you need to set things up, right then and there, so that you're protected. What I think you might want to say to them [the IP and the wife] is that they have a lot of passion to get out of themselves and that you understand that. Tell them . . . use the word "passion" . . . that way you don't sound like you're ordering him around. Say that it's not good for that much passion to come out and, especially, not good for the session . . . that it makes it all that much harder and will take more time . . . you know, be more expensive than it should be. That way, you're elevating them and telling them that they've got something real special. You know, play on the positive side and then stress that all that passion can get out of hand . . . and under the circumstances, you're required to make a formal agreement with them that the violence must stop. If it doesn't, say you won't be allowed to help them anymore. What you're saying to them, too, is that that's something [the passion] they should keep to themselves and not bring to the session. Just say, "I realize you folks have a lot of passion and deep feeling for each other" and that you don't want to get involved with that in the session. One of the goals you should set for yourself in the upcoming sessions is to feel that you control this couple, that you don't feel intimidated by them. [Elaborates] I forgot how they were sitting. Were they sitting apart facing each other . . . like confronting each other? That's what you'd expect from . . .

CANTOR: [Interrupting] No, they were sitting next to each other like Kelly and me.

BILLINGS: Oh, I thought one was here and the other was [motions toward the other side of the room]. Well, that's good then. You've got something to build on.

Relations of control between Westside clients and referring agencies also are used to make sure things are set up to go as planned. Most of the IPs court-referred to Westside for drug and family counseling have been "popped" for possession of marijuana or cocaine. Referral may require regular attendance at counseling sessions and screening urine for drugs. Family members who refuse to cooperate with counselors may be warned that the court will not look favorably on failure to attend counseling or on so-called dirty urine (positive urine tests).

The threat of direct reports of a lack of cooperation to community control agents is common. Counselor Nancy Cantor explains that the possibility of reporting an IP to his or her probation officer gives families incentive to attend counseling sessions and pressure the IP to do likewise.

It's like this. What they call "community control" is the highest level of control by the criminal justice system of a person not in jail. There usually are restrictions on where the guy can go in the community. Like . . . let me give you an example of how it affects us here. I have this dame and she's pretty overweight. So we thought she might go to Weight Watchers . . . you know, to improve her self-image. I had to call her probation officer to get permission for her to go. Having that leverage helps. She doesn't want to get into any more trouble than she's already in. We like community control because it's a way to pressure the IP and the family. I just tell the family that if . . . well, if any of them don't continue to cooperate, I'll just have to mention to the probation officer that so-and-so is out of bounds.

Court liaison officers also may be used to put pressure on whole families. Again, the setup for taking control ostensibly comes from the outside—from the legal system that sends the family to Westside in the first place—as shown in the following extract from a group soup deliberation over an especially stubborn client named Curtis.

CANTOR: The urine I got out of him [Curtis] has been negative ... for coke.

BILLINGS: You're not testing him for marijuana?

CANTOR: No, but I only got one test for coke. Curtis is stubborn. I tried telling the family what'll happen if he doesn't cooperate but I don't know how much control they have over him. I don't know what to do if he doesn't come. I don't think I can get the family to put pressure on him because he's out of control. I talked to Phil [court liaison officer] earlier and he said to work it out in counseling.

NELSON: Did you explain that he wasn't coming in for counseling?

CANTOR: Not really. Not yet. I don't want to get him [Curtis] in any more trouble.

NELSON: I'll tell you what Phil will do if he [Curtis] doesn't show up. He'll just put him in jail.

CANTOR: [To Billings] So you think I should get Phil to put pressure on him?

BILLINGS: I think we have to be a bit careful here. There's a tendency to want to be real hard on this kind of guy because he's manipulative ... and I understand that. On the other hand, he's lost both of his parents and only has the aunt and uncle he's living with. Work on control. He's out of control. His whole life has been out of control. He had no control over his mother's car accident and his dad being killed [in the accident]. It's a theme that you could work on. If we could build on self-control, you might convince him that he could profit from what you have to offer.

NELSON: You can bet that Phil would help to convince them of that. I think we're being too easy on this guy. I think the aunt and uncle would react to a little pressure. Just say that you won't be able to do much to protect Curtis if the court gets wind of what he's doing.

Urine screenings are scheduled according to a drug's metabolizing rate and are paid for out of pocket by clients. Screenings are done more frequently for drugs that do not remain very long in the body, which is both a monetary and legal incentive to remain free of drugs. Nancy Cantor explains:

[The urine screening schedule] depends on the drug. Mostly it's coke here [at Westside]. Coke metabolizes in 3 or 4 days. So we usually tell the client that we want them to come in twice a week for a urine sample. And we make sure that they pee here right in front of us . . . like so they don't bring in someone else's clean pee. Some of them don't like it because they have to pay $7.50 out of their own pockets for each screening. [Chuckling] Some of *us* don't like it either. We ask the male staff to accompany the male clients to the bathroom to make sure it's their [the clients] urine. It was so funny . . . yesterday I asked Keith [counseling intern] to watch Grover [client] pee and when I saw Keith later, I nearly died laughing when he said, "Hallelujah! I must be a full-fledged counselor now because I watched a guy pee."

Counselor Donna Reddick notes that urine screening is especially useful in "heating up" the family, which in this case means pressuring family members to join the Westside staff in keeping the IP free of drugs:

We use the urine screening results in different ways, depending on the situation. When the screen is positive, which means that's dirty urine, we can use that to really heat up the family. It's a way to promote a crisis in the family system if we say that they had dirty urine and we can warn them about different things, like their son will go to jail or something worse.

But not all court referrals require Westside to screen for drugs, nor is it always clear what the actual community control consequences of dirty urines will be. Still, the mere threat of dire consequences is a source of control.

Of course, we don't really know if anyone will go to jail, but the family gets scared and we can use that to shake things up and get them moving on doing something about it. We can use it to shake up the enabling. It can change the dynamics. [Explains drug metabolism] Sometimes we're court-ordered to do screenings and to report the results. We try to get a handle on the reporting for our own advantage. The amount of screening depends on the drug. It's part of the treatment file. So we can just casually explain that we may have to do urines and that can help to set things up so they cooperate.

It is considered especially important that the whole family system, not just the client, be set up. To warn an IP alone that he or she will go to jail if the drug use continues is no guarantee that the system will respond. Yet, threatening the entire system can sometimes backfire, depending on its power structure. Counselor Kelly Seever points out:

> You have to get them all involved, so that they all have an investment in him [the IP] being drug-free. That way the whole system works on the problem. If it has any authority intact at all, you can elevate that and *it* works on the problem. The real problem comes when the IP is empowered. Then the system can work against you . . . like it works to protect the IP from any threats and that can be really, really bad.

Taking control also means running the show during therapy sessions and not letting clients get the upper hand, but keeping on top of the system. Displaying a confident and imposing demeanor is an important ingredient, mirroring a common sign of domestic authority. A halfhearted performance risks letting an overbearing father dominate the proceedings just as he does at home. A weak presence allows the impropriety of a commanding son or daughter to define the course of treatment according to his or her personal judgment.

Beginnings are especially important. According to its nature, the system has momentum. If the control status of the system is initially set at a level at which family members run the counseling process, system momentum is likely to overwhelm treatment. The received wisdom is to take control at the first encounter by setting a commanding tone. Inasmuch as the system's momentum will respond to the counselor's initiative, this is likely to hold the counselor in good stead for some time.

The counselor's verbalization discursively guides the session. The counselor who primarily responds to family members' talk permits them to direct the flow of interaction. The counselor who assertively engages the system stands to speak with authority and manage the system according to plan. Verbalization takes many forms, which variously affect the status of speakers. As a rule, those who speak the most are perceived as commanding the floor and, in turn, the system. It is believed that an effective counselor makes certain that he or she is repeatedly heard in the session. The effective counselor does not permit family members, especially those considered to have domestically inappropriate authority, to monopolize the proceedings. The effective counselor draws out family members who should be in command and attempts to discursively contain those who should not. Only those who should be in command are privileged to interrupt. Likewise, the volume and cadence of verbalization are managed. The counselor should be heard above others in the session and noticeably control the pace of the proceedings.

Although there are different strategies for discursively running the show, the basic rule is, as consultant Al Borba routinely cautions, "Don't tolerate therapeutic chaos." This is touchingly evident in Kelly Seever's plea in a group soup for help with a verbally "abusive" family, for whom she nonetheless has great affection.

SEEVER: I'd like to talk to you [Borba] about the Wallace family. I don't know if you know them. They're so close that they're constantly all over each other. But it's all wrong. Mom lives in the house with her children and her friend, Robert, who's come to be very close to the family. Unfortunately, he has AIDS and that, combined with everything else, has put a real gray cloud on everything. The kids are doing a lot of blaming. Mother has been keeping an eye on her 11-year-old daughter. Mom is concerned that the 11-year-old is having sex. [Mom is concerned] because they've already had two abortions in the family. It's wild.

BORBA: Two different daughters have had abortions. Amazing.

SEEVER: No, one of the daughters has had two abortions. [Elaborates] It's very sad. He's [Robert] become very close to the family and gives the mother a lot of support. I've talked to him. He's been in with the family and I have him on tape. He's told me a number of times that he hates sex because sex caused his AIDS. It's a real pity that anyone can say that they just outright hate sex. And Mom was sexually abused as a child. The real basis of the whole household seems to revolve around its sexuality. In one way or other, that's the theme you hear over and over, and it's not a pretty picture. [Elaborates] It screws up everyone's priorities and, of course, that makes the sexual thing all the worse.

CANTOR: I can see how difficult it must be for you, Kelly. I know you really care about them.

SEEVER: The homework for Mom was to go to Planned Parenthood with her daughters and get information. I wanted Mom to be more decisive, not just blab about everything. I told her to get some condoms and bring them home and have the kids play with them, to get a real feel for what they have to do, and to talk about prevention up front. [Elaborates]

BORBA: That's sounds about right . . . good processing.

SEEVER: My problem is that when they're in here, I can hardly get a handle on what's happening. The kids keep acting out. Every time I start talking about things with Mom, one of the kids'll yell at her about why she brings those things up. They don't want her to talk about them. They keep talking loudly and running in and out. I can hardly hear what Mom is saying. It's very, very difficult to do the session. I'm just drained by the end. [Elaborates] It's not that they're hurting my feelings or anything like that. Mom can be a wonderful lady and poor Robert . . . it's just that I feel verbally abused. It takes all my energy to get through the session . . . and it sometimes goes on and on. The last one lasted an hour and 45 minutes.

BORBA: So what are you going to do with them? Maybe you want to work on that with them.

SEEVER: What?

BORBA: The sound level. This family sounds very chaotic to me. It must be a real zoo at home. And they're bringing it here with them. It's a way of not getting to the heart of their problems. They just talk away at each other. You should remember that that kind of thing is exhausting for them, too. What they're doing . . . the dynamics of the thing . . . is they're very good at keeping the dynamics going and some-how they know that the more they keep it going, the farther and farther away from their sexuality they are. And, of course, the system is right in there with you and it's sucking you in, too. Don't tolerate therapeutic chaos. You have to break the cycle—the sound level, the interruptions. It's a way to bring some structure to this family, building on something that they can have to deal with their problems. [Elaborates] Maybe there are two structures you can provide . . . one is the sound level and the other is the length of time in the session.

SEEVER: I know what you're saying, Al, and I'll try to get things more under control. Believe me, I know that's the only way I'm going to make it. I've got to keep my cool, get a handle on them, and not let those kids motor-mouth me to death.

BORBA: That's what they're doing to Mom and, whether they know it or not, it's making it very difficult for the system to function.

SEEVER: It's just, . . . well, . . . you know how you get involved and all. The friend was dying of AIDS, but then he stabilized. I've been seeing them for a while. When they were in the throes of the problem, there was a lot of hurting and I've been seeing them since. The friend, Robert, has been very important because Mom's been counting on him to keep things running smoothly at home. He's kept them going since he's been with them. He's a real supportive influence.

BORBA: I know, I've been there, too. But that's a good way to lose control.

What is particularly striking about this discussion in relation to the Westside understanding of the basic reality of the home is the way in which considerations of how to run the show are affected by the sentiments of counseling. Although Borba and others sympathetically acknowledge the existence of emotions and the affection felt for families in the therapeutic process, the basic sense of the reality under consideration places a premium on maintaining therapeutic authority. Indeed, Borba states at the end, sentiments are a "good way to lose control," even as he admits that he, too, has been affected by such feelings.

SHAKING UP THE SYSTEM

The nature of the system suggests "shaking it up" in order to effect change, not just tinkering with individual parts. Working

on individual members' attitudes leaves the larger system intact—
a father who mentally reorients his overbearing attitude toward
his wife and children does not necessarily alter his interaction
with them, for it is fueled by the social inertia of custom. Although
education can provide personal insight, dysfunctional families
are sick in their own right, and educating individual family members about domestic relations does not directly alter their overall
dynamic. Least of all do changed sentiments affect the system.
According to the local understanding of system functioning,
authority underpins the family's interpersonal feelings; at most,
the emotions of domestic disorder reinforce or exaggerate their
foundation.

In shaking up the system, a counselor initially aims to "join"
the family, that is, the system comprising it. The counselor may
actively join Mom against an overbearing dad by openly siding
with her in a session. This is believed to shake up the entire system's
sense of Mom and Dad's relationship with each other and with
other members of the household.

The live soup of a suspected wife battery case highlights how
disconcerting the shake-up can be to family members, who expect Dad to be Dad and Mom to be herself. Dad has been monop-
olizing the conversation, several times demanding that his wife
Cora shut up. At one point as consultant Al Borba and other counselors monitor the proceedings, Borba remarks that Kelly Seever,
the working counselor in the adjacent room, "could really shake
up that system if she sided with Mom right now." In the following
exchange, note how staff members' subsequent remarks reify the
system ostensibly under consideration, eventually telling of change.

NELSON: Man, oh man, does that guy [Dad] like to hear himself talk.

CANTOR: Talk?! You call that talking. I wouldn't put up with that
crap. I wouldn't take that from anyone. He tells her [Mom]
to shut up every time she opens her mouth . . . like he
doesn't want her to say anything he doesn't agree with.
What kind of crap is that?

KORSON: Did you notice how he looks at the kids? Kelly can hardly
get a peep out of them. Does he ever have a mean look.
Would I hate to have that look come at me in a dark room.

It makes me shiver just thinking about it. It's so hateful, like he wants to bash out their brains.

Proceedings in the counseling room heat up when Dad yells at Mom for not keeping the oldest daughter in line. At one point, he screams, "You're [Mom] just a big fool!" at which Mom seems to cower.

HORTON: Look at her [Mom]. She just sits there, the turkey. Why doesn't she say something? She lets him go on and on and just takes it. And the kids just sit there like they better not open their mouths, or whack! You saw what happened a minute ago when Jimmy [son] tried to explain to his father what happened at school . . . that poor kid started to say something and Dad gave him the meanest look.

KORSON: He [Jimmy] said, "I'm sorry."

HORTON: He should have said, "I'm sorry for living." There's a self-reinforcing system if I ever saw one. They all feed right into it. Like they all have their sick roles to play. It's classic.

BORBA: And none of them knows what to do about it. You can't really blame Mom, now, can you? Look, she's just used to being beat down. She's playing her role. She knows that if she shuts up, he'll quiet down. It's automatic.

KORSON: And the kids know it, too. They play right into it.

BORBA: And something else. Now don't get me wrong, but Dad doesn't know any better either. We can't excuse what he's doing . . . what he might be doing to his kids and to the wife. But, in a way, he's not to blame either because they're all feeding right into it. The system's orchestrating everyone.

KORSON: Like puppets.

BORBA: That's right. And now's the time that I think we've got to get Kelly to pull some strings.

Borba telephones the counseling room and directs Seever to provoke Dad, to get things going and then openly join Mom against him.

BORBA: [Ending the telephone call] Make sure that you heat things up a bit before you join Mom. I'd be really firm, because this guy's really weird and doesn't know what he's doing. No one in that family's ever confronted him.

The staff members gathered in the monitoring room watch for and distinguish two entities: Seever's and each family member's individual behavior on the one hand and the conduct of the system as a whole on the other. As Seever attempts to heat things up, the observers scrutinize the proceedings for signs of change, in particular, clues that a more proper balance in domestic authority is being achieved. Dad has just told his wife to shut up, to which Seever responds.

SEEVER: Hold on there, Mike [Dad]. Have you ever listened to yourself, to what you're saying? I'm Mom right now and you've just told me to shut up. I don't like that. I don't like it at all! What if I told you to shut up? Shut up, Mike! Just shut right up!

There are immediate expressions of amazement in the monitoring room. Mike is overheard responding that he does not really mean to tell his wife to shut up in so many words. Seever explains that that is the way he is heard by the whole family. She continues the provocation.

SEEVER: [Speaking directly to Mike] I'm going to be Mom whenever you tell us to shut up. [Turns to Mom] We're not going to let it happen. Okay?

Again, there's an approving response in the monitoring room. Two counselors actually applaud Seever's courageous stance.

REDDICK: That-a-girl, Kel. That took a lot of guts, grabbing the bull by the . . . horns. [Laughter] I don't know how she does it sometimes. What if that guy gets violent? That would always be in the back of my mind.

They pause for observation.

NELSON: Man, like, listen to them. It's like they got hit by a ton of bricks. Mike doesn't know what to make of it. [Pauses and then suddenly points to the monitor] Listen up! Just look how they're looking at each other, would ya, like they're being yanked around.

BORBA: Now, if Kelly can just manage to keep things going, they'll have to adjust to a new way of dealing with each other. That's the way to shake things up. But she'll have to keep after them or the system'll just pull them back to where things were before. There's got to be a new equilibrium built up.

Borba telephones Seever.

BORBA: [Speaking to Seever] Good work. Good joining with Mom. [Briefly elaborates] I think we're getting somewhere. You should see them . . . like a cloud came over them. You've got to keep the heat on. Don't let them slip away from you. Get them sucked into a new dynamic. Keep being Mom, but play it carefully. You don't want to elevate Mom so much that Dad gets blown off like a lead balloon.

As live soup continues and the onlookers discuss the proceedings, talk and interaction in the monitoring room affirm the separate realities evidently being observed. Speaking of the system, staffers indicate its effect on Seever and individual family members. Ordinary words and expressions such as "a cloud [coming] over them," a "new dynamic," and "[getting] blown off" reference something discursively distinct, an altered entity standing over and above the individuals participating in the counseling session and, as staff would hope, the family troubles being treated.

Not all interventions have such immediate or obvious results. Still, attempts that seem to fail or provocations that yield undramatic effects after repeated intervention are nonetheless construed as operating at two distinct levels—as the system itself and in its individual role players. Whether or not attempts to shake up the system succeed, the entity being treated and scrutinized is understood to be something larger than Mom, Dad, and other individual members of the household, something to be managed in its own right.

The system also may be shaken up by "paradoxical provocation." Because the resilience of the system keeps it on an even
keel, a movement, poke, or shove in one direction produces a reaction in the opposite direction. In particular, movement in an undesirable direction will produce a countermovement. As long as
the paradoxical provocation is not too strong, making things worse
should work to make things better.

Haley (1976, pp. 72-73) presents the case of a 9-year-old boy
who is referred to a clinic for compulsive public masturbation. The
boy masturbates at school and at home in front of his mother and
sisters. According to the mother, the habit is so pervasive that he has
worn holes in the crotch of his pants and has been hospitalized
for blood in his urine. Psychotherapeutic techniques ranging from
insight to rewards and punishments meet with no success. Then
a child therapist refers the boy for family therapy, on the assumption that the home situation is an important ingredient of the problem. The family live on welfare; the father died some time ago, but
other, extended kin live in the household.

The family therapist takes the approach of encouraging the boy
to increase his masturbation. From study, it is evident that the boy
enjoys masturbating most on Sundays. The therapist's directive
is to do it more on Sunday, when he enjoys it, and less on other
days. Haley writes, "[The boy] was asked to do it eight times on
Sunday, twice as often, perhaps getting up early to get it done"
(p. 74). The family is not to get upset over this, but treat it noncha-
lantly. In time, the boy finds that the regimen interferes with his
recreational activities. What is more, it does not seem to draw
anyone's attention, least of all his mother's, for she acts indifferent. The boy loses interest in masturbating. Meanwhile, the therapist continues to work on other issues in family counseling sessions, such as the boy's sports activities and girlfriends, the daughter's problems, and the mother's personal concerns, all of which
divert attention from the boy's presenting problem.

Westside counselors adapt the social logic of such cases to their
own needs, emphasizing the paradoxical manipulation of authority. Counselors sometimes speak of sharply "escalating" a paradoxical authority. For example, in domestic situations in which
it is believed that Mom or the children are making decisions that

Dad or the parents together should be making, the strategy is to elevate Mom or the children so much as to spark a reaction.

In group soup, counseling intern Roger Savage reports using an IP's claimed control over a cocaine habit as a paradoxical strategy for change. The IP is a 20-year-old single woman who lives with her parents. The parents are self-referred, hoping to get help for their daughter, who, according to the father, "has lost all direction in her life since this thing [the habit] got ahold of her." Savage comments on his initial failed attempt to "get Dad to be more forceful in the family." It seemed that part of the underlying problem was the daughter's subtle overdependence on parents who could hardly work through their own difficulties.

> At the beginning, I thought I read them as Dad was, you know, like really ineffective. Mom wasn't too swift either. She let Jack [Dad] make all the decisions because . . . like she's always saying, "He's the man of the house and he should decide." Huh! Jack's one of those . . . there's-this-and-there's-that types. You know, any time a decision has to be made, there's this and there's that. He brings up so many conditions and creates such a maze for himself that he can't find his way out. Can you believe what it's like living with someone like that? [Elaborates] It would drive you up a wall. That's what Cheryl [the IP] is up against. So at first what I thought I'd do is elevate Dad . . . you know, get him to recognize the firm decision he did make [bring his daughter to Westside] and get, especially Cheryl, to realize that he could be very helpful in dealing with her addiction. Needless to say, that didn't get me anywhere.

Haley's chapter on paradoxical intervention gave Savage the idea to "try something really weird," which seemed to work. According to Savage, it was weird because it suggested getting Cheryl to make her habit more systematic, smoking on a fixed schedule rather than when it suited her. Savage reports, "When I mentioned what should be done, even the suggestion got a rise out of them."

> When I told them all to keep track of it, for the first time . . . Dad just fell all over himself and started to like gush

over with this and that. Like he said, "Hey, I thought we came in here to get her [Cheryl] off this thing [the habit], not to make a game out of it." You should have seen it. The more I put him down, subtle-like, the more Cheryl defended him. I really got a kick out of Jack, too. He got all huffy and decisive for a change. Cheryl didn't like what I was saying to Dad because, like she asks, "You've got to depend on your parents . . . real parents. Who else do you have to help you keep your life together?"

The responses from consultant Dick Billings and the other counselors to Savage's achievement shows how central the system entity and domestic authority are to their understanding of intervention.

BILLINGS: I'll bet you didn't realize how powerful that system could be, did you?

SAVAGE: I just fell into it. Like I said, I was just reading some Haley and this weird idea kinda struck me . . . that I should try something really different. So, . . .

BILLINGS: So you "paradoxed" it. It's totally illogical, but that's how the system works. It's not reasonable. You think . . . when you want to get rid of a problem, you naturally work to get rid of it. Right? Wrong! You can work on making it worse and I guarantee you that that old system will respond and balance itself out. It does it every time.

SAVAGE: I think it just made Dad mad as hell [to hear that drug use was being encouraged, not discouraged]. That was too much for him and that old id of his gushed right out at me.

BILLINGS: Let's not get too hyped on old id. What you were seeing is the system shaking out. Dad was reacting like you'd expect he would. [Elaborates]

REDDICK: When you showed them that you were going to . . . like join the coke, they reacted. Like Dick said, they had to react. Dad had no choice. He was being forced to be Dad for a change, even though his old lady [wife] likes to say he's the man of the house.

SAVAGE: Oh, her . . . all she sees is the drugs. She doesn't think anything is wrong at home. She thinks that everything is just peachy . . . you know, like Dad's in charge and Daughter's having a bit of a problem.

SEEVER: The poor ignoramus doesn't realize that she's part of the problem herself. She's so sucked into this image of Dad's at the helm and we all follow the great white father that she's just a big dope being led along. I've seen a lot of women like her. They don't realize that Dad's a poor excuse for a father and that makes it all the worse. Talk about head in the sand.

Once again, staff members are reminded that what is going on in the system is not the brewing and interplay of feelings but the dynamics of authority. It is not that Dad's id bursts forth to vindicate his concern, but that a system's mechanics are programmed to respond to Savage's disequilibrating provocation. Even the daughter is quick to support an otherwise ineffective father, because, as she is reported to have claimed, one needs "real parents" to help one deal with life's problem. The outcomes of paradoxical intervention are not rational individual responses. Dad, it is thought, has no choice. He is forced to change, because of the power of the system of which he is a part, a system the wife apparently is unaware rests on the inertia of ineffective authority.

By and large, Westsiders keep the concrete reality of the system in focus, but the search for ways to shake it up occasionally brings the social construction process to the fore. Staff members sound like the new social constructivists in family therapy (see *Family Therapy Networker*, 1988), who question the epistemological priority of domestic reality, implicating therapists in creating the reality of systems otherwise taken to be objective and implying that the system is a product of the therapists' own making.

Deliberations over "reframing" are notable in this regard. According to Simon, Stierlin, and Wynne (1985, p. 286), *reframing* "refers to a therapeutic strategy that effects an alteration in a client's or family's internal model of the world." The authors explain that since frames shape conduct, "when reframing is effective, a change in behavior is to be expected." The notion is informed by Erving Goffman's (1974) conception of frame as a way of viewing the organization of experience—for example, approaching a family system as if it basically is closely knit although its members claim to be distant, is an attempt to reframe their view of domestic life.

Consider a group soup discussion of how to reframe a mother's sense of her relationship with her children, especially a 14-year-old daughter who the mother claims is "totally alienated" from the family. After extended videotape viewing and a lengthy and belabored exchange over what the mother actually thinks is occurring in her family, counseling intern Sara Brighton summarizes what she takes to be staff's conclusion. Al Borba is the consultant.

BRIGHTON: It's obvious we all don't see this mother in the same way. Tammy [Horton], I know you think the mother has other things in mind besides how Shana [the daughter] fits into the family picture, and, Roger [another intern], your point is well taken about Shana's trying to con Mom sometimes. But I think we all agree that Shana is a very troubled young lady. She's all wrapped up in herself. She skips school. It looks like she's sexually active. [Elaborates] Mom sees the situation like this. She really believes Shana is depressed because her daughter is slowly realizing that Mom doesn't belong to her alone, that Mom's got other responsibilities . . . like trying to make a living and keep the kids with a roof over their heads and food on the table.

SAVAGE: I don't know, Sara . . . . Shana sounds like a pretty sharp kid to me. That girl's no fool. You saw how she spoke up [on tape] and spilled her beans about how guilty she feels sometimes when she gets Mom to think she's sick and depressed when she really isn't. I'd call that pretty sneaky and Mom snowed.

BRIGHTON: Yeah, . . . I guess. But maybe you don't have a feel for the whole picture. When Shana says things like that, I've gotten to feel that she's just trying to get Mom's attention. You know, . . . she needs Mom and she apologizes for saying outrageous things and that gets Mom to feel guilty and sorry for her. She gets Mom's attention for what I think is a real problem. And I think Mom sees things that way, too.

Discussion ranges over the different interpretations.

BORBA: We're not going to settle this this afternoon, I can see that. [Laughter] You're all being very perceptive. That's good. You're tracking and seeing things that, to be honest, I didn't even see. The dynamic here is intriguing. Someone [Shana] *appears* depressed and totally alienated from her family, which may or may not be real. It seems she's depressed. Maybe she somehow came to believe she's depressed and convinced Mom of that, too. Who's to say she's not really depressed?

SEEVER: Oh, come on, Al. Do you really believe that that girl's depressed? I think Mom's letting her believe that so Mom can show she cares and that makes Mom feel that she's on top of things.

BRIGHTON: I can see that we're back to Square 1.

CANTOR: I think the problem here is that we're each framing this differently. Sara's making Mom out to be the good guy, and Kelly sees Shana as really thinking something else. What's real here? Who are we going to believe. [Chuckles] Look, guys, I'm having a rough enough time right now just figuring where you guys are on this. [Turns to Brighton] Sara, this is a black family and, . . . well, . . . maybe we're not reading it the right way. How would you frame it as a black person?

BRIGHTON: [Long pause and puzzled look] I guess I never even thought of it that way. Black families get depressed, too. [Laughter] They sure do. Whatever, . . . I still see Mom as pretty much on top of things here.

The focus on the differences in framing slows down a bit as Al Borba compliments Brighton on her work with the family. Eventually, with considerable irony, Borba returns to the question of framing.

BORBA: But that doesn't take care of *our* problem, does it? What's really going on in this family is the question? After listening to what we've each said, don't you all get the feeling that if *we* could just settle our differences, we'd have an agreement on what's real here, sorta like reality by democracy? [Chuckles]

SEEVER: They say, Al, that truth is in the eyes of the beholder.

BORBA: That's what they say. I know. [Pause] I'm serious. That's where some family therapists are right now. It's all about framing and reframing and reality. Very philosophical.

[Pause] But very important, I think. I think what's at issue here is how are we going to reframe this family? [Pause] Let's create a reality for them . . . the whole ball of wax. Never mind what's really real. We're never going to get to the bottom of that. I guarantee it.

NELSON: You're not telling us that this family is not really sick, are you, Al? That we have to frame them as sick to give them therapy? I don't accept that. These families *are* sick. I've heard that argument, and I don't buy it. I mean, . . . what are we doing here then, just spinning our wheels?

Nelson's earnest objection briefly turns the group soup into a philosophical discussion of the nature of framing and the relation of reframing to the reality of domestic disorder. The social constructivist movement is referenced tangentially. Attention is focused on the part the counselors themselves play in producing the reality of this particular family. With due respect given to the "very interesting questions" being raised by the movement in general, all nonetheless repeatedly return to the issue of how to reframe *this* family's reality. The philosophical issue is eclipsed as the proceedings concentrate on methodology.

BORBA: It's important to see this in the right perspective. We . . . each of us . . . you can work the reframing like you always do. Reframe what's happening and just process it out. [Elaborates] It's another counseling strategy. Just think how you can really shake things up if you go in there just thinking and acting in a completely different way. Talk to Mom like she's always been in complete charge of things. It's important that Mom be treated like everyone knows that Shana is just a child.

SEEVER: I'd frame it to take the focus off Shana and put it on Mom's power.

BRIGHTON: Yeah, . . . I like that. Mom does need a lift.

BORBA: You've got to try to get Mom to make the decisions. It's real important to elevate Mom when she takes over. Compliment her and tell her how wonderful it is that she has been able to arrange to make time for Shana. Tell Mom that. Like I said, it's important that Mom knows that Shana is still a child. That way you contaminate the power the child has. Frame it with Mom at the top of the hierarchy. Don't ask Shana what she wants to do. Ask Mom what she believes is best for Shana. If you can get Mom alone . . . like when Shana goes out of the room . . . ask Mom like, "Can't you see that you're asking a 14-year-old what she should do this summer? *You* need to make that decision for her." If Mom describes the child as being depressed, when you build on that, reframe it to help Mom set boundaries so Mom can get on top of it. Make Mom the instigator of help to her daughter, rather than just a reactor. You've got to strike the right balance. If you take it as a heavy thing and Mom takes it as a light thing, there's going to be such cognitive dissonance that you won't get anywhere. [Elaborates] This mother is giving this daughter permission to be a sexual being at age 14 and what you have to do is reverse that. Reframe it by asking if Mom really thinks it's right for Shana to make those kinds of decisions.

BRIGHTON: So I should just see Mom?

BORBA: I would see Mom for the first 15 minutes or so. Let Shana wait in the lobby. Then I'd bring her in.

The remaining moments of the case review dwell on the procedure for reshaping the system. Reframing becomes a strategy for restoring hierarchy, just as joining and elevating are indicated elsewhere in the process. As in other cases, it is suggested that Sara assign Mom and Shana "homework," in this instance comprising assertively giving directives for the Mother and attention skills for Shana. Shaking up the system has become a method, domestic authority returning to the proceedings as a therapeutic aim.

PART THREE

Fairview Hospital

Domestic Sentiments and Control

The fundamental reality of the home at Fairview stands in dramatic contrast with that at Westside, family troubles being embedded in the respective organization's very different images of domesticity. At Westside, attention focuses on the system, an object separate and distinct from individual members, operating over and above them. In the background are feelings, unconscious desires, and felt needs, among other less significant personal paraphernalia. System references at Fairview are not so much to a separate and distinct entity as they are a kind of shorthand for the mutual feelings and related interactions of the home. Family treatment at Fairview is a therapeutic encounter with emotional beings and the bonds of sentiment among them.

The feelings of those who reside in the home can have a significant impact on its daily life and rhythms. This includes live-in friends and lovers. Anyone residing in the home may be considered family, just as there are some, it is claimed, who should not be resident because they are not "being family." In the Fairview understanding, the feelings of each person in the home should be taken into account in dealing with domestic problems.

This is not to say that other settings are bereft of feelings. The husbands and wives who participate in the evening program for families at the addictive diseases unit speak in passionate detail of work, leisure, and community settings in which feelings are not properly expressed or unappreciated. The adolescents who join parents, other family members, and significant others in multi-family group ("group") discussions on Sundays or who, following discharge, participate in aftercare sessions one evening per week share the felt setbacks and successes of school and work as well as home. Hospital life itself presents feelings that bear on the home, such as the familylike bonds that adolescents form as inpatients.

Still, as Lasch (1977) puts it, the home is considered to be the final "haven." According to Fairview staffers, home is unique in being the only setting held together by feelings, in particular, the mutual and gratuitous sharing of self or love. If, for better or worse, other settings appropriate feelings to their activities, the home is where emotional life is first formed and where, it is hoped, it freely develops and crystallizes. In essence, the healthy or loving home is the bedrock of life. Other settings sharing these characteristics are accordingly said to be "homelike" and their memberships "familylike." As family therapist Dave Shindell explains in a parent effectiveness training group:

> Family operates on a real emotional level called "love." That's the bottom line. You've got it other places, of course, but the family's unique because that's the source. That's what family is all about and that, unfortunately, is also where all the trouble comes from. Then expectations work on in over that . . . like "You do this and if you want me to do that, then you'll have to do so-and-so." So expectations fall in there. There are all kinds of conditions put in the way, like power trips. [Elaborates] That, my friends, is when you fail to love, . . . to recognize the other person for themselves, deep inside. You've got feelings and you've got love. What happens when unconditional love is there, the child starts to grow . . . and others grow and trust, too. It's real, real important to be consistent with your adolescent in this way. [Elaborates] That's what makes a home a home. There's no place quite like it. You know it. I know it. If you're inconsistent, you risk questioning that basic love that's the family and that holds things together.

For some, the truly loving home is hard to find. Family therapist Tim Benson describes existing homes from a quasi-statistical standpoint. Similarly linking home and love, his remarks in an ADU family group indicate that there are few really functional families.

> If you ask me, I'd say, offhand, that 95% of the homes these days are dysfunctional. You name a family, and I'll bet you I can show you a home where feelings are all screwed up. I'd say there are probably fewer than 2% of the homes that you could really call loving homes . . . you know, where everyone has respect for the other guy's feelings and shares feelings and knows how to give when someone is hurting . . . you know, recognize feelings. [Elaborates] And, ladies and gentleman, that's what we're up against and what we're here for: to help you share those feelings, . . . get them out on the table, and try to rebuild your families. Love's where it's at. When love breaks down, that's when the trouble starts.

THE ORGANIZATION OF DOMESTIC SENTIMENTS

The home comprises two primary components that distinguish it as an entity. First is its essential substance: individual members' sentiments. Although reason and household rules affect or articulate sentiments, feelings are fundamental. As Dave Shindell noted, more than any grouping or institution, the family's basic structure is a sentimental order.

The second component is the social glue that holds together the collection of characteristic sentiments: the love of family members and significant others in the home. Love is a mechanism of social integration at Fairview, but it lacks the phenomenological status the system has at Westside. At Westside, the system is taken to be an entity distinct from individual members of the household, virtually a separate being with its own life force; what Fairview staffers call "love" and sometimes "trust" is understood to be a gratuitous personal offering, an open orientation to the other, not a condition of experience standing over and above individuals. Love has no distinct system, but is, rather, an expression noticeable and denotable in a person's empathetic action.

Social integration or functionality exists in a home to the extent family members love and trust one another. Because these are characteristic of individuals, anyone can threaten the whole. In addition, women, particularly, can "love too much" and, as a result, so forcefully bind themselves to others as to control them and destroy the gratuitous mutuality of their respective sentiments. Given the voluntaristic quality of the social glue, a problem for one is a problem for all. Personal troubles are by definition domestic issues. According to the ADU program director, this requires a family orientation:

> I guess we could have them [patients] each in here alone . . . you know, just take them out of, away from, those unhealthy settings [homes] and place them each into full-time treatment. The problem is that you might turn him or her around and, bingo, when they return home, it starts all over again— the accusations, the yelling, the outbursts, overdependence, the suspicion, enabling, you name it. You've got to have a give-and-take feeling there that's shared . . . basic trust between all of them. One rotten apple'll spoil the bunch. It's not going to work to have one learn how to express feelings and be open and concerned for others and you get nothing but grief in return. That's why we have to get the whole family in here. They all have to learn what it means to love each another . . . that everyone has needs and feelings, not just this or that son or daughter or husband who happens to be in here for treatment.

The unhealthy home is a "heartless world" filled with sentimental strangers, where the feelings that surely exist in each member's experience are ignored or unknown. It is a household without love. In such a world, feelings are likely to simmer ominously, build up to the danger point, and eventually boil over or burst out of control, to the detriment of all. It is a world whose members are in dire need of interpersonal recognition and respect. Because love is lacking, sooner or later the situation can only break down into the brutal chaos of uncontrolled individualized emotion.

This heartless world, or dysfunctional home, is metaphorically cold. As Georg Simmel (1950, pp. 402-408) reminds us, strangers are interpersonally "objective," mutually orienting to very general categories of presence; their attention is not aligned to the unique characteristics of others, but to abstract properties. A distressed father's comments in a parent effectiveness training session concretely reference the opposing characteristics of home and the "cold nasty" world. Comparing what his son, Jack, "seems to prefer," the father defines the home by what it is not.

> I don't understand Jack sometimes. We try to make a good home for him. But he seems to prefer the streets. My God, tell me, who really can say that they prefer that kind of life? Huh? It's a cold and nasty world out there. You find a lot of wolves that'll eat you up just like that. He seems to prefer the company of strangers. They don't know him like his family does. How could they? To them, he's just another Joe Blow. All they're interested in is what they can get out of him. They don't care how he feels deep down inside. They could care less. [Pause] And I hate to say that I think Jack's become one of them. He's like a stranger to us. When he's home, he treats us like he doesn't know us. He looks right through us like we're just a crowd of people . . . real cold-like. That's not the Jack we knew. [Details the old Jack] And [whimpers] you know what's sad, I think we're becoming the same. I don't ask him anymore, "Hey, Jack, how're you doing, boy?" No more. I don't care about my own son. I figure he's empty. [Pause] Just like strangers. We just come and go. It's just not home anymore.

The home ideally is warm and loving, but not "hot." In Fairview talk and understanding, *hot* can signify the personal turmoil and explosiveness generated by the home that has become too cold. Even strangers have feelings. If feelings are not given their due respect, they grow in intensity, covertly heating to the boiling point and eventually steaming forth. Jack's father explains:

> Sometimes, I just can't stand it. It makes me so mad to think that here it is my home and I feel like a stranger. What kind of life is that that you can't tell someone how you feel or don't dare to ask your own son, the stranger, how he feels. We all have feelings. I'm not a fish. It's no wonder I blow up sometimes. Who wouldn't? And it can get pretty hot, I tell ya.

A heartless world is metaphorically calculating. In this respect, the dysfunctional home is made up of people who orient to each other instrumentally, each figuring what is required to achieve a particular end. The other is not approached for him- or herself, on his or her own terms. As the father in the preceding example described, it is a world of "wolves," operating by a calculus of individual gain and loss. An adolescent hospitalized for depression and alcohol abuse portrays her "dog-eat-dog" household this way, again defining home by what it is not.

> There's no love at all there. My mom . . . all she cares about is herself. She's just too, too busy for words . . . for me or anyone else, really. She's always trying to figure out how she can get what she can out of me. My stepdad's the same. Really. Who cares how I feel? No one really gives a shit. I have feelings. I'm not a goddamn machine . . . cleaning up the house, washing the car, being here and there at just the right time so Mom can get on with her life. You've got to watch out for her, because everything's got an ulterior motive. For Mom, . . . well, as long as things are real down pat and everything is in its place and neat and all tacked down, that makes her happy. Does she ever ask or even wonder how *I* feel . . . like just for *me?* Hell, no! I'm just a goddamn dog and my home life is dog-eat-dog. I can swear to that.

Domestic sentiments escape control when the home becomes a heartless world. This is the kind of home that presents itself at Fairview in the empty, unloved lives of family members. Therapy aims to restore love or the mutual recognition of feelings, the hallmark of the functional family. The program director of the adolescent services unit explains:

> They [the adolescents] come in here or they're put in here because no one knows what to do. They're hurt. Mom and Dad are hurt. They're all hurting. Their lives are in shambles. They've tried everything. What we try to do is put those lives back together again or at least give them another chance. The way we see it, Hillary's doping because her home life's a wreck. Michael's drinking because no one loves him and he doesn't feel like family. Karen's high as a kite because that's

her way of getting away from, well, nothing. Ken is hot under the collar because Dad treats a friend more like a son than he does Ken. It's all the same, really, when you get down to it. It's feelings and it's trust. If we can get those things going again, we feel that we have a chance of licking their problems. The key is the home situation. So we try to teach them ways to understand each other and to recognize their own insides. No one is going to control those feelings by letting them get bottled up. That's just going to explode. That's why they're in here.

THE HISTORY OF DOMESTIC SENTIMENTS

ASU family therapists especially like to place the fundamental reality of domestic life in historical perspective. The family comprising equal and independent members who freely love and trust one another is today's functional family. Yesterday's functional family is altogether different, based on authority, not primarily love, with the rule of tradition and hierarchy paramount. Mutual regard is vertical. Children respect their parents for the leadership and good common sense they provide out of the wisdom that comes of experience. It is not so-called book learning that warrants parents' leadership, but the proverbial school of hard knocks. In the context of yesterday's family, children have much growing up to do; they have a long way to go to become responsible family members.

In yesterday's family, age, too, designates social order. Wisdom of years justifies older siblings' claims for respect from younger brothers and sisters, just as adult children respect their older parents. Generations hold sway over each other in due order: Grandparents possess authority over parents because of their experience in living, and parents rule children because parents have been "around longer" and have "learned the ropes."

Gender also secures yesterday's family. Because the father is "the man of the house," he commands the greatest respect in relation to authority. A good wife looks up to a good man, and no good husband would let down his spouse or his family. References to yesterday's domestic order usually feature the familiar effective older brother, rarely an older sister, as parental substitute when the father is missing. Families without an older brother to "take over" in the father's absence are destined for trouble. It is exceptional for an older sister to fill this role, considered contrary both to her own nature and to the natural domestic order. Indeed, the mother without a husband who succeeds in keeping her family together and the children out of trouble, or the older sister without parents who keeps the home front under control, is considered exceptional, effectively "filling big britches."

Work, too, figures in this retrospective. In the traditional family, father works and mother remains at home. Yet, father is the man of the house, his decisions on behalf of the family as a whole are informed by experiences in the wider world, not to mention the resources and formal recognition he commands for being the breadwinner. Mother's decisions are limited to her area of expertise, namely, the management of the household. When this division of responsibility breaks down, trouble arises. In yesterday's home, an unemployed father serves to explain as many family troubles as a working mother. Today's functional family is different. With both parents working and sharing in the family economy of responsibility and sentiment, it is the lack of mutuality and an undemocratic attitude that causes problems.

The "olden days" had their share of domestic disorder, perhaps not drug related, but certainly evident in excessive drinking, domestic violence, and sexual promiscuity. In the Fairview understanding, these were by-products of a breakdown in authority. Families without the full complement of parents were unstable, and the children of "broken homes" were likely to get into trouble. The death of a parent meant the loss of a role model who would otherwise have provided the wisdom of experience. Daughters became pregnant before marriage and sons became delinquent or criminal. Again, exceptions proved their rules.

This conception of the family of yesterday is frequently used to define today's functional family and the hospital's aims in treatment. It is said that in today's world the traditional family is anachronistic, if not problematic. Today's functional family is *democratic*, with equality and mutual respect for individual feelings, based on love or trust. Yesterday's functional family was *autocratic,* with authority the basis of domestic order. The terms—democratic and autocratic— reference models of the currently preferred and the currently undesirable as well as the present and the past.

Actual families are compared to the models. In a parent effectiveness training class, therapist Dave Shindell uses the models to make points about such matters as punishment and preferred parent-child relationships.

> We don't use the word *punishment* anymore. Punishment is old-fashioned. Punishment is jail. If you listen carefully and read the materials I handed out, you'll see that we talk about *consequences* now. It's not like "If you do this or if you do that, you're going to get smacked or get a beating." That's negative. That's power. That's the autocratic model speaking. It's based on control and punishment. We find it's more appropriate to talk about the *consequences* of misbehavior. We talk about the consequences because consequences can be positive or negative. We use the democratic model . . . you know, we're all involved in agreeing on the rules and talking out differences and feelings. It's not just "That's the way it is!"

Following a discussion of various aspects of the models and their historical relationship, several parents remark that the autocratic model is "still very much around," to which Shindell responds didactically, using his own family experience as illustration.

MOM A: Oh, I don't know, Dave. I find that that model is still very much around. What did you call it?

SHINDELL: The autocratic model.

MOM A: That fits my sister's family to a T. I mean it's like whatever Tom [the father] says is the law. Boy, does he lay down the law. I don't know how my sister stands it. I ask her sometimes, "Andrea, how can you and the kids live like that? None of you has any opinions or says anything." She just shrugs her shoulders. I take the hint; I don't think she wants to talk about it.

SHINDELL: But that's the point. Right there! You have to talk about it and that's the problem with the autocratic family in today's world. I'm not saying that those kinds of families aren't around. I'll bet that most of you here know families like that. [Several nod or agree] They're real old-fashioned, with Dad right up there, godlike, and Mom doing the dishes in the kitchen listening to him spout off. That's the way the family used to be. I remember from when I was a kid, my dad had nothing to do with negotiation. He laid down the law and that was that. That was the autocratic model. You didn't think, like "What's the worst thing that can happen to me if I do that? What's the best thing I can do?" You just did what you were supposed to or you got the consequences. Here we do things differently. We want to lay out the consequences very clearly and try to treat the adolescent as a young adult.

MOM B: You mean like an equal, don't you, Dave?

SHINDELL: Yeah, kinda. An equal in the sense that you respect your son's or daughter's opinions. Like you listen for his or her feelings and try to respect where they're coming from . . . like you'd expect from them.

DAD A: In other words, you don't just tell them to shut up when they're mouthing off.

SHINDELL: Well, it's like this. Did you ever stop and think that they might not mouth off if you took the time to listen to their feelings? The autocratic model . . . it probably was effective in the past, but now it's a different story. [Details the past and its support for autocracy] Nowadays, if you talk punishment, some people hear that as child abuse. Nowadays, everyone, including kids, has their rights. It [autocracy] just doesn't wash anymore and, frankly, it doesn't pay not to listen.

MOM A: I don't know, Dave. I try my darnedest to listen to Susan [her daughter who is a Fairview patient], but she acts like I don't matter, that I don't exist. I try to show her how much I love her. God knows! But it just doesn't work. That's why she's in here.

SHINDELL: Well, we're here to show you *how* to listen carefully and how to respond to Susan. We're going to give it our best shot. And she's in here for the same reason. She'll learn that you have feelings, too, and that you love her, but, . . . well, love is a two-way street and she needs to know that.

The contrast between the two models not only introduces family members to a preferred vision of domesticity, but follows them through treatment and after. For example, one evening in an aftercare session for adolescent former patients and their families, what therapist Ken Olsen calls the old value system eventually distinguishes the old and the new family as autocratic or democratic. The discussion follows a bit of lighthearted persuasion as Olsen responds to the report of a mother and her daughter Missy fighting during the week.

OLSEN: Okay. Let's go for how things are going. How've you all been the past week since we met last time? Missy, what's been happening in your life?

MISSY: Oh, we [mother and daughter] were fighting, but we better not talk about it.

MOTHER: I don't really want to get into it right now.

OLSEN: Can we skirt the issue and deal with the feelings underneath?

MOTHER: Well, I don't know, Ken. I think I've just gotten all talked out about it. Anyway, I get a bit tired about talking about *my feelings* all the time. . . .

OLSEN: [Humoring her] Oh, come on now, Mom, we all know you've got to feel something about what you and Melissa [Missy] have been going through. Let's hear it, Mom. You can do it.

Olsen persists in coaxing the mother, who coyly resists.

MOTHER: I can see that you're going to pull it all right out of me, Ken. [Pause] You've got to beg. [All laugh] No, just kidding. One of the issues is that Missy still can't sit and be home. She's always on the go. She says it's boring at home. She doesn't want to watch the same television programs Calvin [husband] and I do. I wish we could just have a pleasant evening at home once in a while as a family. I work all day and I don't see Missy very much. [Elaborates] But she's been pretty good about letting me know where she is. I guess being here [Fairview] did her some good in that regard. She can call me up to five times a day at work and wants to go out. She's real good about telling me where she's at. [Elaborates] Maybe the problem is me.

Missy is the last one [child] at home. I have three boys and Missy is the baby and I'd just like to see more of her. I think she thinks I'm boring. Like she says [imitating Missy], "You're so bo-o-o-ring, Mom." [All laugh]

MISSY: You're not boring, Mom. It's just that it's boring at home.

Missy and her mother bicker and banter at length about Missy's so-called platonic boyfriend, who never comes into the house to introduce himself to the mother, but waits for Missy in his pickup truck.

MOTHER: I can't seem to get it into her head that it's important for a parent to know who their daughter is going out with. We've been arguing about it all week. She says he's just a friend, just platonic. Heck, we have more communication when she's not home, because she calls me all the time.

MISSY: Oh, Mom, you don't even know how I feel. You don't even listen when I tell you he's just a friend.

MOTHER: Look, Melissa, it's a parent's right to know. I'm just going to have to demand to know who he is. That's all. Or you'll be grounded and there'll be no buts about it.

OLSEN: Missy, . . . Mom, . . . you both remember that old value system we talked about. It used to work very well. Parents ruled and the children followed orders . . . or else. Mom, . . . I think we have to remember that in this day and age children have feelings and a certain freedom that we didn't have when we were their age. These are new times. And Missy, . . . you've got to remember, too, that Mom has feelings just like you do. She's not just a parent, way up there on a throne, lording it over you. Did you *really* listen to what she was saying to you a few minutes ago? She'd like to see more of you because she loves and cares for you. You've got to give that back to her. [Elaborates] I don't think that old autocratic model is very useful these days. No matter how much you try to force the issue, Mom, Missy's not going to listen if you don't try to understand her side of it. And Missy, don't you think you should try to put yourself in your mother's shoes and ask yourself, "How would I feel if I were her?" Society is not set up for the old value system anymore. No one is going to look favorably on parents treating their children harshly. [Pause]

> Of course, I'm not saying that's what's happening here, but . . .
>
> MOTHER: [Interrupting] Yeah, I guess I'm being a bit old-fashioned. Cal tells me I'm out of step with the times when it comes to my daughter: I don't listen. Well, maybe I am. It's just, well, she's the last one and she's all I have now. Maybe it's because she's a girl. You know how a mother gets.
>
> MISSY: But, Mom, you don't have to lay down the law like that. The boys [her brothers] say you did the same with them. It makes you so hateful sometimes. What about the way I feel? Do you care about that?

As Missy and her mother's exchange grows in intensity, two senses of their relationship come to the fore. Both Missy and her mother recognize the distinction under consideration, called the old value system, tradition, or the autocratic model on the one hand and modern times, nowadays, or the democratic model on the other. Several participants eventually convey separate experiences with "the times." Olsen repeats that it is important to keep in mind that today's adolescent is different from yesterday's, just as parenthood has changed since the olden days, suggesting that if parents and their teenagers realized this, they would not have the kind of trouble Missy and her mother have. Missy's mother seems to encapsulate the entire discussion when she confesses, "I guess I'm just being old-fashioned." She eventually admits, "I've just got to put that old-fashioned mind-set behind me, because it's just alienating Missy and wreaking havoc with my peace of mind." As if to reinforce the change in historical preference, another mother concludes:

> I think we know that our best bet is to keep a modern attitude. The kids, too. We all need to keep reminding ourselves that each of us is an individual with her own feelings. In olden times, you weren't supposed to have feelings. You just followed the rules. Point-blank. Kids stayed out of trouble because they had to or else. Nowadays, everything is set up so that that kind of attitude doesn't work . . . although, believe me, sometimes some of us wish it worked. It just makes everything that much worse. Nowadays, it all really gets down to feelings and trust.

The local view of the general history of domestic sentiments is as a movement away from the autocratic to the democratic model of control, but not everyone agrees about which model works best in particular circumstances. The old value system might have predominated in the past, the new one in so-called modern times, but, according to some, the old values still can be useful. Some family members suggest that the old values never should have been abandoned. For them, domestic sentiments have had an unfortunate history, in which a mode of relating that worked for parents, grandparents, and great-grandparents broke down and gave way to today's domestic chaos—disrespectful children, unruly adolescents, drug and alcohol abuse, and domestic violence. An angry and anxious father complains:

> I know things have changed, how we're supposed to respect each other's opinions and all. But I think it's gone too far. It really has. And it's too damn bad, too. I can't relate to having to explain everything to Tad [his hospitalized son]. He's bent on being out of control no matter what I do. I'm mad as hell about it. I've gone the full nine yards with him and I still haven't gotten to first base. [Elaborates] I'm totally frustrated and a nervous wreck and that's why he's in here. I'll try anything, even all this feelings and sharing stuff, if it works. But sometimes I think that, with this guy, what he really needs is the firm hand that my father and grandfather had with us. What he needs is a solid kick in the butt and his neck wrung. All this moral decay around us . . . that's what's making these kids the way they are. My son has no morals— drinking and drugging and never listening to jack shit.

Family and staff members admit that the past had its share of domestic troubles, that it certainly was no golden age as far as home was concerned. But a desire for control in difficult circumstances sometimes makes the efficient resolution of command that seemed to work in the past more attractive than the slower contemporary strategy of sharing. It is argued that if domestic chaos did exist in the past, it was either exceptional or limited to particular classes of people. Some family members consider the focus on individual feelings to be self-indulgent and, in the final analysis, detrimental to the efficient rule of the home. Bitterly complaining that her inpatient husband cannot seem to control his gambling and is not trustworthy, a wife cries in an evening ADU family group:

> I've lost all patience with him. I'm at my wits' end. [Weeping] I love the hunk but he just doesn't seem to care or even hear me. Everyone's too soft on the guy and he just eats it up . . . and look at what it does. He can be very, very sweet sometimes, but he's out of control underneath it all and it's just wrecking all of our lives. He needs to be chained down, that's what. [Details control required] He doesn't need to know how I feel. I've told him a million times. [Regaining her composure] But, look, . . . hey, I'll try anything. I think what he needs is a good dose of old-fashioned reality. You can't tell me that there was always this kind of trouble we see nowadays. If there was, it was just bad seed or them low-life classes. Today, it's affecting everybody. It's awful. [Weeps]

By and large, however, those who occasionally tout autocracy are pragmatic. Distressed about the problems of their hospitalized family members, they are willing to try anything, as we just heard one wife state, that offers the hope of relief from domestic troubles.

HOW POWER SPOILS

Anything that infringes on domestic love and respect for feelings spoils modern family functioning—not just blind allegiance to authority, but any attempt to "lord it" over or otherwise eclipse a family member's feelings is dysfunctional. So-called power trips routinely spoil domestic order.

If parents' arbitrary authority causes domestic chaos, adolescents have their own way of producing the same results. It may not be entirely adolescents' own doing. Peer pressure and the attractions of teen life and culture outside the home easily displace the mutual respect and love of any modern family. As is often noted at Fairview, in today's world, external pulls and attractions combine with the resources readily accessible to adolescents to avail the teenager of more power than he or she ever had before. Therapist Dennis McDonald explains:

> It's different today. My parents and their parents didn't have all the things these kids have nowadays. Look around. They've got a hundred malls to hang out in, a thousand movie complexes, all kinds of theme parks and joints just for the teenager. TV gets to them, too. You know, ya got to have this and ya got to have that, or else you're out of it. God help them if they're out of it! And they have tons of dough now, too. And if they don't have it, they find a way to get it . . . peddling dope and what have you. And do they get around! It's not just a bomb [jalopy]. It's like a brand-new Beemer [BMW] for some of them. Have they got it good. Too good. That kind of power really plays havoc at home. Some of them could care less. Everything plays into it. I mean, just look at the tube any night and you'll see an old man who's a dope and Mom is an airhead. Guess who's savvy?

Power trips spoil the recognition of others' feelings, creating resentment and an escalating suspicion and manipulation likely to spiral into domestic outbursts and violence. The important thing to note is that power easily gets out of hand, causing the modern family to go out of control. The spoilage is poignantly illustrated in group, as one parent or teenager after another relates how power trips affect their home lives. In a session composed of eight parents and their inpatient adolescents, child psychiatrist Robert Henderson (Dr. H) and ASU nurse Daisy Jackson discuss hospitalized teenager Carol Emery's progress in interacting with her mother, stepfather, and others, eventually focusing on the insidious intrusion of power into the household.

DR. H: Okay, Carol. Now your turn.

JACKSON: How do you feel about the strides you've made?

CAROL: Being able to talk to him [stepfather seated next to her] and him to me and express our feelings. That's an important thing, I guess.

DR. H: You guess?

CAROL: No, what I mean is that, at first, I didn't want him to be there . . . you know, be in the house and everything. He used to yell all the time. I didn't want him to come here [Fairview] either. Then they [mother and stepfather] used to come together. And now he's here alone sometimes and we're a family together now.

DR. H: You say you're able to communicate now, to express feelings better?

CAROL: I guess. Yeah.

JACKSON: That's real progress, I'd say.

DR. H: [To mother and stepdad] Now, here's a tough one. What have you learned new about each other?

STEPDAD: [Pause] I've noticed how Carol has changed and I'm beginning to see that she has feelings and I try to understand them. She's starting to take notice of others, too. Like her mother and I aren't just bumps on a log. You know, we have feelings, too. She used to think, I think, "Well, he's not really my dad, so I don't have to listen to him and I don't care how he feels." Remember, Carol?

CAROL: I guess.

MOM: I think she's more considerate now. I was really surprised. She really blew our minds a couple weeks ago when she asked her dad how he felt about being laid off work and not to worry because he'd find another job. [Elaborates] Wow, that sure wasn't the Carol we knew!

CAROL: Oh, come on, Mom, I really worry about you guys.

DR. H: [To Carol] So, you've been aware of others' feelings?

CAROL: At first, it was all yelling. [Elaborates] But what I guess I've learned new is that he [stepdad] was willing to change, to make a family together. I learned that he had feelings, too, and was willing to talk about how he felt. It really made a difference.

Carol's mother snickers. Irritated, Carol turns to her and complains about being made fun of. The mother immediately hugs her daughter and teasingly but tenderly describes what Carol was like "before."

MOM: I'm a power person and we were having a power struggle, my daughter and me. I think she's a power person, too, and that seems to present us with a real problem because each of us is always trying to get her own way. [To Carol] I thought at first that you had the problems and you were

              disrupting the family and so we put you in here. [De-
scribes the decision at length] I don't know. I thought I
was doing a good job. But now I know I wasn't. It [group
reading material] says it was a power trip.

DR. H: There's a lot of ways of being powerful. Describe it, Mom.

MOM: Well, it was always kind of the same. We'd come home
from work and be real tired-like. We wanted to have a
drink and relax before I got dinner going. She'd [Carol]
have her records blasting all over the house. He'd [hus-
band] yell at her to turn it down.

STEPDAD: I had to yell. She couldn't hear me over that crap.

MOM: Well, anyway, . . . one thing just led to another. It was
always the same. She'd have this little power fit. Like
she'd slam the door, it seemed with all her might. God,
you knew right away that would set him [her husband]
off. Sometimes she'd slam the door as soon as he walked
in the front door. You can imagine how he felt. It was like
a slap in the face. Well, needless to say, that would set
him off. He'd charge in there [Carol's bedroom] and start
yelling at her and she'd tell him to stop yelling. [Imitat-
ing Carol] "Why are you yelling? You're always yelling!
This is my room and you've got no business being in
here. Close the door!" That kind of stuff. It just made him
madder. And she'd get started, too, and get bent all out
of shape and walk out. She had a great habit of slamming
every door in the house on her way out. Didn't you,
Carol? [Hugs her]

CAROL: Look, Mom, it wasn't just me. You two do a lot of yelling,
too. You're both out of control most of the time. You never
listened to *me*.

MOM Y: I've been through it, too. We've all been there. It sounds
just like home sweet home to me. This one wants to do
something her way or doesn't want anybody to bother
her. Like she's a princess or something. They like to test
. . . like to see how far they can go. It's a power thing.
That starts it. I see it coming every time. I grit my teeth
and figure that I've got as much reason to get mad as she
does. I figure I'm not going to let her get away with it.
Why should I? It's my house! My food! [Turns to her
daughter] It's you against me, baby. [Turns to others] You
just start to lose control and you get mad and she gets
mad and you get madder. I just want to pull her hair out.

Several parents and adolescents join in and describe similar domestic scenes of uncontrolled emotional exchange. Emphasis is on the spoilage of power. Dr. H interrupts.

DR. H: There are a lot of ways of being powerful. Can you be powerful by being silent?

Several agree and briefly share instances of that form of domestic power.

DR. H: Can you be powerful by doing nothing?

Again, there is agreement and additional examples.

DR. H: They all are powerful. Each of them eats away at trust so that the only way anyone can express herself is a blowup. Feelings get hurt and have to be expressed and there's an outburst. Another feeling gets hurt and there's another explosion. One thing leads to another. That's the way power works to spoil family relations. The modern family doesn't know how to handle power trips. All it takes is one rotten apple to start a chain reaction. That's why you're here, . . . to learn how to share feelings and to really listen to one another. I know that several of you have a made a lot of progress in that regard.

The power that particular family members wield over themselves also can spoil domestic life. Rather than directly lording it over others, an individual member mistakenly feels he or she is fully in control of his or her personal affairs—a ruinous personal power trip, as it were, drawing unlimited attention to the individual and away from other family members. According to Fairview staffers, these are the hallmarks of, respectively, addiction and codependency.

For the addicted, the sense of control is false. For example, the husband who is addicted to alcohol claims that drinking is an activity he freely chooses to engage in and can schedule for his enjoyment and convenience. He is said to be unaware that the addiction has taken over his life, affecting his ability to make rational choices and, indeed, to control the habit itself. A false belief in self-control

overrides feelings and concern for others, making the addicted
completely self-centered. The addiction becomes the consuming
force in his life, to the detriment of love and trust. The woman or
young girl who loves too much has a similar psychological profile. She centers attention on the love object, typically a husband
or boyfriend who does not reciprocate or understand her zeal,
which is portrayed as pathological because it is obsessive. Like
the alcohol or drug addict, the "drug"—in her case love—consumes
her, even while she believes that she is in control of her emotions.
The obsession blinds her to other, equally important feelings,
particularly her helplessness and inner need. Giving her all to someone, she, like other addicts, inadvertently becomes self-centered,
unable to be genuinely open to, and concerned for, others' feelings.

As with addiction in general, in both of these cases a fundamentally emotional being falsely assumes that he or she controls
life. The assumption spoils, or masks, the self, expropriating the
person's basic humanity. This image of the addict, informed by
AA and the other As, aligns with the local image of domesticity.
Domestic life being what it is—a configuration of emotional bonds
—the family is functional when bonds are secure and dysfunctional when they break. It is said that the self-centered power trip
severely strains love and trust. The self-consumed addict cannot
genuinely love, for love requires gratuitous openness to others.
At the very least, the addict damages the modern family's social
integration. At worst, he or she destroys it altogether.

Originally associated with AA, the twelve-step philosophy is
the recovery approach of all the As. The recovery process is envisioned as twelve progressive steps of eschewing false personal
mastery, placing one's trust in a higher power, morally invento-
rying the self, and sharing the philosophy with others similarly
addicted (see Alcoholics Anonymous World Services, 1939/1976,
pp. 59-60). Twelve-step educational material is much in evidence
at Fairview, especially in the ASU and ADU, where addiction is
a common family problem. The twelve steps are not an exclusive
treatment resource, however. The clinical director explains:

> We use whatever works. The AA approach and the twelve
> steps stuff is fine, but we find that toughlove, for example,

is handy, too. They use STEP [Systematic Training for Effective Parenting] on the ASU and that seems to work out real well. We have our point program in there, too. We're always looking for new ideas and new treatment modalities. Right now, I'm looking into a computer-assisted program that might help us to more efficiently get at these folks' emotional lives. I guess the point is that we're not stuck on any one methodology. These folks [patients and family members] have *real* emotional problems and we use whatever we need to help them.

The clinical director emphasizes, it is *real* emotional problems, not any one recovery strategy, that is the central commitment.

What is more, Fairview staffers are not equally partial to the twelve-step approach. ADU therapist Tim Benson seems to be sold on it, dealing as he routinely does with a range of adult chemical addictions. The therapists on the ASU use it and its terminology in the course of working with similar adolescent addictions, but tend to ignore it in dealing with behavioral problems such as truancy or domestic violence. The psychiatrists are less professionally committed, often applying more standard psychotherapeutic techniques. Still, the twelve-step approach is likely to emerge when issues of personal obsession and their related feelings come under consideration.

Although addiction is personal power gone awry, its effects ripple throughout the family and strain the emotional life of every member. Fairview staffers borrow heavily from the language of codependency, seeing it—in contrast to Westsiders' view—as a vocabulary that spells out how family members inadvertently yet systematically support a problem and magnify it. The wife of an addict who both loves her husband and attempts to contain his problem, covering for him in public and attempting to ease the effect of the problem at home, is "enabling," further empowering the addict. Not facing up to her own feelings, which are considered to be in dire need of attention, the wife selflessly devotes herself to her husband's problem. Her commitment may be an attempt to keep both him and the family operating effectively, but it supports and exacerbates the problem, perpetuating the household's dysfunction. Other members of the household feed into the problem as they, too, ignore their own feelings and needs to engross themselves in "keeping things going as long as possible, for the sake of the family." The result is an unwitting by-product of sheer interpersonal momentum. None seems to realize that what is kept going is founded on unrequited love, love given but not returned. This, according to Fairview staffers, is dysfunctional, bound sooner or later to destroy itself from within. In such families, all members become addicts, as it were, equally "codependent" on the obsession that uncontrollably eats away at home life.

In the opinion of those Fairview staffers who consider most, if not all, contemporary families to be dysfunctional because of "pressures" of modern living, nearly everyone is an enabler. ADU therapist Tim Benson routinely refers to his own background in this regard. In his family groups, Benson describes how as a child growing up in a home with a self-centered alcoholic father, he was drawn into an enabling role in attempting to keep things under control at home when his father got drunk. Reflecting the statistics of dysfunctionality that Benson often recounts and a "sixth" sense of the matter, Benson remarks:

> My sister is a recovering alcoholic, and she says she can walk into a room and pick out the sick, most dysfunctional family. Codependents have a sixth sense like that, and they're attracted to dysfunctional people. Like me, some of us become therapists. [Laughter] Adult children of alcoholics and codependents have a real tendency to know what people really want to hear. If you watch soap operas on TV, those families are all dysfunctional. They're all enablers. All adult children of alcoholics are codependent. Anyone involved in any kind of relationship with anyone who's dependent is codependent. [Presents several other instances] Have I missed anyone? You find me any family nowadays, with all the pressures, and I'll find you a codependent and dysfunctional family. And if they don't want to admit it, . . . like they don't want to call themselves enablers, . . . they're denying.

Even the unwillingness to apply the vocabulary of codependency and enabling is a dysfunction, making for a limitless patient population.

The family figures into the spoilage of power as both source and magnifier. As far as source is concerned, it is not the family as a separate and distinct system that causes the breakdown of home life, but the power trips of particular members, who selfishly withhold or otherwise infringe on trust. From Fairview staffers' standpoint, the delicate social glue that keeps the modern family together is easily dissolved, held together as it is by members' democratic attitude, not the systemic rule of tradition or authority. The surrounding heartless world, with its many pulls and pressures, lures members away from the home with myriad material enticements, whose ready rewards easily overtake the nonmaterial inducements of domesticity.

Today's family is its own worst enemy, yet is not to be replaced by the family of yesterday. When the modern family works or is functional, it provides the ideal setting for building personal wherewithal and encouraging independence, both necessary traits in an equalitarian, diverse, and competitive world. But these very traits can infringe on the family's gratuitous democracy. The modern family must constantly be apprised of, or treated for, the consequences of excessive or misguided independence, the selfishness of addiction, arbitrary authority, and peer pressure, among other power trips. A self-centered family member weakens the very entity that provides a defense against the selfishness of modern life. Weakened, the family loses hold of its members, who are cast adrift, only to fetch up on the shoals of drugs, alcohol, delinquency, sullenness, rebellion, promiscuity, and other forms of self-indulgence.

The modern family magnifies its own spoilage. As members adjust to selfishness through obsessive attachment and support, "love" falsely and dysfunctionally affirms itself. The basic integrative ingredient of the modern family becomes self-destructive as codependents unwittingly persist in loving and trusting those who have torn the domestic fabric, enhancing dysfunctionality.

Fairview offers a two-pronged solution. First comes help for self-indulgent or addicted adolescents, parents, and other family members in getting a realistic hold of their feelings by confronting the hurt generated by their actions. The idea is to get the troubled to be assertive, not passive or aggressive, about their emotions—in effect, to "relate" their feelings and restore the grounds of modern domesticity. Therapist Dennis McDonald comments:

> The biggest problem we find in these patients is that no one relates to anybody. They're hurting but they don't know how to express it. They withdraw or they just get all hyper and aggressive about their kids or the parents and that makes them wacko. We try to work on techniques that get to those feelings, to make them see what's happened to them, how everyone's hurting. Hopefully, they realize that they're not alone in the world. They have to learn to trust others and recognize that everyone has feelings and that the problem comes when, by hook or crook, they selfishly close themselves off from others.

Second, Fairview seeks to apprise enablers or codependents—all others in the home—that they have feelings, too. Unfortunately, those who most desire to affirm love and trust often find themselves dysfunctionally mired in the patient's troubles; thus, every member of the household needs treatment. ADU therapist Tim Benson explains:

> As you can see, they're all affected. They're all part of the problem. They just can't see it. If we don't get them all involved, the patient goes home and the others just launch into their old habits and start enabling, like they just love him too much, and the old habits come alive and they hang themselves again. They've all got feelings and they've got to realize that. They're all dysfunctional. As much as they love and worry about their kids over there [in the ASU], those parents are part of the problem. Over here [the ADU], all the crying and sobbing wives . . . they've all got to see how each of them is involved.

If anything signals progress at Fairview, it is communicative evidence of an ability to share sentiments and contain the authority and power trips that make equitable sharing difficult or impossible, leading to emotional explosiveness. Therapist David Shindell pithily and repeatedly reminds parents, "Autocracy sets up the conditions for rebellion." Parents, spouses, and other family members learn to speak of domestic power as ruinous of the fundamental character of today's home life. As at Westside, language and the reality of domestic disorder are bound together in a special way.

The Rationalization of Feelings

At Fairview, feelings are believed to reference the depths of experience. When an adolescent druggie complains bitterly that his father favors an older brother, therapist Dave Shindell questions how the adolescent really feels underneath it all. The assumption is that beneath the complaint lies a domain of possibly contrasting emotional facts. When an addictive gambler shouts that his family does not understand him and thinks he is a loser, ADU nurse Bev Simpson asks him whether, in his heart of hearts, he does not feel otherwise. It is taken for granted that beyond the yelling and resentful comments is a domain of more authentic responses.

Some emotions are deeper than others and more genuine. Beneath fleeting emotions about such passing matters as the day's unsuccessful attempt to clearly communicate with a visiting company supervisor lie depths unencumbered by affectation or errors in seeking authenticity. But surface layers can also comprise feelings about deeper feelings, such as the guilt a teenaged girl has about her real hate for her father and the "secret" pleasure a cocaine addict has in feeling glad his wife is suffering from his habit.

Feelings also may be "mixed," convoluted with other feelings. The comments of patients, staff, and family members indicate that guilt, for example, may so confound hate that the two almost become inseparable, as when a teenaged patient starts to hate herself for how much guilt she really feels for despising her father. The gross affection of a woman who loves too much may be so diffuse as to drown all her feelings in a deep pool of sickly ardor.

Because dealing with feelings requires knowing them, Fairview staffers, family members, patients, and significant others face the enduring challenge of recognizing and communicating the depths of experience. Concerning every family member's implication in domestic disorder, ADU therapist Tim Benson states that all must "see how each is emotionally involved," pinpointing one of the two central problems of treatment at Fairview, namely, the rationalization of feelings. (The second problem—facilitating emotional expression—will be considered in the next chapter.) The rationalization of feelings is the process whereby emotions are put into words—denoted, connoted, or acknowledged through language—if never fully expressed. As child psychiatrist Robert Henderson reminds those gathered in multifamily group on the ASU, "You've got to learn how to put those feelings into words, even though we all know how difficult that is . . . or else no one'll know, even be aware of, what you're going through."

PRERATIONALIZED EMOTIONALITY

The vocabulary for conveying "raw emotion"—what is felt but not conceptualized—is ordinary and metaphoric, borrowed from familiar usage. Undistinguished or raw feelings are more hot or cold than they are warm or cool. The rational or rationalized has a moderate temperature, namely, temperate. The emotional family member usually comes to Fairview all hot—but sometimes very cold, "cold as ice," it is said. It is thought important that there be a "cooling-off" period following admission. This is especially indicated for adolescents, who, more than children and adults, are believed to be naturally volatile. In a toughlove session, ASU therapist Dennis McDonald describes the cooling-off period:

You know these kids; they're your sons and daughters. They're real hot under the collar when they come in here, full of hate and bitterness. You know the story. "No one listens to

me!" "Mom and Dad don't give a damn about me!" "No
one in my family loves me!" "No one cares!" They act like
nobody, I mean nobody, has ever listened to them. Of course,
you've heard this time and again. They hate everything and
everybody. They're mad at the world. They're angry that you
forced them to come here. They're a bundle of uncontrolled
emotion. That's why we feel it's important that there be a 72-
hour cooling-off period right after admission. No phone calls.
No visits . . . from anyone. They've got to chill out.

Therapist Dave Shindell ties this need to cool off to what he
calls the teenage mind. More than any other age period, the teen
years are said to be a time of pure emotionality energized by
"glands," unprotected by the emotional innocence of childhood
and unbridled by the leavening norms of maturity. Shindell
explains:

> The adolescent mind is unique. It faces a mass of new feel-
> ings . . . all glands. All of a sudden, they have these feel-
> ings that seriously connect with the world and they don't
> understand what it's all about. For many of them, it goes
> to their heads. They act out. They spout off. You know what
> can come out of their mouths. God knows, you've heard
> them enough. They're not children anymore, but they're
> not adults either. They don't know how to express what
> they feel. [Elaborates] That's the problem. It's a new phenom-
> enon, really. The autocratic family took care of the prob-
> lem. No one had feelings, point-blank. But, nowadays, with
> the democratic family, the teenage mind goes wild. It's sup-
> posed to express itself, but doesn't know how to. It doesn't
> know what to do. Parents don't see the problem right away.
> Some never do, and things go from bad to worse. The only
> way that hot, seething mass can go is to boil over and act
> out. That, ladies and gentlemen, is your typical dysfunc-
> tional teen of today. When the home can't handle it, you've
> got your dysfunctional family.

Less commonly, dysfunctional emotionality is described as icy
cold. The teenager arrives at Fairview numb and inexpressive,
considered unusual for an adolescent. The adult addict enters the

ADU with nothing to say and seemingly bereft of feelings, as if he or she were drained of emotional life. In either case, emotional problems are evident in the unhealthy sign of undue chill. The more usual hot unexpressed emotions are subject to exploding. The disturbed teenager may be compared to a volcano, likely to blow his or her top at any time. A woman who loves too much is said to be a walking or ticking time bomb, ready to go off without notice. The emotions of an alcoholic's spouse are likened to a pressure cooker, whose lid cannot be expected to hold against the mounting tension from the alcoholic's self-centered willfulness and other family members' codependence.

Whether it is blowing up, boiling over, about to explode, or ticking away, the deep self is out of control, in need of the moderating influence of controlled expression. Control of expression does not mean heavy-handedness: That is the language of autocracy. In the democratic model, control means facilitation. To control feelings, or learn how to do so according to Fairview guidelines, is to have a rational basis for emotional expression. In the context of yesterday, the support of traditional "ruling" institutions for the autocratic family enabled the suppression of individual family members' feelings, to such an extent, it is said, that members did not even recognize they had feelings. Although the modern family lacks rule in the traditional sense, it nonetheless can provide rules for rational, emotional expression, the hallmark of contemporary domestic order. Even the application of AA's recovery philosophy is rule-like facilitation, with the twelve-step approach to emotional health under the ultimate control of a higher power.

A healthy emotional life is calm and collected. One is said to be warm or cool—warm with others and cool in various situations. The functional family makes this possible. In a functional family, emotions are not given an opportunity to heat up, but allowed to thaw or chill out as necessary. By this analysis, it becomes reasonable to focus treatment on the home and family living, and accordingly, at Fairview, family members and others encounter a staff who greets them with open minds and hearts, prepared to address and name feelings, paving the way to emotional health.

THE DEMOCRACY OF EMOTION

Linked as emotions are to the democratic model of the family, it is understood that everyone has feelings, not only parents, or women, or adolescents. Each person is frequently reminded that he or she is not the only one who is hurt, offended, or ignored by other members of the household. Parents' feelings are important and need to be recognized, and children's also. The old adage that children should be seen and not heard lacks application here, as does the autocratic model that informs the adage. Even the youngest, most helpless member of the household has feelings and is not to be overlooked or thought to be too young to take seriously.

A parent effectiveness training group coordinated by therapist Ken Olsen shows how mothers and fathers are taught the democracy of emotional life. Participants have been discussing teenage sullenness and depression. Parent Mike Diaz scoffs at the idea that his son, Kenny, a 14-year-old inpatient, has deep feelings of any kind. As the proceedings unfold and Olsen insistently describes "everyone's" emotional depths, other parents join in to affirm the need to rethink what often is taken for granted, namely, that "kids don't have any real feelings to speak of."

> DIAZ: Jesus, I don't really know if I buy some of this stuff . . . you mean, Kenny? That kid is tough, real tough. You know what he's like . . . another one of those tough hoods you see on the street. [Elaborates] I know he's my son, but, Christ, that kid's as hard as nails. That's his problem. I wish to God the kid had feelings. Most kids his age . . . they haven't got any feelings or thoughts about anything. All they're interested in is smokes, drinking, and tearing ass around town.
>
> OLSEN: I hear what you're saying, Mike. Most of us here, I'm sure, have had similar thoughts. Kids these days have too much: too much freedom, too many things, easy access to booze, too much money. You name it, they've got it. [Elaborates] I've seen the toughness, too. The big act. The big bad dude! They all want to be dudes! But . . .
>
> DIAZ: [Interrupting] That's Kenny! He's the runt of the family but he sure thinks he's wearing the pants—big man. The little

weasel'll work circles around you if you let him. [Elaborates] That guy doesn't care. He doesn't know what it feels like to care. It's not him. They're all the same, these kids.

OLSEN: What I was going to say, Mike, is that I think we have to be a bit careful here. Stop and think about it. I know it's hard to do sometimes, especially when a kid is giving you a lot of headaches. I know how you'd never in your life feel that they have feelings of any kind . . . but they do. You say, "How can *he* feel anything?" "Why should I pay any attention to *him*?" But they really do feel. Everyone does. Each of them is an individual, like you and me.

DAD A: You know, Mike, I used to think like that. My kid Andy was always in trouble. He hustled dope and was always running into the law. It got to the point that I thought, "They can have him." That kid doesn't give a shit about anything or anyone. I won't listen to him anymore. Why should I? He treats his mother and me like turds. No one like that could feel anything for anyone. [Elaborates] It got worse and worse. We didn't know what to do. He was driving us up the wall, like nearly wrecking our marriage. But, you know, after we got Andy in here, we learned that maybe some of it was us. Sure, a lot was him, but maybe some of it was us. Before that, we'd decided that Andy was just a regular street kid: no feelings, no cares about anyone but himself.

MOM A: That's when the trouble starts. You turn your ears off. Whatever they're saying, you think, it's more of that big talk. There's nothing behind it . . . best to ignore them.

MOM B: You know, it's funny. Like my Billy. He's an 8-year-old and he's a rascal, like his older brother [an inpatient]. You'd never think . . . I mean, this little guy . . . I never thought *he* felt anything about anything. Him? Nah! Just the other day, he asks me, "Mom, I kinda feel sad that Ronnie [the older brother] is away." I told him that Ron is away to get better. You know what he said then? He sorta choked up and said, "I feel like I'm all alone, Mom, and you guys [parents] are at work or at that hospital and . . . "

OLSEN: [Interrupting] That's the way it is a lot of times. We keep going along with our lives or get so busy with this and that, that we forget that that little guy in the corner has feelings, too, . . . and they *do* matter. It really could matter if we continue to act like he's, well, "just a kid."

DIAZ: Maybe you're right. Right now, I don't know. It's hard for
         me to think that a kid like Kenny thinks about anything
         besides dope and girls.

OLSEN: I think it's important to remember that everyone's got
         feelings. Sure, sometimes they act like they don't, but
         they're there. You can bet on it. Yeah, even a half-pint like
         Billy. The problem is that sometimes parents . . . we get so
         busy and we *are* busy . . . we just don't bother to think
         about it. [Elaborates] Especially that little guy that doesn't
         give us too much trouble. We think, "Why bother to spoil
         a good thing; just let him be." Right? Everyone's got feelings.

Boys may be thought not to have as many, or as deep, feelings
as girls, but, according to Fairview staffers, a boy's feelings are as
real and deep as anyone's. Gender bias in the recognition of
feelings is sometimes said to be the reason why boys get into
greater trouble and act out, because boys' feelings are thought to
be minimal and left unrecognized or unattended. As the distressed mother of an inpatient teenaged daughter states in comparing her daughter's milder behavior with the "real" trouble her
older son causes, "Boys do; girls feel."

The teaching and affirmation of ubiquitous feelings also applies to adults and spouses. The teenaged patients on the ASU
often complain that their parents have no feelings and that, if
parents did, maybe the children would not have the domestic
problems they do. The spouses of addicts who are inpatients on
the ADU likewise decry the cold and calculated conduct of husbands and wives whose lack of consideration for others spoils the
home. However, as psychiatrist Henderson informs the inpatient
teenagers gathered with their parents for group one Sunday
afternoon:

I know it's difficult sometimes for you to believe that your
parents have feelings just like you do, but they really do.
You think, "How can *Dad* have feelings?" "Mom never stops
to feel anything about *me*." Believe me, your parents are no
different than you are. [Elaborates and then turns to a teenaged girl] Like, Jenny, you might think, "How could *my* dad
feel anything? *He* doesn't feel sorry. *He* doesn't feel embar-

rassed. *He* doesn't get lonely." But he does. And you all have to recognize that. Try asking them some time.

In the context of codependency, therapist Tim Benson speaks similarly to the inpatient adults, husbands, and wives who participate with family members in the ADU evening family groups:

> All family members are codependent. There's no use thinking that one or the other is not involved. Everyone's got feelings in every family. [To inpatients] You guys and you gals in here, . . . don't go around thinking that it's only you that's hurting. The whole family's hurting. Like we all have feelings? I think the hardest thing to ask is what do *I* feel. Most times, most of us wouldn't know an emotion if it slapped us right up the side of the head. Your wives aren't just out there thinking you're being treated. They're worrying. They've always worried about you. That's codependency. The trouble was that *you* didn't recognize it and *they* didn't recognize their part. Parents, too, have feelings, even though you might think that they've never had an emotion in their lives, that all they want to do is get you in here to dry out and straighten out so that you don't give 'em any more trouble.

Emotional ubiquity translates into a highly personalized language of reference, underscoring the individualistic basis of the democratic model of the family. Personal pronouns designate the essential location of the family's emotional life: in you, me, him, her, us, and in them. It is emphasized that *I* have feelings just as much as *you* have them. Decried are the power trips that keep others from knowing *me* and *my* feelings. Family members are taught and, in turn, advise each other, to take *his* feelings into account as much as *hers*. Parents collectively assert that *they* have feelings; children and adolescents claim the same for themselves. Spouses indicate that *they* suffer as much from a family member's addiction as the addict him- or herself. The family as a whole does not have feelings, nor is the home's atmosphere referenced as an emotional entity in its own right; comments about warm families and cold atmospheres are shorthand phrases for the ways individuals relate to one another.

Touching, for example, signals thoughtfulness by *you* for *me*. A family that hugs publicly affirms *each* member's feelings. Affection of any kind shows that everyone is an emotional being worthy of attention. Tim Benson put it this way in a Sunday afternoon support group for codependents:

> People need touching. People need intimacy. [Cites the dying of babies from lack of touching] That's the importance of nurturing. We all need to be nurtured. It's a way of relating that's part of the functional family. A warm family atmosphere shows everyone nurturing everyone else. When you hug your husband or your wife, it says, "I care about how you feel." When your kid comes up to you and gives you that unexpected little peck on the cheek, she's saying, "Mom, I love you and I understand how you feel." The dopehead who all of a sudden breaks out of his self-centered attitude and puts his arms around you is saying, "Please understand how I feel, that I need help." In dysfunctional families, people are so wrapped up in themselves, there's no time for nurturing. How can anyone hug anyone else if they don't care about anything but themselves? They don't even know what they feel themselves, they're so wrapped up in their little . . . big . . . power trips. It's like living with a stranger. What each and every one of them needs is to be recognized and loved for themselves.

THE ULTIMATE DEPTH OF FEELING

In the final analysis, the personalized language of emotion references the socially noncategorical, reaching beyond roles such as adolescent, parent, wife, husband, spouse, breadwinner, homemaker, addict, codependent, enabler, troublemaker, truant, druggie, dopehead, crackhead, and drunk. Roles indeed sometimes are said to "get in the way" of knowing the individual's true self, screening an appreciation of the person "just for" him- or herself. The phrase *just for* is signally important in suggesting that language itself—notably the ordinary categories we share and use to communicate self and experience—can hamper authenticity.

Ultimately, authenticity is presumed beyond language, achieved when we get to know each other "just for" ourselves, not as mothers, fathers, sons, daughters, spouses, codependents, drunks, and the like. As a distressed daughter once yelled at her mother in aftercare, "Did you even stop to think what it feels like for me, or do something just for me!"

Reflecting what David Silverman and Michael Bloor (1990) describe as the attempt in patient-centered medicine to penetrate the subjectivity of the new sick-man, or the patient as person, the aim at Fairview is to clear away surface, public roles or categories (or debris, in the case of dysfunctionality) to disclose and affirm the subjectively meaningful and emotional. As Michel Foucault (1978) might put it in this regard, the object is to *really* incite expression. Yet, as Silverman (1985) argues elsewhere, this romantic goal nonetheless implicates language, its subject matter—emotional life—knowable neither behind or below communication. Although the home is believed to be the final venue of domestic authenticity in today's uncaring world, the home's distinguishing characteristics—love and emotional being—are recognized in and through communication, the hallmark of public life (Gubrium & Holstein, 1990). To argue, as Fairview staffers in effect do, that "home is where the heart is," is to, well, argue, convince, and believe that the only genuine location for knowing our inner depths in modern life is in the context of the loving family or the trusting home in which each member expresses his or her true feelings.

The attempt to get beneath the surface, beyond the categories that Frederic Jameson (1972) calls the "prison-house of language," in order to authentically know one just for him- or herself is an enduring Fairview aim, but its elusiveness can be poignant. A multifamily group discussion centered on "self-disclosure" reveals the difficulty of attempting to communicatively penetrate the nondiscursive. As is customary, prior to group, inpatient adolescents have decided the particular topic of family life and dysfunction they would like to discuss with participating parents and significant others. In group, psychiatrist Hal Gomez encourages several adolescent patients—Chuck, Paul, Lamont, Heidi, and Lenny—to "identify feelings" and relate them to their problems. The idea is that the recognition and appreciation of the true feelings central to domestic disorder secures love and trust. Responses are initially terse.

GOMEZ: [To Paul] So what are your problems?
PAUL: Drugs, alcohol. I have problems at home and at school . . . and in life. [Elaborates]
GOMEZ: [To Lamont] Lamont, talk to me about your priorities.
LAMONT: Drugs.
GOMEZ: What got you into drugs?
LAMONT: Peer pressure.
GOMEZ: Just peer pressure? Doesn't your family and your feelings fit into this somewhere?

In an extended exchange, the other teens prod Lamont to provide and elaborate on the reasons for his drug abuse, in particular the feelings that led up to it. The proceedings become confessional, with the teens personally castigating themselves or others for the emotions behind particular problems having never been "really" disclosed or recognized. The discussion soon centers on Chuck's feelings and home life, especially his past and his mother's attempt to get help for his problems. At one point, Chuck's mother despairs of all the dead ends she's encountered.

MOTHER: Look, I've been through it all with him [Chuck]. I'm not sure I'm getting anywhere. I'm not sure I'm going to get anywhere here. It's been 7 years of this and that treatment with Chuck. He's into one program and out of another. It's so inconsistent. One place says that you've got to be tough and another place wants to get into feelings, . . . like they want to work out the past in 20 minutes. My feelings are all mixed up right now. Chuck's past . . .
CHUCK: [Interrupting] Mom, would you cut it out! I don't want to get into the past! Just drop it!
MOTHER: One counselor says to do this and another says to do that. They've also broken confidences here, right here in this place, about a lot of things. [Elaborates and then abruptly changes the subject] I was told by a psychiatrist that I was the problem and my other counselor said that he's [Chuck]

the problem, that he has to open up more, that he's not relating the way he really feels.

Gomez sympathizes with the mother's reaction to inconsistent therapeutic experiences, then concentrates on her current problem.

GOMEZ: I can relate to how you feel. The problem is between you and your son. You have a problem. I guess what I'm saying is that you've got to forget what you've heard in the past and face the present . . . get to the problem. You know how these kids were talking about "attitude." You're just frustrated and I know just how you feel.

MOTHER: How do you know it's not anger?

All encourage Chuck and his mother to get their feelings out on the table, as it is put. But Chuck again decries his mother's public discussion of their therapeutic history and shouts at his mother to stop bringing up the past. Several adolescents support him, telling the mother to stop dwelling on the past and to listen to Chuck's feelings for a change. The conversation is forceful and animated. The mother repeats that she's been doing just that for the past 7 years and it's gotten her nowhere; she stresses that she knows all about Chuck's feelings, that there's nothing more to know. She complains that no one seems to think she herself has any feelings in the matter, because parents are supposed to always listen for their kids' feelings. She yells that she is totally fed up with everything. Unconvinced, several teens persist in urging Chuck to uncover for his mother what they believe has not yet been recognized—his own, true feelings.

LENNY: [To Chuck's mother] What Chuck is trying to say is, "Mom, I love you, but this is how I feel." [To Chuck] And you're saying, "I love you, but you're not listening to how I feel." That's the problem. [Pause] Oh, I don't know. I'm not a doctor. I can't say for sure.

CHUCK: [To his mother] You never listen to me! I've tried to tell you a thousand times how I feel and you never listen! To you, I'm just Chuck, your son, the kid with the problems. Did you ever wonder what it's like just for me?

Several adolescents shout, "Tell her! Tell her!" Lenny makes an impassioned plea for self-disclosure, arguing that now Chuck has the chance he's always wanted to tell his mother exactly what he feels "deep down," intimating that perhaps Chuck has something to hide. There's tension in the air.

CHUCK: What do you mean? I've got nothing to hide! You're full of it. Jesus, she [mother] knows everything there is to know about me. How *can* I hide anything? You want me to tell her how I feel about school. She knows all about it. You want she should know about my friends? She knows. Believe me. She knows how I feel about her. I'm not afraid to say that I love my mom, although I know I don't always show it. What's the use of getting into that?

HEIDI: Well, now's the time, Chuck. She's listening. Never mind all that other stuff. Forget that you're her son and she's your mom. Just tell her how you really feel, deep down inside.

Lenny breaks the tension as he explains that the roadblock is an inability to communicate, pointing out that if Chuck and his mother would "only *tell* each other what they *really* feel," the problem would be resolved. Repeating Heidi's request, Lenny urges both Chuck and his mother to speak to each other, not as son to mother or as mother to son, but as "real people." In effect, Lenny asks the two to talk from unrecognizable standpoints, as ostensibly real people; he uses a computer analogy for their communication breakdown: wires unplugged and in need of replugging. Others join in and expand on the analogy. Chuck's mother interrupts, returning to her family's therapeutic history:

Let me tell you all a thing or two! You think it's just a matter of Chuck's feelings? Well, the doctors are bringing up all kinds of things. Not one of them has said the same thing twice. I've listened and tried to follow their advice, but it's completely opposite all the time. Anyway, how do you know I haven't tried to communicate, that I haven't sat down for the last 7 years and tried to communicate? It's not that simple.

The mother describes the other problems she faces, especially her recurrent cancer. She reports that the cancer is now in remission, but she has been told that stress may reactivate it. She complains about her husband leaving her in the midst of her difficulties, although he has since returned. She concludes:

How'd you like to have that hanging over you and try to communicate? I've got doctor bills and have to think about that. Anyone can see there's more to it. To tell you the truth, I don't know why I even came today.

Several adolescents empathize. There is commiseration over all the problems a parent has to cope with these days, especially Chuck's mother. Chuck is reminded that he has to think about his mother's situation and be open to her feelings, too.

The conversation flags. Eventually, another mother returns to Chuck's feelings and, with due respect for Chuck's mother's situation, asks Chuck now, finally, to tell his mother how he feels. Several others underscore the request. Again, Heidi urges Chuck, "Okay, Chuck, you have your chance. Tell her how you feel. Now's the time, man." All eyes are on Chuck. Briefly pausing, Chuck responds:

I guess I don't know what to say. What can I say? What more can I say? She's heard it all. [Turns to his mother] Mom, I don't know that there is anything more to tell you. I feel like . . . what do I feel? It's just going to sound the same. Shit, I don't know what to say. [Weeping] Mom, you already know I love you. You know that. [Mother nods] Is that what . . . you know me . . . . [Pause] I really . . . no, I really do want to say how I feel. [Chokes] God, I feel so stupid. But I don't know how . . . what to say. [To others] Help me, you guys. Help me tell her how I feel. Please. Please, you guys. You gotta help me. I don't know.

His mother reaches toward her son and embraces him. She, too, weeps and, through her tears, softly cries:

Never mind. Never mind. That's okay. You've said enough, sweetie. You've said it all. I know how you feel. I love you, too, honey. Cry all you want, baby. You can't say. No one can say. I know you love me, baby.

NAMING FEELINGS

Short of what is finally unspeakable, the naming of feelings is the critical step to shared emotional recognition and healing. It guides feelings into discourse about the family and domestic disorder and thereby establishes rational grounds for the resolution of troubles. The functional family is the family that routinely attends to members' feelings, recognizes (names) the feelings, and takes their distinguishing characteristics into account in organizing domestic relations. The immediate problem for Chuck and his mother is that, because of their extensive contacts with individual and family therapists in a variety of treatment settings, they already have voiced all there is to say about feelings. Having said it all and knowing all about each other, they have difficulty casting that veneer aside to discern how they, especially Chuck, "really" feel, beyond their roles as mother and son. Although analytically important, the problem is momentary, as Chuck, his mother, and others eventually invoke the language of love to show and acknowledge what Chuck really feels—even though love already has been conveyed. The process of public realization through words may be as dramatic as Chuck's confrontation with emotionality or as fleeting as responding to the simple directive, "Name a feeling." As learned and independently applied by patients and family members, the process realizes contemporary domestic order, an entity believed to comprise systematic and steadfast communicative exchanges in the home centered on feelings.

The direct naming of feelings is highlighted in multifamily group sessions, although similar designations are undertaken throughout the Fairview treatment program. On one occasion, psychiatrist Henderson asks ASU nurse Kay Mandel to go over the confidentiality rules, which specify that parents, adolescents, and others are not to discuss session proceedings with outsiders. Mandel then turns to the concern of the day, as established by the adolescents in their meeting before group; it is feelings and communication, a frequent topic of discussion. As the proceedings unfold, a "seething" feeling is named and eventually placed in the context of healing.

MANDEL: Our pre-family group kept coming back to feelings and lack of communication. As you might guess by now, it's a major concern with these kids. Anne [patient], why don't you jump in with both feet? You're an old-timer and have been around a while. What are your feelings?

DR. H: [Interrupting] Before we get into that, let me explain something a bit for the newcomers. The format of this group often changes, even week to week. Sometimes, like Kay mentioned, we go around and ask for each of you to state your feelings. Sometimes, we just let it all hang out and freely discuss a problem that seems to be important that particular day. Sometimes, we mix it up. Actually, we leave it up to you, pretty much. The goal is always the same, though: to open those blocked pathways of communication. [Elaborates] The other thing I'd like to say, mostly for the newcomers . . . the old-timers have heard this before . . . the thing to remember is that all families have problems. When a person is hospitalized, the symptoms are often laid on the patient. This hides the fact that the patient lives in the family and connects with other family members. What this means is that what we mistakenly take to be individual symptoms are really symptoms of a dysfunctional family. So the business here is to learn communication, particularly how to express feelings and especially what to do when negative feelings are expressed.

Again for the benefit of newcomers, Dr. H asks participants to introduce themselves. This done, he returns to Anne and repeats Mandel's question.

ANNE: Oh, I don't know.

MANDEL: Anne, you must have some feelings. Your parents are here and would like to hear from you.

ANNE: Well, I was sorta thinking . . . we talked about this yesterday. I was sorta thinking that maybe some of the problem is that Mom is sorta too much of a Goody Two Shoes. Like she feels that whatever she thinks, that we all should feel the same way.

MOM: Ah, come on, Anne! Goody Two Shoes? I'm just trying to get you guys to do the right thing.

The mother compares herself to her brothers, who, she says, did not turn out very well. There's a lengthy argument between Anne and her mother and father about the family differences.

MOM: If you mean, am I more of a Goody Two Shoes than Harry or Dan [two of her brothers] . . . yeah, I'd have to say I am. So what of it? [Elaborates] Like I said, they turned out to be alcoholics. The other two [brothers], well, . . . judge for yourself.

DAD: I wouldn't call them angels either.

ANNE: Mom! You're getting off the subject. I was talking about you, not Uncle Harry and Uncle Dan. You have to admit that you're uptight all the time. Right?

MOM: No, I'm not!

ANNE: Yes, you are! You're always uptight!

MOM: Damn it, girl, I'm not!

ANNE: You are!

The accusatory exchange goes on for a short time, with evidence put forth by both Anne and her mother. As the exchange spirals, Dr. H interrupts.

DR. H: Is this a lot like it is at home?

MOM: It's funny. Like at home, the conflict is usually more between them [Anne and her father].

Anne raises the issue of manipulation at home, which both her mother and father elaborate on.

DAD: Look, I know what she [Anne] says sounds like we try to manipulate her, but she's got it all backwards. [Turns to Anne] I'd say that you do a good bit of manipulating . . . especially of your mother. Right?

ANNE: I'm sorry I brought it up.

MOM: Look here, Anne, . . . you brought it up and I think you should do your part to talk about it.

DAD: I'm tired of this. Let's go on to another family.

ANNE: Well, like when Dad starts yelling at Mom about not trying to get her way . . . oh, never mind.

MOM: What do you mean my getting my way? How do you think I feel when . . .

ANNE: [Interrupting] Just drop it.

MANDEL: Anne. Why don't you explain what you mean?

There's a long pause. Mandel repeats her request, coaxing Anne.

ANNE: Well, alright . . . like Mom is usually so uptight about
          where I can go and when I come in. It's really . . .

MOM: [Interrupting] Look, Anne, we've talked about this a
          thousand times. We're more liberal with you than any of
          the other parents [of Anne's friends] are. You bet we are.
          What we feel is . . .

ANNE: [Interrupting] Just drop it!

MOM: Damn it, Anne! Stop interrupting me. You brought it up.
          What do you mean, "Drop it."

ANNE: [Yelling at her mother] Never mind, Mom!

DR. H: [To Anne] Name a feeling! Name a feeling!

ANNE: Feeling?

MANDEL: Anger.

ANNE: Anger? No! I'm PO-ed [pissed off]! You're driving me
          crazy. And that's why I'm in here. [Pause]

MOM: [To Anne] Please don't get all excited. The hardest thing
          I've had to do in my life is leave you here. [Elaborates]
          Boy, do I remember that first morning after we brought
          you here. When I got up in the morning and you weren't
          in your room, it scared the life out of me, especially when
          I realized what had happened and that you were going
          to be in a . . . a psych hospital. I broke down and just
          cried and cried. [Elaborates her feelings]

Anne puts her head down on the desk where she's sitting, folds
her arms in front of her, and begins to cry. Dr. H talks to the entire
group.

DR. H: Feelings are very, very important in the family. They're
          bedrock. Understanding this in each of us is hard to do,
          but you have to learn how to do it. That's what family is
          all about—love, trust, and understanding. We saw some
          pretty powerful things coming out here this afternoon. I
          was beginning to see a feeling being expressed and then
          it was cut off with "Oh, never mind." and "Drop it."
          That's power. Things begin to seethe and, in time, "Bingo!"

MANDEL: Boy, does that kill the trust. [Addresses all the adoles-
          cents] When someone . . . Jim, Anne, Heidi, John? Any of
          you. When you ask each other about feelings, you think
          you're going to be able to talk about feelings, right? So,
          you've opened up a channel of communication. What
          happens when that channel is suddenly closed off by the
          person who opened it up in the first place?
JOHN: I'd say that's a power trip.
DR. H: You bet it is.
MANDEL: And, folks, that doesn't mix with love and trust. If you
          get into that kind of thing, people figure "What's the use."
DAD: It kinda reminds you of Lucy and Charlie Brown [comic
          strip characters] and the football. Like Lucy keeps getting
          Charlie Brown to run and kick the ball while she holds it
          in the tee. Boy, . . . just as he takes the bait and is ready to
          kick, she swipes the ball and he falls flat on his back.
DR. H: Yep, but the problem is that Charlie Brown never learns.
JOHN: He's a dunce. [Several adolescents elaborate Charlie
          Brown's and Lucy's characters]
DR. H: Here we know that that's power. Lucy power! [All laugh]
          If they were a family, they'd be dysfunctional as all get
          out . . . because the family is essentially built on trust.
          [Elaborates] Here, we're in the business of building com-
          munication, naming our feelings. You've got to get those
          feelings out and name them. We've got to know what in
          all get out we're dealing with. That's the healing process.

There is little to "deal with" until feelings are designated in some
way. The directive to name a feeling, although seeming contrived,
is a standard feature of group sessions. Naming can also come in
response to requests for self-disclosure from fellow patients or
family members, answering questions such as "Tell us how you
feel?" At times, feelings are freely offered or a particular family
member or patient demands that others, especially other family
members, now listen to how he or she feels. It is not uncommon
for an adolescent, adult, or significant other to state flatly that he
or she will describe exactly what is felt, when, where, with whom,
or why. Naming can be highly formularized, even humorous, as
when Bob LaPointe, an ex-ASU patient, remarked in aftercare:

It's like this. *What* I feel now is anger. A-N-G-E-R. I'll tell you *why*. Because my old man gets drunk all the time and never learns. I take him with me to AA and he gets all holier than thou, but he's right back on the sauce the next week. When? I get really angry when he stands there and tells everyone . . . and me! . . . that I've got to trust in a higher power if I want to stay off the bottle. Get that! It's like the boozer talking to the booze. Now, ask me again how I feel. It's anger! Right down here in my gut.

Another participant, the mother of an ex-ASU patient, immediately lightened the mood, even as she confirmed the seriousness of naming feelings and LaPointe's formula for doing so:

Well, Bob, there's no doubt in my mind that you were a patient in this place. [Laughter] You've got the recipe all down pat. You told your feeling. I'd say that's really telling it like it is. [Turns to others] Spelling it out, even! [Laughter] But, seriously, folks, that's where it's at. You've got to say how you feel. The reason I come back here is that it's good to hear, over and over, that there's a way out of this. There's no way around those feelings.

Feelings are less directly named through exemplification, in which patients and family members publicly identify with role models' emotional lives. Role models are exemplified in four ways: through written materials in which dysfunctional roles and role relationships are diagrammed and described; in videotapes in which roles and relationships are acted out; in related interpersonal experiences described by staff members; and by means of exemplary experiences that family members present to each other.

ADU therapist Tim Benson's family sessions illustrate all four means serving together to exemplify emotions. Benson frequently uses a "role chart" to help members of dysfunctional families to share feelings. The chart is distributed to session participants following videotape presentations that usually focus on addiction. Depicted on the chart are six circles representing the dysfunctional family's typical roles: the chemically dependent person, the chief enabler, the family hero, the scapegoat, the lost child, and the mascot. Listed outside the circles are the common defensive responses of each role. For example, the chief enabler, who usually is the spouse, is said to be self-blaming, superresponsible, and manipulative, among other characteristics. Listed within each circle are the feelings typically associated with each role. The chief enabler is hurt, fearful, angry, pained, and guilty.

The chart provides a common basis for naming, communicating, and comparing feelings. As family members consider their domestic troubles, they are encouraged to name feelings of their own according to the roles depicted on the chart, thereby exemplifying particular but shared experiences. The chart serves to concretely "read" a generalized pattern of institutionalized emotions and domestic disorder into each participant's family troubles.

Consider a session in which participants initially view a videotape presentation of "family sculpturing," a performance with actors positioning themselves on stage in such a way as to physically embody the different responses and feelings of the typical dysfunctional family. For example, standing precariously on a kitchen chair "sculpts" personal insecurity. After this presentation and the distribution of role charts, Benson asks the participants to consider the different ways family members effect domestic dysfunctionality. Participants include Pete, a chronic gambler; Becky, a young woman who loves too much; Wayne, an alcoholic; and several family members.

BENSON: Let me say, once again, that *no* family is completely functional. No family is perfect. There's the ideal at one end and no one is like that. At the other end is the totally dysfunctional family. Most of us fall somewhere in-between. You just saw the typical roles of these families. Let's look at the chart you have in your hands. It's very easy to recognize yourself. Is there anyone who sees himself anywhere on the chart?

Family members and patients peruse the chart. No one answers at first, prompting Benson to review each role.

BENSON: I guess the cat's got all of our tongues today, so I'll start. [Pause] Historically, we've identified the CD [chemically dependent] person as the problem. Using this model [the role chart], you can see that we now view the whole family as sick. Overall, there are three "rules" that govern CD families: never trust, don't feel, and don't talk. [Elaborates] What we hope to do while you're in here is break the cycle and get you to express your feelings, talk about it. [Elaborates further] Let me see, now. . . . Raise your hands. How many of you come from a CD family?

A few participants raise their hands. Benson repeats comments he made before the videotape presentation regarding the extent of dysfunctionality. Several participants start in.

PETE: My mother was dependent on prescription drugs and my father was a workaholic. He didn't drink much or anything like that, but he sure sounds a lot like this here [points to chart] chemically dependent guy. [Reviewing role characteristics] Yeah, he was aggressive, alright. He was a perfectionist, too. I guess he felt ashamed about how he never paid any attention to any of us, just his work. [Elaborates] These others [roles] . . . yeah, I guess you'd say we fit in there. My mother really fed into it. I guess she was the chief enabler. I'm in there, too.

BENSON: Codependency is a family disease that is passed on from one generation to another. They're not sure yet if the interface is biological or learned or a process of identification. [Elaborates] It's not clear yet. Let's look at the chart again. Each of you, see if you can identify with one of the roles. Ask yourself, "Which one of these am I? Which way do I feel?"

Before anyone answers, Benson uses the terms on the chart to describe the family in which he grew up, particularly his own role as family hero.

BENSON: The family hero typically is the oldest kid. That was me. You know, just like it says, I worked hard for approval. I was super responsible. I focused in on success away from the family. So I made it through college and became a therapist . . . and I'm still not finished. What did . . . or do . . . I feel? Hurt. Confused. Inadequate. Lonely. Do any of you play any of those roles?

WIFE A: I guess all of them. I guess I've played one or some of the others at one time or another. Like, well, I was definitely the chief enabler. I was hurt. Hell, I'm still hurt. He's [her inpatient husband] no charmer, believe me. Oh, is he a jerk sometimes! But, you know how you feel . . . you think to yourself, "Well, maybe he'll snap out of it [drinking] and come around." So you try your damnedest to keep him and the rest of the family going. But he lets you down.

WIFE B: And you're mad as hell because of it. That's me! Like you trusted him and he let you down. And he doesn't want to open up . . . like nothing's really wrong, that he can't handle. Right?

WIFE A: You got it, babe! And I'm the scapegoat, too. Like I get sucked into his sweet talking and his promises and, when things don't work out, he dumps on me. What do you think of them apples?

BENSON: How about you, Becky? How do you feel?

BECKY: I really don't know. It's hard to say. They're all a bit like me.

WAYNE: Come on, Beck, you sound like the lost child to me, like in the movie [videotape presentation].

BECKY: Yeah, I guess. Put me there. [Pause] Wayne, I thought you were saying last night that you felt like a lost kid. Isn't that what you said?

WAYNE: I don't know. You tell me.

BECKY: Well, if you're the lost child, *I'm* surely not the lost child. We're night and day. I must be the mascot. [Reads the mascot's emotional characteristics] Yeah, that's me all right. Being super cute. Clowning. Doing anything to attract attention. Deep down, feeling insecure and lonely, but you try to hide it. That's me.

BENSON: How about it, Wayne? Which are you?

WAYNE: I think, to be honest, I'm the scapegoat. [Looks at his Dad] I got more of that than any other one. I'm the CD person, too. I'm guilty and charming.

All laugh. Several family members and patients join into a comical role-playing exchange. Wayne's father eventually changes the mood of the discussion.

FATHER: Seriously, folks, . . . I don't really believe Wayne is the
          scapegoat. [Turns to his son] Wayne, now . . . you can't
          seriously tell me that you're hurt or rejected [characteris-
          tics of the scapegoat]? If anything, we spend all our time
          tryin' to help you out when you're on the sauce or in a jam.
WAYNE: Ah, come o-o-on, Dad! Gimme a break, will ya!
FATHER: Break nothin'! That's all you get is breaks. You ain't no
          scapegoat, man.

As father and son continue to express disagreement over which
role typifies the son and specifies his feelings, it is evident that,
although the chart, the videotape, and interpersonal comparisons
do not determine emotional life, they nonetheless serve as a set
of mundane, experiential templates for designating affective possibilities. In their practical application at Fairview, related affective
categories combine to rationally constitute the felt basis of family
troubles.

THE GOOD SESSION

Whether feelings are directly or indirectly identified, the good
session is considered to be discursively expressive, with emotions
in some way made public. Conversely, the poor session does not
communicate the real "me," "you," "us," or "them," respectively,
for "myself," "yourself," "ourselves," or "themselves." Rather
than giving voice to what she "really feels," an alcoholic woman
dwells on her children's irresponsibility. Rather than speaking
openly of what bothers him, an adolescent druggie acts the
haughty, uncaring kid his father has always known and despised.

The good session takes many forms, from being outwardly
affectionate to being elaborately confessional. The session quoted
earlier, which focused on Chuck feelings, was thought successful
because it was "heartfelt," "pure gush." A unit nurse indicates
that it finally showed how Chuck feels about his mother:

It was really good. Heartfelt. Pure gush. I felt that for the
first time Chuck came right out and told her how he felt.
Not in so many words, but it was written all over his face.

Somehow he just couldn't say it. But you knew how he felt.
It got pretty heavy in there. You can't help getting involved
yourself. [Elaborates] It was hard for *me* to hold back the
tears and I've been through this sort of thing many times.
When it gets heavy like that, you know it's all coming out
. . . and sometimes it really gushes. But that's good. That's
what we're looking for . . . the chance for people to get to say
. . . show what they feel, to show what they are, just for
themselves, without all those pretenses they get into.

Dr. Gomez adds:

Yeah. Finally. Chucks spills his guts. I was waiting for that.
We all were. Chuck, the cool kid that nobody understands.
Chuck, the dude that has it all together. Today, we saw the
real Chuck: the vulnerable kid who has real feelings like
everyone else. It was real emotional in there, but that's the
only way they're going to know what's underneath . . .
what's causing their problems. These people have to learn
that they have to *show* their feelings. When they do, well,
they're on their way to recovery. Those that can't have a
long way to go. I think we made some progress today.

Elaborately confessional sessions also are good. When family
members come together in aftercare, group, and other sessions,
they may voice their innermost thoughts and emotions in detail
far beyond the momentary expressiveness Chuck and his mother
displayed. As expatient Bob LaPointe did earlier, they may explain at length how they privately feel, why, when, and about
what or whom. Sessions sometimes take the tone of a dramatic
reading, in which the feeling under consideration is described in
its varied subfacets, say, according to imagined scenes of daily life.
Speaking for a parent, Dave Shindell provides an example by relating the real feelings of the mother of a sexually active, chronically
runaway daughter to a parent effectiveness class:

Let me tell you how it feels. I remember . . . it wasn't that
long ago. We had a mother whose teenaged daughter was
sexually active and was always taking off. She just took off.
Her mother never knew when she left or where she went.

She was gone. Zip! Just like that. At first, Mom hardly said anything about how she felt. She'd share some things, of course, like how she had called the police and she called all her [the daughter's] friends to see if she was there and all that. At first, Mom talked like she was a machine. You could tell she wanted to give the impression that she had it all together. She never panicked. She just tried to find her daughter. Real cool-like, but determined. [Elaborates] You just knew that, underneath that cool exterior, she had her own feelings, but she hardly ever let on.

Then, one afternoon, she got in here and heard another mother talking about how she felt when her son took off like that. Well, . . . that did it! You should have heard her. It was confession time. You'd have thought that this mother had no feelings about anything, but, man, did it come out. She told us how empty she felt when Diane [her daughter] left and all the thoughts and emotions she felt. She imagined all kinds of things. What an imagination! Like she'd imagine that Diane was walking under an overpass and that a car sideswiped her and then dragged her along for a mile and she'd [the mother] panic that her daughter was lying somewhere in a ditch bleeding to death. She kept saying that she was embarrassed at herself for having such morbid thoughts when her daughter was probably safe somewhere. I mean, talk about detail! This lady was panicking, guilty, embarrassed, morbid, and everything else all rolled into one. [Elaborates] And no one knew it!

After a lengthy and sympathetic discussion of the mother's situation and feelings, Shindell comments on what a good session it was:

It was a good one. Memorable. I feel it's important that each of us here attempt to own up in this way. It's good for you and it's good for the other members of the family. Feelings are very subtle and complicated things. They get all twisted up and wrenched apart. They get bent all out of shape. You've got to be willing to talk them out in all the gory details, get to the bottom of things where those deep emotions really are. That way, you let them know what you're going through. They've got to know. It's part of the healing process.

EIGHT

Facilitating Expression

The ideas of a democratic domestic order and fundamental feelings combine to center on an overall healing goal of facilitating expression. In the functional family or healthy household, the process is maintained naturally by the principle of trust or love. But how does the principle translate into treatment? Trust or love must in some way be concretely extended and received—displayed—to produce functional effects.

The facilitation of expression at Fairview is guided by sets of more or less explicit communication rules. Dinkmeyer and McKay's (1983) manual for parents, *STEP/Teen*, provides one set of highly rationalized rules, although it is variously adapted by staff members. York, York, and Wachtel's (1983) book, *Toughlove*, gives another set, typically recommended as a last resort, when "rational" rules prove ineffective. The twelve steps offer yet another set, interwoven with still other rules. Overall, the rules specify how to organize and extend communication, realizing love or trust and, in turn, the sharing of feelings.

PASSIVE AND AGGRESSIVE RESPONSES

As is often noted, communication is a two-way street. Messages not only are extended, but are received. To be effective, domestic communication must be formulated so that others not only are informed about feelings, but also hear what has been conveyed. Assertive communication is a set of rules about how to inform so that what is conveyed is clearly stated and heartfelt, unhampered by either the reticence or the exuberance of the speaker. Assertive communication is, in effect, a set of positive speaking rules.

Reticence to communicate prevents others, in particular other members of the household, from knowing how one feels about domestic matters. One keeps feelings to oneself or passively expects others to "read" one's mind or heart. This tactic may temporarily prevent trouble, but in the long run it is believed likely to be highly troublesome, not only suppressing the healthy realization of particular feelings, but possibly affecting the domestic integrating function of trust or love.

The problem of passive communication is a common topic of discussion at Fairview, said to cause some families considerable frustration because certain members "just won't talk about themselves." Focal in the following proceedings of an ADU evening family group is one such passive communicator, alcoholic patient Tad Williams. According to Williams's wife, Janet, his greatest problem is that he refuses ever to say how he feels about anything and "makes understanding what's behind the drinking that much worse." Nurse Bev Simpson underscores the "more important negative [domestic] consequences of clamming up," which therapist Tim Benson later links directly with trust. The group has just finished viewing a videotape presentation of communication strategies in problem families.

SIMPSON: Jan, what's your reaction to the tape?

JANET: I guess I felt that the couple at the end was a lot like us. The husband came home from work like he'd had a really rotten day, but he wouldn't talk about it. I think his wife suspected something was wrong, but the guy just clammed up, real tight-like. Tad's a lot like that. Aren't you, Tad?

TAD: Oh, I don't know. I tell you things.

JANET: Well, . . . he tells me things and he doesn't tell me things.

BENSON: What do you mean?

JANET: [To her husband] Tell them. You know what I mean.

TAD: Nah. [Pause] You go ahead and talk.

JANET: It's not that he doesn't talk. He's a great talker. The guy can be the life of the party. But, man, oh man, you try to get him to say how he feels and zilch. He refuses to say how he feels about anything, and that just makes trying to understand what's behind the drinking that much worse. How am I going to know what makes him drown himself in the stuff if he doesn't say? I've always known Tad was like that, but he didn't use to drink so much before. And now all this. It's hard to take.

BENSON: [To Tad] I think what I hear her [Janet] saying is that you're making it that much harder on her and the kids because you guys don't talk about what's bothering you.

TAD: It doesn't matter. I'm trying to get off the sauce and I'm going to get off. Period.

SIMPSON: That's not what she's saying, Tad. Everyone's got feelings. You have feelings. I have feelings. Tim has feelings. Jan has feelings. Even your 4-year-old has feelings. You just can't brush it off with you're getting off the sauce. There's something real basic going on here, whether you know it or not. I've seen it wreck many marriages. The more important negative consequence of clamming up is not just that you're not telling her things, but how it makes her feel when you do that.

JANET: Bev's right, Tad. How do you think it makes me feel when you don't open up to me? [Elaborates] I'm not a stranger. I'm your wife. At least that's what I thought I was.

TAD: Oh, come on, Jan, don't go getting overly dramatic on us.

JANET: I'm not being dramatic. [Turns to others] See. That's the way he always responds. I try to get him to speak up and he blames me . . . me . . . for getting all dramatic.

BENSON: I've seen a lot of marriages like this. Some say it's the old male ego working itself out. You know, a guy's not supposed to want to get into feelings like a woman does. Right, Tad? [Tad shrugs] So the drinking becomes a problem. Right? What's she think, Tad? [Pause] She's beginning to think that you don't trust her. She starts to feel that maybe you don't care? Maybe she excuses it for a while, like she thinks that you're just having a lot of trouble at work. She'll sit tight until things blow over. But things don't blow over. So you start drinking more . . . because she's nagging you? Sound familiar? And you get real uptight and clam up tighter. You're real upset inside but you don't say a thing . . . maybe because you don't know how to? Or you feel funny talking about how you feel? So you land up in here before things blow completely apart.

SIMPSON: But you know what could have happened? You could have just wrecked your marriage, that's all . . . if there's anything left of it.

JANET: I don't know . . . I don't know if I trust him anymore. How can I, Tad? You never tell me how you feel. Maybe you don't feel anything at all for us. If that's it, then I hate to tell you . . .

TAD: Come on, Jan! I never said anything like that.

JANET: Well, saying nothing is no way to show that you care a hoot about us. I'm talking about love, Tad. Love. I don't mean just in bed. [Pause] You act like we don't love you or something. People who trust one another tell each other what they feel. At least that's what I always thought. Why should I go around feeling guilty about it, like *I'm* doing something wrong?

BENSON: You know what that is? [Pause] That's a subtle form of power. [Turns to Tad] You're not just clamming up, you're *making* her feel like she's the problem. [Turns to others] Remember what we said about problem ownership? When you fail to communicate or you're very aggressive about it, you turn the tables and, Pow! someone else owns the problem. Communication and power work together like that. I've seen it many times, like would you believe in 90% of the families?

As Benson suggests, aggressive responses likewise spoil communication. Aggressiveness signals emotion bursting out of control, such as when feelings have been "bottled up" for too long and not permitted to "vent" or because of a dysfunctional switch in problem ownership between two partners in communication. ASU therapist Dennis McDonald routinely cautions patients and family members that no expression of feeling need be conveyed aggressively. By its nature, aggressive communication makes difficult matters worse. An initial problem, such as an adolescent's domestic slovenliness, gets "blown out of proportion" when what a parent feels about it is aggressively conveyed or when what the teen thinks, in turn, is related angrily.

Responding to an exchange between teenaged former patient Bobby and his stepfather Matt in an adolescent aftercare meeting, McDonald distinguishes several features of aggressive communication.

McDONALD: Bobby, it's your turn. How was your week? You were visiting your grandparents this week, weren't you?
BOBBY: Yeah. It was a lot of fun and I didn't get into any trouble the whole week.

As usual, participants clap in response to a report of successful abstinence.

McDONALD: That's good. How'd you do it?
BOBBY: What can you do to get in trouble in an old people's [trailer] park? [Laughter] No one gets on your back. There's not much to do anyway. They're real nice.
MATT: You should be so nice at home! [Turns to McDonald] All I've been getting from him lately is a lot of shit. He was pretty good for a while after he got out of here, but that didn't last too long, believe me. The kid gives me shit every time I ask him to do anything around the house.
BOBBY: Aw, come on, Matt. You're always on my back. [Turns to others] Give *him* shit . . . listen to him. *I'm* the one's getting shit. Like last week . . .
MATT: [Interrupting] Yeah! Tell them about last week. [Turns to others] He's supposed to take out the garbage cans on Wednesday because it's pickup day Thursday, first thing in the morning. He knows that. God knows I've told him enough times. So what does he do? He tells me he's going to do it right away. So I wait. Like I'm watching the little shit completely forget what he's supposed to do. So I tell him again. [Imitating Bobby] "Yeah, okay, in a minute, okay, in a minute." This goes on for a couple hours. I finally tell him that it's now or else. [Elaborates] I hear him go out the door and the cans moving. I think to myself, "He's finally moving his ass." The next day, I walk out the door and the

garbage is still in the yard. The lids are knocked off and there's shit all over the place. I really tore into him.

BOBBY: Yeah. And that tells you how much he listens, too. I tried to tell him that Tiger [his dog] ran out the door before I could get the cans out there. So I had to catch her because . . . she bites. . . . [Elaborates] I didn't want her to be put in the pound again. I tried to tell him [Matt], but would he listen? Heck, no! [Sarcastically] He just yelled his mouth off as usual.

MATT: [Shouting] Someday I'm going to shove a can down your throat! That sarcastic mouth of yours . . . you're always mouthing off to your mother and to me. This Tiger excuse of his is a bunch of bull! You don't give a shit how anyone feels! Your mother doesn't know what to do with you! [Turns to McDonald] That's why we sent him to my in-laws for a week. He was too much.

BOBBY: [To Matt] You're always on my back! Why don't you lay off!

The angry exchange expands as Matt boisterously accuses Bobby of irresponsibility and Bobby, in turn, just as loudly voices hatred toward his stepfather. Bobby's facial expressions are anything but relaxed; Matt's are livid.

MATT: [To McDonald] What this kid needs is a good dose of child abuse.

McDONALD: Whoa there! Let's not get carried away. I hear you both loud and clear. You're blowing things all out of proportion, both of you. [Elaborates] Just stop. Let's stop a second . . . okay . . . listen to yourselves for a second. Do either of you stop and ask yourself what the other one might be feeling? It doesn't sound like it to me. Man, Bobby, you're sitting there just like you have a chip on your shoulder, just waiting for Matt to set you off. You don't even look at Matt when you're talking to him. No eye contact at all. And, Matt, look at you. The anger's written all over your face. That's aggression. Did you guys learn *anything* when Bobby was in here? You both know better than that.

MATT: Aw, Dennis [McDonald], it's his sarcastic attitude!

McDONALD: I hear your anger, Matt, but I think it's imperative that you approach Bobby so he hears how you feel. All he's

> hearing now is the yelling. [Turns to Bobby] And all
> he's [Matt] hearing is the mouthing off. Neither of you
> is really listening to each other. [Elaborates]

As McDonald elaborates on the characteristics of aggressive communication, he repeats that Matt and Bobby's interpersonal relations would improve if they stopped shouting and actually listened to each other. McDonald explains that angry talk is a "perfect way" of falling into one of the vicious traps of dysfunctionality:

> I'm not saying you're not angry. I hear the anger. We all
> hear it, from the both of you. There's nothing wrong with
> telling someone you're angry. It's imperative that you do.
> That's not the problem. The problem is when the *message* is
> angry, the first reaction is to respond with anger. You know,
> "Why should I listen to that bull?" When the whole family
> gets to yelling like that, it's a perfect way of falling into a
> trap. The whole thing twists around and you get this vicious
> circle of aggressive communication. No one can say any-
> thing or do anything before they get their head chewed off.
> There's a lot of shouting and people are waving their arms
> around and shaking their fists at each other. Forget the eye
> contact. There's no such thing as sitting back and telling
> your side of the story. Everyone's on the edge of their seat
> . . . if they're sitting down, that is. Everyone's having tem-
> per tantrums. Sometimes there's violence; hopefully not.
> You can bet that's not the way to facilitate the expression
> of feelings. What that kind of family needs is quality time
> and that ain't it.

ASSERTIVE COMMUNICATION

The term *quality time* often is used to describe periods of inter-action in which emotions are functionally expressed and family members effectively convey their individual feelings. As an ASU nurse states when a mother and daughter describe their mutual joy and satisfaction in talking straight to each other and laughing about their feelings, "So you've had some quality time together."

The rules for producing quality time guide assertive communication. There are three groups of rules, for seating, posture, and
verbalization. Family members who communicate with each other
in the right tone of voice and with the proper, equalitarian demeanor, assertively convey their feelings and thereby maintain quality time, a hallmark of domestic order. Those who repeatedly ignore
the rules, mounting the power trips that "lord it" over others, are
dysfunctional families.

An interesting parallel with Westside House emerges. At
Westside, seating, posture, and verbalization comprise the chief
signs of authority, traditional authority being construed as domestic
order. A father who, in the context of a therapy session, seats himself
prominently in the room, presents confidently, and speaks author-
itatively is interpreted to be the power in the home, as is believed
he should be. As a rule, fathers counseled at Westside do not present
in this way—or overpresent, as the case might be—which serves
to explain their families' domestic troubles. At Fairview, seating,
posture, and verbalization do not so much refer to ruling as to facilitating the expression that supports domestic order. Tied to a liberal,
democratic model of the family, ruling is eschewed at Fairview
and rules of expression touted.

The sense of excessive authority or overdomination at Westside parallels at Fairview the set of communication rules considered to be too complicated to apply. Emphasis is placed on traditional authority at Westside, but too much authority signals possible domestic violence, in particular, spouse battery or child abuse.
By the same token, although the functional family at Fairview lives
by rules that show trust or love, too many rules make it difficult
to be relaxed and spontaneous, and are especially cumbersome to
sort through and rationally apply in times of crisis. This last concern
bulks large in Fairview families, especially parents attempting
systematically to contain the turmoil of their domestic lives according to the comparatively tepid rules of assertive communication
taught at the hospital.

The seating rule is not the most important guide to assertiveness, but it is taken to be a concrete basis for effective communication. The rule is familiar, borrowed from a common view of
rational discourse. Time and again, Fairview treatment staff speak

of the need to "sit down" and put assertive communication into effect. Of course, family members and patients readily recognize the rule, but they become more adept at systematic, even formulaic, application as they progress through the program. A "canned" quality can prompt good-humored mocking.

One Sunday afternoon in group, ASU therapist Dave Shindell responds to an angry teenager by elaborating on the need to sit down and talk in order to effectively convey feelings. Ricky Watson, the teenager, has just stood in the middle of the room and hostilely told his mother that he is not going to "take it anymore," that neither his mother, who is present, nor his father understands what it is like to be "grounded" because of the "littlest" infraction. Before Ricky finishes, Shindell interrupts and several parents as well as fellow teenaged patient Bill join in the discussion.

SHINDELL: Okay, Watson, I think we've heard enough. We've . . .
RICKY: [Continuing] It's not fair. I get grounded just because . . .
SHINDELL: [Interrupting] We *heard* you, Ricky. You can sit down now. You've told your side of it.

Rick slowly takes his seat. There's a long pause. All eyes are on Ricky and his mother. Shindell continues.

SHINDELL: [To Ricky] You've come across loud and clear. [To all] I think we should ask ourselves, "Has Ricky really communicated what he feels?" [To Ricky] You say they ground you for the littlest thing? But do you bother to ask them how they feel about what you did to deserve that? I don't think so. Maybe the more important question is, "Did you really *tell* Mom how you feel?" I think all of us would agree that we heard you loud and clear. The question is, "What did we hear?" [Pause] Think about it. [Looks around the room] Anyone. What would you hear if someone was standing there, just 3 feet away from you, yelling at the top of his voice at you about something?
DAD A: I'd say I'd be hearing a lot of screaming and yelling.
MOM B: I'd say, "There's a pretty disturbed teenager."
RICKY'S MOM: That's what Ricky's like lately . . . shouting, racing around the room, mouthing off, standing right in

front of me and his dad and swearing like a sailor. It's a wonder his dad doesn't haul off and brain him when he's like that. Ricky never sits down and tells you what's on his mind. No, sir. He's got to be on a soapbox with a loudspeaker.

SHINDELL: I think what we're hearing here is the first thing about how not to communicate. No one is going to say anything to anyone when he's standing there yelling. I'm sure that's not what any one of us believes is effective. I think the first thing is that we have to learn to just sit down and . . .

BILL: [Interrupting] You have to sit tight for 5 minutes, Ricky-boy, and think about what you're doing instead of yelling and starting into it right off the bat like that.

SHINDELL: That's the first thing. If you don't sit down and deal with this rationally . . . get down to business . . . no one's going to hear anything you're saying, no matter how much you say or how loud you say it.

BILL: [Chuckling] That's right, Ricky-boy. [Singsong] You got to sit a little; smile a little; put your feet on the ground a little. [All laugh] Seriously, Watson, you got to put your feelings on the table, man, or you're gonna get nowhere fast.

This first rule for assertive or effective communication conveys the likeness of a business meeting. The family member who wishes his or her feelings to be heard sits down at the proverbial table, with the others, it is to be hoped, similarly sitting. Sitting is a sign of tranquility; standing represents an aggressive attitude. Passive communication avoids the table altogether, wrongly presuming that feelings will be conveyed by inference. Ordinary language actually links rationality with seating as Fairview staff, patients, and family members speak of having "sat down and been reasonable" and "sitting back and thinking clearly," among other mundane connections of order and discourse. And exceptions prove the rule. As Shindell once noted, "You take a kid who reluctantly sits down, but doesn't get down to business; that kid looks right, but the attitude underneath has a long way to go."

According to a chapter entitled "The Family Meeting" in
Dinkmeyer and McKay's (1983, p. 157) guide for the effective parenting of teens, "A democratic family thrives on making decisions
together." The family meeting is a businesslike forum for learning
that each individual opinion and corresponding feeling matters.
Sitting down together as a family allows participants to "be heard,"
to "express positive feelings about other family members," and to
"express concerns, feelings and complaints" (p. 157). Fairview
staff routinely urge family members to hold such meetings to talk
over differences or get their feelings out on the table. In turn,
family members report on attempts—failures being treated as
exceptions to the rule, caused by such extenuating circumstances
as some member, particularly the patient, not knowing how to
behave in a meeting or the meeting turning into some other type
of gathering, such as a "circus," "zoo," or "war zone."

ASU and ADU addict patients are encouraged to attend twelve-
step meetings in the community. There are Alcoholics Anonymous meetings for teens, just as there are special groups for the
spouses of adult narcotics addicts. Some family members are sold
on these meetings because, as one spouse put it, "They get you
away from the craziness and give you, and everyone, a chance to
sit down and tell what you feel." The mother of a recently relapsed
teenager, a former patient in the ASU, speaks at length in aftercare
about how "meetings" help to break the cycle of addiction, because they "get you down to business" in an open and systematic
fashion:

> AA says that you have to go to 90 meetings for 90 days and
> then you can decide what you need. God gave us church
> groups and God gave us AA and NA too. We all need those
> meetings. [Pause] I'd like to go on record and say that this
> Wednesday night meeting [aftercare] is not enough. Sure it
> helps, because it gives us a chance to sit down and talk out
> feelings. You don't get much chance like that at home, es-
> pecially when everyone's running in and out and all hell is
> breaking loose. But the hospital [Fairview] should know
> that one night of aftercare a week is not going to do it. There's
> no hope without the meetings [the As]. [Elaborates] Par-
> ents need to go to the meetings, too. There are Alanon pro-

grams [for family members]. We all need to stick to the twelve steps. Those meetings really do get you down to business. It's a system and, God knows, these kids need a system. This drinking stuff is a disease. It's a disease of the attitudes. It's simple things. It's the attitude . . . like when something makes you angry . . . is that okay? So you get to feeling it's not okay and what do you do . . . bang . . . you shoot up or you get drunk. The attitude is that you've got to feel good about yourself. That's got to be built up, but you can't do it on your own. You've got to surrender your feelings to something greater than yourself. That feeling that you can do it on your own and that you've got control . . . that's false confidence.

Others, like ASU patient Bill, quoted earlier, mock the formularized character of the twelve steps. Although it is generally agreed that a businesslike atmosphere is a basis for assertive communication, the atmosphere can become stifling, or "too hokey," "too planned out," and "not free floating enough." It is said that the As are contrived—which gets stale—and not naturally related to the emotional contours of particular domestic problems. Former Fairview patient Jack Dillon argues in aftercare:

Shit, you can get addicted to AA. Right? I don't think the meetings is where it's at. They're useful. I'm not saying they're no good. But they're not the total answer. [Elaborates] And they can get pretty goddamn stupid. All that surrender-to-God stuff. [Mocks self-disclosure] I don't buy that. Serenity bullshit. Sure the meetings help. They keep those guys who've decided to go straight on the wagon. Right? I tell ya . . . it's not my thing. When I get low for some reason and start to relapse, I don't want to hear about those fucking twelve steps. I want to sit down and talk about me! My shit! Not their fucking shit! They had me coming and going. [Elaborates] I didn't need that on my back on top of everything else.

Indeed, at one point in an extended discussion and debate focused on the rules for rational family discussion, Dillon takes issue with the idea that getting down to business itself is desirable for everyone or in all circumstances. This time, Dillon comments less about the contrived ineffectiveness of sitting down to talk than his felt need at times to "just break loose and raise hell"—not talking out feelings, but simply acting out. Still, as Dillon finally remarks and others confirm, he may be exceptional in this regard.

> All I hear is that you've got to put a lid on it. You know, [mockingly] "Sit down and talk about it real rational-like." Everyone's got to tell how he feels and that makes you feel better. Well, shit, . . . what if I want to raise hell? I mean, that's what I *want* to do. Okay? I *want* to do it! You want to just break loose and raise hell! I don't want to talk about it. Talking about it's going to be a drag. You want to act out, that's all. So? [Pause] It's not that easy. To me, it's like a circle. Being dry is only a high for a while for me. So then, you drink or drug and get high and you feel good. And you're into that for a while and that gets old. You don't get anything out of it. So you go straight. I did that. And you feel good about that for a while . . . until that gets old. You want to raise a little hell again. [Pause] I guess I'm just different. [Several participants react, one sarcastically with, "Yeah, Dillon, you're sure different."]

Perhaps the ultimate formalization of getting down to business is the family contract. Contracts are also part of Fairview's internal programming, especially on the adolescent services unit. The contract normally is written, although formal verbal agreements are occasionally struck. In addition to matters such as when and where domestic privileges and responsibilities apply, contracts specify the facilitation of expression, in particular attending family meetings.

One contract, for example, is divided into five categories: chores daily and weekly, responsibilities, privileges, Sundays, and behavior. The entry under Sundays reads: "Family must have a family talk and discuss what they have felt through the week." The phrasing under behavior features the agreed upon consequences for the adolescent should he or she not properly communicate with other family members, notably parents. It reads:

There will be no back talking or cussing or any lying from me. If so, I will serve a 15-minute TIME OUT in my room. If I get two within a day, I will be grounded for a weekend. After TIME OUT is served, then Mom and Dad and me will discuss the reason for getting the TIME OUT.

Another contract specifies the consequences for misbehavior. Regarding school, it states that "intentional skipping" results in "weekend restriction," and "failing grades" requires "consequences to be determined by a family meeting." The entry under "family" is a list of domestic understandings:

1. Sunday family dinner: Everyone home by 4 PM on. . . Take turns on cooking; the other two [family members] do dishes. Family meeting.
2. One Saturday each month—Family Day . . . All day, all evening.

Contracts are considered to be an effective means of organizing the household division of labor when there is considerable contention in the home. But, according to some family members, when it comes to the heat and turbulence of some domestic disagreements, contracts may be too complicated to apply. Details are forgotten. The particular interpretation of consequences is unknown. Written contracts themselves may be mislaid and cannot be located when needed. As with all contracts, ultimately required is an agreed-upon way of interpreting the meaning of phrasings and their applicability in particular circumstances. That, it is claimed, is what is often found missing in the discord of domestic disagreements, even when contractual specifications have been arranged. A distressed mother put this succinctly one Sunday in group:

You're asking me to be judge and jury at the same time and I just can't do it. It's enough that we have to keep track of these contracts, but, believe me, when she [daughter] starts to act up and we all get into it, no one thinks about sitting down and figuring out what we agreed to. You just want everyone to do what they're supposed to or get the consequences. She [daughter] starts yelling that that's not what this means and that's not what that means . . . and, of course, her dad and I think differently. We even disagree. So who's to judge? That's the problem. You're back to Square 1.

Although intended to facilitate rational expression, in practice the contract itself can turn minor domestic discord into complicated disorder.

Posture also supports assertive communication. In figuring the quality of communication, Fairview patients, staff, and family members take a broader view of posture than Westsiders do. Westsiders read authority from body carriage and demeanor; posture at Fairview references attitude as well as physical bearing. Assertive communication not only emphasizes a calm demeanor, typically represented by sitting down, but also highlights discursive composure, placing equal value on "sitting back." Raised voices, screaming, yelling, grunting, sarcasm, mocking, verbal abuse, and violence, among other animatedly aggressive actions, have no place in rational discourse. Anger, for one, need not be conveyed loudly, with fists shaking and arms waving, but can be stated forthrightly, with equanimity, by sitting down and sitting back.

The view of posture as communicative attitude is significant, according to some, for it can "make or break" the facilitation of expression. ASU therapist Dave Shindell explains:

> That basic attitude can make or break what these families are all about. You have a kid like Frank Hoffman [an ASU patient], who really needs to tell his mom and his dad how angry he is and he just doesn't know how to do it and you've got a volcano. All's Hoffman knows is how to . . . you know what he's like . . . [Imitating Frank] is "tell 'em how he fucking feels" and he's "fucking mad as hell." It's that foul mouth of his. You know as well as I do that no one in hell is going to listen to that. All they're going to hear is his fucking this and his fucking that. [Pause] He's so damn funny sometimes. He'll sit down and you can just see how he's trying real hard, like in group, to talk about his feelings. You know, he gets to first base. He's sitting down, like real calm and laid back. But the kid goes bonkers when he opens his mouth. [Elaborates] He's just going to have to learn to change his attitude, that's all. We're working on it.

Shindell suggests that, although it is important to establish a businesslike atmosphere within which to communicate feelings, the rest depends on communicants' attitudes.

Fairview staffers depict vividly what happens when posture prevents expression. Metaphors are mixed to present the potential for, or the actual expression of, emotive storms. Dave Shindell is especially graphic in portraying the process in parent effectiveness classes. Speaking of the expression of feelings, Shindell draws a funnel on the blackboard to depict the emotional domain:

> Inside here [pointing to the funnel] are all the feelings. Mom, here's your impatience with Suzie. Dad, here're all your worries about Jimmy. That's where Suzie's and Jimmy's feelings are, too. They're all churning and swirling in there just waiting to come out. Feelings that just stay in there ... Wow! They've got to come out. [Elaborates] All of these pressures go into the system. The computer gets all clogged up. They're bugs in the programming. There has to be a bleed-off. [Draws little holes in the funnel] When there's a bleed-off, things cool down a bit. If this is an adolescent [pointing to the funnel] and there's not much there yet by way of some way to bleed-off the pressures ... that bad attitude ... like when you don't have a system of processing, then you have a tornado. [The funnel becomes a tornado] You have slamming doors, stomping around, screaming bloody murder. That there's your basic democratic family shot to hell.

That, too, is the mundane realization of domestic disorder.

Shindell, like others, describes how Fairview works to establish the right attitude for the expression of feelings. An important step in taking a properly assertive posture is "thinking twice before you speak." According to psychiatrist Robert Henderson, "This is one of the most important variables: that ability to distance yourself from your feelings so that you can say what you feel with clarity, so that others will hear you." ADU nurse Bev Simpson explains to new patients and family members in an evening family therapy session:

> We can provide the kind of controlled environment that they [patients] don't have. Hopefully, we can teach both you and your patient how to build that at home. You're going to have to be patient. Learning to stop and think and not shoot your mouth off at any moment isn't easy. Some of you might

think, "Heck, that's nothing." But, you'll see, it isn't that simple. It's a matter of attitude really, and you all know attitude can get you into a mess of trouble. To me, that's the basic problem in most of the families we get. That attitude screws them up so bad that they just drink or drug it off, whatever their pleasure, even before anything gets said. It makes a difference.

Still, when things eventually are said, "It's how you say it that counts." Sitting down and sitting back are pertinent and form a basis for the proper facilitation of expression, but the voice conveys the actual feeling. Someone has to state or declare what is being communicated, even if it is a sober inference, such as we saw Chuck's mother make in the last chapter in response to her son's inability to "really say."

The rules for the effective verbalization of feelings are tonal, structural, and substantive. It is important that the proper tone of voice be used to state how one feels. One risks being ignored, for example by using the angry tone that "turns others off" to the recognition of an emotion. It also is important that statements regarding feelings be structured so that they are emotionally factual, not precipitously accusatory or otherwise judgmental. It is imperative that the words used be substantively appropriate to the voicing of feelings—so-called feeling words. Stated in the proper tone of voice and factually, the use of feeling words should turn attention directly to the heart of domestic matters, namely, the emotions that the words expressly reference. Therapist Dave Shindell explains, indirectly distinguishing tone, structure, and substance:

> I guess what I'm telling you is that if you're sounding cool, like real calm-like, it's not everything. You're just going to sound real funny if you keep beating around the bush. No one's going to know what you're needing to talk about. You've got to use all those feeling words. Love, anger, guilt, hate, jealousy, what have you. [Elaborates] I know it's not easy for many of you; you're not used to using words like that right out. But that's where it's at in the democratic family. You have to put it the right way, too. You can't go around accusing everyone for the way you're feeling, like "you this"

and "you that." Those are those ineffective you-messages. They put people down. Just get to the point and tell them, easy-like, how you feel inside . . . like "I hear you telling me that . . . whatever." Use I-messages.

ASU therapist Ken Olsen is particularly adept at illustrating verbalization rules—some say comically so. Like other therapists, Olsen takes some of his material from Dinkmayer and McKay (1983), but he also provides examples drawn from his own experience, adapted to meet the needs of his patients and family members. Still, in sharing ideas and assertiveness techniques, the therapists together have formed a lively culture of communicative responses to family troubles that make their individual styles and exemplifications as much variations on a common approach as they are idiosyncratic.

The following exchange from an aftercare meeting illustrates Olsen's particular style. After the usual introductions and casual comments about the week's domestic experiences, Olsen mentions that he has heard a great deal of accusing, especially from Blake Summerfield, a former adolescent patient, and her mother, Mrs. S. A few parents have encouraged Blake to seek help from Alanon, but she sees her problem differently. Additional accusations prompt Olsen to zero in, in a highly modulated style of voice, on what "all should have learned during treatment," namely, how to state feelings and use feeling words. At one point, Greg, a former patient, laughs and mocks the tonal rule, to which all respond with amusement.

OLSEN: Sounds like there's a lot of accusing going on here. Do you hear what I'm hearing? Blake [a former patient], did you try to tell your father [who is absent] how you feel?
BLAKE: No, because he's real frustrated and he's gotten really picky.
OLSEN: What do you mean?
BLAKE: He [her father] gets mad when we put too much ice in his drink. He's drinking more than he used to. He's trying to run three businesses. [Elaborates] He acts like no one's around and no one matters but him. [Explains] You try to do something for him, like get him a drink, and no matter how hard you try, he finds something wrong with it. You

can't please him. Like he wants three cubes in his drink, not two. It's stupid because it's our house, too. He should be happy that we even make him a drink.

DAD A: [To Blake] So it's a drinking problem?

BLAKE: No, I just used that as an example.

MOM A: [To Blake] Have you been to Alanon? Because they teach you that it's his [Blake's father] problem. In families, when you've got someone drinking a lot, the whole family gets into it and tries to protect each other because you can't reason with a drunk. I know. [Elaborates] And [to Mom B] you know, too.

MOM B: I sure do. Whenever my husband got into his thing, you just knew you wouldn't be able to say anything for the rest of the night. If you just mentioned the wrong thing, he'd be off on one of his loud fits and you couldn't stop him until he fell asleep or passed out. I used to try to go halfway with him, like you're doing, Blake, you know, try to please him because you feel sorry for him because he'd had a hard day. That's when you become a codependent; you make it your problem.

MOM A: [To Blake] They're [Alanon] good because they let you vent your feelings.

OLSEN: [To Blake] I think it's important to look at problem ownership. How much of it is your problem?

BLAKE: I said it's not his drinking! I just used that as an example. He's not a drunk! He's just picky and gets real moody. It's like all he cares about is the business. He's driving us all crazy.

MOM C: Of course, you have to look at the other side, too. I had a business once and I got in over my head. For months, I tried to make a go of it and it wasn't easy, boy. Every night, I'd come home and all I'd have on my mind was if we're going to make it. I didn't have a husband either to fall back on. All I had was my kid, and she really didn't understand what was going on in my head. [To Blake] Don't take it personally, like it's an attack on you. Believe me, I went bankrupt and it can be devastating. That's probably what's happening with your dad. Ya come home and who else is there to pick on but you kids. I didn't have a husband to pick on, so Joyce [her daughter] got the brunt of it. I'm here alone tonight.

OLSEN: Why isn't Joyce with you?

MOM C: I don't think she'll come back. She's sounding a lot like Blake . . . frustrated and mad . . . a lot of accusing.

BLAKE: I said I'm not mad, damn it! I'm just trying real hard to make it easy on Dad. But he's not trying.

MRS. S: I can tell you right now, Blake, that yelling's not going to get you anywhere . . . not with your dad anyway. You're just getting yourself in deeper and mad over nothing.

OLSEN: I guess some of the problem here is what we all should have learned in treatment. [In a highly modulated, monotonic voice] Mom [Mrs. S], I think . . . first of all . . . that you might . . . ask yourself . . . how Blake feels about how Dad reacts. I hear . . . a lot of you-messages. "You're getting mad for nothing!" [Elaborates] "You this and you that." [To all] How does that sound? [To Blake's mother] How does that sound to you, Mom?

MRS. S: It sounds like I'm accusing her. [Pause] I know, I know.

OLSEN: [To Blake in his modulated tone] I think . . . I hear you saying . . . "I'm trying real hard . . . and that no matter what, Dad's picky." I hear deep frustration.

BLAKE: Yeah! And I'm not mad at him! [Pause] I guess I'm . . .

OLSEN: [Interrupting] I take it . . . you're . . . disappointed because . . . he doesn't realize . . . how much . . . you're concerned about him.

MRS. S: She [Blake] jumps to conclusions too fast. She tries to do something for him [Blake's dad] and he lets her, of course. . . . But she doesn't roll with the punches. He's had a hard day. If he raises his voice and complains about something, she goes stamping off, yelling at him . . . and he gets mad at that, of course.

OLSEN: It's those judgmental you-messages again. [Pause] Blake, I'll make you a deal. When he comes home from work tomorrow night, try *saying* how he feels. Like, "I know . . . you're tired, Dad, and . . . that when you come home . . . you're frustrated about the business." Like that. Get those I-messages in there, nice and easy. That shows you're placing *his* feelings first, not your own.

MRS. S: Hah! She yells at him if he so much as peeps about anything.

BLAKE: Mom! Would you please stop! You don't know what you're talking about! You don't give a damn about him. All you care about is that he goes to work and gives you your allowance each week!

MRS. S: You don't know how I feel. Why don't you just shut up!

OLSEN: [To Blake and Mrs. S, in a modulated tone] I sense you guys
          are . . . pretty mad. I hear . . . you . . . both saying . . . that
          . . . you . . . both care. Mom, try this with Blake: "When you
          [Blake] feel frustrated, I worry . . . that we're not trying to
          understand how you feel." Blake, try to get more feeling
          words out. Don't run off all mad. Try saying to Dad: "I
          think I know . . . how you feel, Dad, when you get home
          from work. But when you get all stressed out about work,
          I feel that . . . you're not seeing how much we care about
          you." Get those feeling words out on the table.

MRS. S: She [Blake] really should try to use more of those assertive-
          ness skills. That's what I've been telling her.

BLAKE: I hate that stuff. . . . I can't say that stuff, like that book
          [STEP/Teen] says. Dad'd think I'm flaky. You can't talk to
          him like that. I hate that tone of voice anyway.

OLSEN: Blake. No one said that you *had* to quote the book chapter
          and verse. Just use what you think'll help. You guys know
          Dad better than anyone. Be creative. When I talk with my
          own kids, I don't have the time to look things up either.
          Who does? Sure, a lot of those things [in the book] don't
          apply to you. Pick and choose whatever works the best.

GREG: [Laughing] But ya got to tell those old feelings, Ken. [Whis-
          pering] Now don't raise your voice. As long as you're real
          slo-o-ow-like, you're okay. [With levity and sarcasm] Blake,
          didn't they teach you assertiveness training around here?
          You know, like Ken does it, "I . . . feel . . . like . . . you . . .
          are . . . making . . . me . . . angry." Re-e-e-al slo-o-o-ow, but
          not aggressive. [All laugh]

OLSEN: [Chuckling] It might sound funny, but it works.

MOM C: Greg's always the joker. [Pause] But seriously, it [the phras-
          ing] does catch them off guard.

As the discussion continues, Olsen concentrates on the tailoring of assertive expressiveness to particular personalities and
circumstances. The tone, structure, and substance of verbalization are important general guidelines, but ultimately "you pick
and choose" whatever works, according to Olsen. There is an
implicit meta-rule in operation here that links general guidelines
with what actually is applied. Just as every rule operates in relation
to a tacit as-a-rule clause, providing for exceptions in practice to

what is generally sustained, a pick-and-choose clause permits tailoring of verbalization and other techniques to individual needs without negating the overall relevance of verbal tone, structure, and substance.

Picking and choosing or being creative in facilitating expression is encouraged across the board. In informing family members how to read parent effectiveness training materials, Dave Shindell routinely underscores the application of selective imagination. Shindell responds to a father's frustration over not being able to use *STEP/Teen* exactly as presented:

> I tell all my parents not to use this as a textbook. I don't want you to go from the beginning and through each and every chapter until you get to the end. There's going to be some topics in this book that you don't buy. It's just not you. We're all different. [To frustrated father] Fred, the kind of trouble that Ben [Fred's son] has I think might require something firmer than *STEP*; maybe not. We'll have to see how it works out. [To all] Go through the book and when you find things that apply to you and that you think you can use, that's what I think you should concentrate on. Be creative. It's a whole new ball game today. You have the democratic model of parenting skills, not the autocratic model that we had when we were raised, when I was a kid. No one would have bought the book in the fifties. Today, you've got to be strategic and get into planning and use your imagination. Look over what the book has to say and try to tie it in with your child and be ready to discuss it.

The pick-and-choose clause also applies to visual media. The many videotapes shown in the ADU, focused primarily on the addictions, are not approached as exact portraits of anyone's experiences, but as examples of "what it's like." Following tape presentations about addiction or about communication and other coping processes, ADU therapist Tim Benson routinely asks family members, "Do you see yourself in any of that?" The conventional wisdom is that there are many (assertive) ways of facilitating expression. ADU nurse Bev Simpson explains in an evening family group:

There's no recipe for recovery. This stuff [videotapes and
written materials] helps you to understand what you're going
through. You might see yourself in some of it and not see
yourself at all in other parts. Pick and choose what fits *your*
situation and *your* needs. No one's going to tell you to do
or say things a certain way if it doesn't fit your family situation. The important thing is to get those feelings out in the
open. Let 'em know that you have feelings, too, and that
those power trips the drunk gets into will not be accepted.
The sooner you establish that basic respect and trust, the
better off everyone will be. Like I said, pick and choose,
because any of it, really, can help. Don't get into that vicious circle that got you into this in the first place . . . the
yelling, the accusing, and the rest. We've all got to learn to
say what we feel, not just keep it inside.

Evident in ASU therapist Ken Olsen's earlier comments, the
other side of assertive communication is effective listening. Assertive communication not only requires the clarity and non-
judgmental tone of I-messages and the explicit identifying function of feeling words, but takes a listener prepared to hear which
is being conveyed. No form of communication can be successful
if its messages are not received. Adolescents are taught to take
the time to listen for their parents' feelings and not rush around
or dwell exclusively on personal or peer concerns. Parents learn
to sympathetically listen to what their children are telling them,
not glibly dismiss them as uncaring and selfish. Spouses are taught
that husbands or wives are not just drunks, drug abusers, and bat-
terers, but "real" people whose feelings require attention, who
need to be understood emotionally as part of building domestic
trust and love.

Two terms of reference are used: *reflective listening* and *active
listening*. Presented in *STEP/Teen,* reflective listening emphasizes
the so-called mirrorlike quality of effective communication. Like
the express overtures to emotional life that come with feeling
words, the reflective listener reacts to a speaker by partially reiter-
ating what has been heard. ASU therapist Dennis McDonald offers
examples in response to two adolescent patients, Sally and Georgia

(George), who complain in a Sunday afternoon group meeting that their parents "never listen."

McDONALD: Okay, we've heard all about curfews and raising hell in the neighborhood. What else is there to complain about?

SALLY: All that stuff that Kim [another patient] was talking about . . . that makes me angry because . . . at least her dad listens to her. [Pause] I don't know about her mom [who's not present]. My parents aren't here today, but are they ever hardheads. [Pause] Sometimes I don't know if they're ever really there . . . in the head, I mean. They don't listen. [Elaborates] You could talk yourself out, all day long, and it's like you're talking to a wall! I don't know what to do! Someday, I'm going to tie both of them down and yell right in their ears, "Hey, you guys! Are you in there?" They make me so *angry!*

McDONALD: I'm sensing that you're angry because your parents aren't taking the time to *really* listen.

SALLY: Damn straight.

GEORGIA: Do you think *mine* do? I wish they were here so you all could see how *they* listen. Mama's always running around with her head chopped off. Daddy's . . . he's my stepdad . . . he's always telling you what to do. He's the man. Blah. Blah. Blah. Just forget listening. No one listens to anyone in my house.

McDONALD: [To Georgia] You sound all alone because your parents don't seem to be interested in what's going on in your life.

GEORGIA: Say what?

McDONALD: I was saying that what I hear you telling us, George, is that you seem to feel all alone at home with two parents who don't bother to remember that you're there, too.

GEORGIA: Yeah. Most days, they don't even act like I'm alive.

Not only should the listener indicate with appropriate recapitulation that feelings have been heard, but the listener should show evidence of being attentive. According to staff, eye contact is a most effective means. As psychiatrist Henderson remarks in group:

My mother once told me the eyes tell all. I've since learned
that there's a lot of wisdom in that. How else can you show
that you're really listening. You look someone straight in
the eyes . . . you know, give that person your full attention
. . . that person knows that you're listening. When you're
looking away or at the ceiling or the floor . . . like a lot of
us do . . . I don't think that's showing interest. Sure, you
might be listening, but the question is does that person who's
talking to you feel the same? Anyway, chances are, you're
not. Eye contact is really important here.

To which ASU nurse Kay Mandel adds:

And I wouldn't think that a good dose of sitting up straight
would hurt either. What parent is going to take any kid
seriously who's slouching in a chair, looking down at the
floor, and like sighing his mind off.

TOUGHLOVE

Even the best of efforts may fail to communicate. After several
weeks of actively listening to a daughter who was in treatment
at Fairview, a mother complains in an aftercare meeting that the
daughter is "still the same old Amy no matter how hard I listen
to what she feels." Midway through a son's hospitalization, a
father remarks that the son "is just as self-centered as when he
first came in here." As a battered wife's hospitalized husband approaches his discharge date, she asks worriedly if he has really
improved. Her relations with him during treatment suggest he
has not yet admitted that his power trips are a weakness. A stepfather, whose adopted son has had extensive experience in treatment facilities like Fairview, speaks frankly in a parent effectiveness class about the virtual impossibility of having a civilized
conversation with the son. After a month of treatment, an adolescent patient complains, "After all this time, my parents still don't
listen and don't give a damn about me."
    Such failures inform the staff and others that the passion and
volatility of the emotions may be beyond rational intervention.

There is a tipping point at which domestic emotions overwhelm rules of reason. Up to that point, rational intervention is possible; goodwill, interpersonal circumspection, and controlled communication will serve to take account of others' feelings and points of view. Beyond the point are persons so "wrapped up" in themselves, so entrenched in their bad habits, that they leave reason behind and "flood out" emotionally in times of crisis. No amount of sitting down, sitting back, I-messaging, or active listening secures communication.

According to staff, at that point, "Toughlove kicks in." The toughlove story, presented by Phyllis and David York and Ted Wachtel (1983) in their book by the same title, reflects the felt failure and despair of getting to the point at which, no matter how rational one is and how hard one tries, it seems nothing further can be done. According to the toughlove philosophy, when reason fails, the troubled must be left to deal with the so-called natural consequences of their acts. The teenager who refuses to adhere to curfew is left to face the legal and community consequences of being out on the streets all hours of the night. The daughter who repeatedly skips school despite all her parents' counseling and communication about how the truancy makes them feel is left to deal on her own with academic failure.

Toughlove is not a return to the autocratic family. According to staff, the idea is that one becomes tough with love, shaking troublesome or troubled family members out of a problem by freeing them to face the harsh rules of life on their own. Dave Shindell comments in a toughlove session:

Toughlove means we are given the responsibility of following through with the ultimate consequences. Toughlove is when all else fails in terms of intervention, when you've said all you can, and you've listened till you're blue in the face. Usually, that ultimate consequence means that the state becomes involved in one way or another—the police, the probation officer, community control, jail, you name it. You [family members] don't become the tough guy; the state does. You're not the heavy like my father was; that's community control's job.

When a disgruntled father remarks that his son needs the back of his hand more than the son needs listening to, Shindell highlights the difference between autocracy and toughlove:

> Don't give up and haul off and hit the kid when you're get-
> ting nowhere. That's what's called child abuse nowadays—
> what my father in the old days used to call straightening
> you out. Toughlove's all about natural consequences, not
> abuse. If that kid wants to be free, toughlove kicks in and
> says he can be free as a bird . . . and see where that gets him.
> There're democratic rules out there too, but, out there, that
> kid learns he's really on his own. He's going to find out real
> quick when he wakes up and realizes that there're laws to
> protect others from him.

Toughlove materials are most visible on the ASU, where parents and adolescents participate separately in formal toughlove
sessions, although the sessions may hardly be distinguishable
from other meetings centered on the sharing of common domestic concerns and their related sentiments. Toughlove on the ADU
translates into the ultimate need to be hard-nosed with the addict,
to be tough enough to break the cycle of codependence and face
the reality that everyone's feelings are important, not just those
of the family drunk or drug abuser.

Just as staff members adapt educational materials and rules to
particular therapeutic circumstances, they tell family members to
read *Toughlove* selectively, according to their individual needs.
Staff members likewise are guided by the pick-and-choose clause.
Adapting toughlove to a presentation in early treatment, ADU
nurse Bev Simpson informs family members:

> Sometime down the line, hopefully, you start to figure out
> that your feelings matter, too, that you can't continue to
> emotionally support his bad habits, that you've got a life
> of your own . . . and, damn it, if he really loves you, he
> should understand that. When you start realizing that . . .
> and I know it's tough, because I've been there . . . that's
> when you're on your way to recovery, that's toughlove.

PART FOUR

The Social Construction
of Domestic Order

Voice and Method

At first blush, one might think that giving voice to experience is a matter of candidly articulating the personal flow of life events. This would seem to apply to the troubled as well as the trouble-free. A young mother who feels betrayed by her alcoholic husband expresses her anguish by stating precisely what goes through her mind when the husband comes home with liquor on his breath. In exacting statements, she points to the domestic disorder that causes her distress. An adolescent girl cries frankly that her mother and father do not understand her and that is the reason she runs away from home and "gets stoned." She passionately laments the reality of her parental problems. A husband speaks openly of the unreliability that causes him to disappoint his children and the fear that his marriage will fall apart because he uses crack, reluctantly disclosing that he himself may be the problem at home, not the family members he often blames. In each case, something experienced is authentically conveyed. One might presume that the troubled who learn to be true to their thoughts, feelings, or relationships are on their way to recovery, or at least that they now have a basis for dealing realistically with themselves and the lives surrounding them.

But is what we know of experience so straightforward? Does honest telling lead to knowing? And does knowing provide a basis for action? The interpretation of troubles and disorder at Westside

House and Fairview Hospital shows that there is more to the voicing of experience than personal authenticity. Truth itself is divided up, so to speak. The truths of family troubles and their related personal experiences as told in one setting contrast with their counterparts in the other setting. The adolescent girl, for one, is heard at Fairview to be telling about a communicative dysfunction and the inability to express emotions. She, her parents, and significant others are encouraged to disclose their feelings in a calm and rational fashion. The girl's counterpart at Westside is heard as self-indulgently infringing on her parents' authority, as lacking sufficient domestic control to get her life in order. Westside staff discourage her from dwelling on her feelings, urging the girl instead to "realistically" attend to the welfare of the family as a whole. They treat her as a minor component in the process of reshaping the social disorder of the home. In either facility, the girl's thoughts, feelings, and conduct take on meaning in the context of their reception and interpretation. What she honestly conveys in one is something else in the other. Context mediates the understanding of what speakers and listeners say and hear about her.

Following the first theme of this book, I have argued that family troubles take on their meaning in relation to interpretations of domestic disorder. This has been illustrated in the family discourse of two treatment settings, whose contrasting images of order and disorder cast personal authenticity in the images' own terms. Following the second theme, I have shown how ordinary and, at the same time, how mundanely theoretical is the process of interpretation. The highly abstract entity that makes such a difference in defining the surrounding truths of troubles—domestic disorder —is circumscribed and constructed in rudimentary and concrete ways, through and by everyday signs such as seating arrangement, posture, and voice modulation.

RATIONALIZATION

These themes reveal microscopic features of a larger design: the rationalization of experience. Broadly speaking, rationalization is the process of adding category and system to the flow of life. Consider two contrasting views.

William James (1890) describes raw experience as a stream of consciousness, his way of conveying that which could not be voiced. Naturalistic as it was, the unremitting stream captured a sense of incomplete, unnamed (untamed) occurrences, now seemingly coming into focus and now fading in a chronology of unknown meter. The stream implied a lack of sort throughout. Helmut Wagner (1970, p. 14) notes that the view applies to the experience of inner time, which, from the beginning to the end of life and in contrast to the outer time measured by clocks, "is as remote from the precision of a syllogistic proposition as is Bergson's duree from the ticking of a metronome." The term *stream* captured the undesignated sense of being enduringly open to living, to time passing, alone or together with others.

In this view, the fundamental task of everyday life is to give order to experience, assigning meaning to life by naming, sorting, and categorizing it. It is the activity of constructing meaning, from life's trivial moments to its dramatic occasions. There is nothing particularly new about the process, being as old, one would think, as humankind itself. Neither James nor the phenomenologists following him, including Henri Bergson, Edmund Husserl, and Alfred Schutz, considered the process historical. Presumably, ancient humans named, sorted, and categorized experience just as medieval humans did and modern humans do. The particular categories may have been different, but they were nonetheless categorical, ways of assigning meaning to the flow of experience. Even the anticategorical mystical experience is nonetheless communicated in relation to what it is not, that is, as being without name, sort, or category.

We might say that the naming, sorting, and categorizing of experience is as old as language. As we speak or refer, the very moment we meaningfully attend to life, silently or audibly, we structure the stream of living. Without language, experience is unarticulated: unnamed and, most important, unknown. This was the communicative problem Chuck, his mother, and others faced in chapter 7. I interpreted their exchange, extracted from a group meeting, to show the communicative impasse of attempting to get to and convey pure experience. Those who urged Chuck on targeted basic feelings, what Chuck *really* felt about his mother, not what he had said so many times in different ways. The aim was to get beyond plain words to the depths of experience. As plain words, every description Chuck mustered was considered inauthentic, not true to his deepest self. Even direct testaments of love were unacceptable. Feelings had to be presented, not just words, in dealing with domestic disorder. According to Chuck's mother, Chuck finally did succeed in conveying what he felt, even though he had not said anything especially new. Weeping and shaken, he finally managed to "tell" his mother, signaling without words what plain words could not. Chuck's mother said as much at the end of the exchange.

On a small scale, Chuck faced an old philosophical problem, the problem of conveying experience, particularly the question of whether plain words, heartfelt though they may be, are adequate to the task when what is considered to be experience's most authentic form is anything but categorical. Although Chuck used no music, poetry, or other common cultural forms for conveying what is felt, he evidently showed enough (see Gubrium, 1988b). What is relatively new about what happens to Chuck and others at Fairview and still others at Westside is that they are urged to give voice to experience in formally designated categories: the express language of feelings in one setting and the explicit language of authority in the other.

This brings us to formal rationality, the second of the two views. This kind of rationality is new in that the languages for assigning meaning to experience are guidelines bound to workings of particular organizations. At Fairview, experience is concertedly made orderly and reliable by way of a language that Westside eschews; at Westside, experience has regularities and a logic that Fairview treats as a mere surface vocabulary or throwbacks to an earlier time. Regardless of the particulars, the meaning of experience, notably domestic experience, is organizationally embedded.

Max Weber was most annoyed by this newness, referring to it as the "universal rationalization" of experience (see Gerth & Mills, 1946). To Weber, it was the key feature of modernization, in which all aspects of life come under the scrutiny and domination of secular categories, contained in a logic of cause and effect, and conveyed under formal or official auspices. Placing rationalization in historical context, Weber considered its eventual consequences for living. Note his pessimism in the following comments quoted by Reinhard Bendix (1960, p. 464) from J. P. Mayer's (1943) book *Max Weber and German Politics.* They apply to formal organization as much as to politics.

> It is horrible to think that the world could one day be filled with nothing but those little cogs, little men clinging to little jobs. . . . This passion for bureaucracy . . . is enough to drive one to despair. It is as if in politics . . . we were deliberately to become men who need "order" and nothing but order, who become nervous and cowardly if for one moment this order wavers, and helpless if they are torn away from their total incorporation in it. . . . the great question is . . . what can we oppose to this machinery in order to keep a portion of mankind free from this parcelling-out of the soul, from this supreme master of the bureaucratic way of life.

In the great transformations of life that took place from the eighteenth to the twentieth centuries, Weber saw the meaning of self and other experiential domains such as family and community, even destiny, increasingly lodged in the meaning-assigning structures of formal organization. According to Weber, the voicing of experience has progressively become the mandate of officials, whose express function is to name, sort, and categorize lives according to administered definition. The question of who voices experience and how has become a matter of "office," contained in an industry of rationalized interpretation. Looking to the future, Weber worried that life, thus defined and known, would be completely devoid of enchantment. As Bendix points out, "Weber was preoccupied with the problem of individual autonomy in a world that was increasingly subjected to the inexorable machinery of bureaucratic administration" (p. 464).

Currently, at the end of the twentieth century, with the great diversity of formal organizations serving to define everyday living—from schools and courts to counseling centers and mental hospitals—is the so-called universal rationalization so dominant and fixed in its life-defining regularities as to totally set the voicing of experience? Is the young mother who feels betrayed by her alcoholic husband automatically defined as a particular kind of human being? Are the poorly understood adolescent girl and the guilty, drugging husband likewise affected? Is each caught in an iron cage of formal rationalization for problems of living?

Although localized understandings of domestic order at Westside and Fairview provide relatively uniform ways of formally adding category and system to the texture and flow of home life, the process is far from automatic. Whatever sense of disorder specifies troubles such as the young mother's, the sense is socially constructed by and through the practical naming, sorting, and categorizing of familial experiences. This ordinary, localized activity constitutes the particular form of her troubled life. Organizationally embedded, rationalization is not of one piece, but as diversely constitutive of troubles and domestic order as rationality's local images. At the level of everyday practice, rationalization is what it always has been, according significantly with the first, or phenomenological, view. If there is to be moral concern over the condition of contemporary life, notably family living, it might more convincingly focus on the local and mundane details of rationalization rather than disparage an ostensibly total design, even though rationality is widely organized.

Weber's concern was understandably pessimistic, given his sense that the historical drift of rationalization flowed forward increasingly rapidly. His was a nostalgia for the past (Turner, 1990). Yet, as I have attempted to show by comparing the social construction of domestic disorder at Westside and Fairview, presenting a process of rationalization that is as diverse and aleatoric as it is fixed by organizational domains, the moral picture is more complicated. Yes, family troubles presented to the agents of an organization become rationalized according to local design, but the process also is guided by interpretive rules—standing rules, made rules, and contingent rules. What is more, the rules have recognizable exceptions. Yes, Westside and Fairview systematically capture and designate family troubles according to separate institutional images of the reality at hand, but the comparison also implies that there are alternate, if not additional, means of rationalizing troubles and disorder. To comparatively document the mundane character and organizational embeddedness of rationalization is to display the morally diverse domain of social construction. The family discourse we encountered at Westside and Fairview indicates that rationalization has several guises. What is mundanely done in one setting can be undone and mundanely redone in another, offering the basis for a more flexible view.

Although we can hardly rid the world of formal organizations, agents, and their collective representatives, we might learn to see and particularly to show that what characterizes their activities, in practice, is made of the same interpretive cloth as characterizes every person's related activity, involving the naming, sorting, and categorizing of experience. Except for the administrative surrounds, the process is as old as history. Indeed, we might continue to compare settings, as I have initiated here, in order to stress formal diversity, which, curiously, Chuck's 7 years of therapy reveals.

THERAPEUTIZATION

Still, as variably rational, if not homogeneously total, as these organizations are, there is something magical about their experiential languages: the enchantments of treatment and cure. Except for a few veteran clients, some of whom, like Chuck's mother, we met earlier, patients, clients, family members, and significant others hear troubles described in enticingly new ways. The young mother who feels betrayed by her alcoholic husband is informed that the feelings are part of a configuration of domestic bonds characterized by emotional dependency, a kind of sickness. Like others in the configuration, she is *codependent.* The adolescent girl who claims to be misunderstood by her parents is said to be *overelevated* in the family system. Contrary to what the girl believes, she discovers that her parents need to be firmer with her, not more sympathetic to her emotions. The husband who feels guilty is counseled to *self-disclose* as a way of communicating with feeling words what he usually keeps under wraps. Unfamiliar terms are spoken by healing professionals—therapists, counselors, psychologists, psychiatrists, nurses, and consultants, among others—whose business it is to specify and treat the disorder of troubled lives. The professionals have their background differences, but they collectively confer the language of specialists. Theirs is not the ordinary communication of the home.

There are parts of these languages that clients and family members do recognize. Fairview organizes family members' domestic troubles in terms of a democratic theory of feelings, but borrows from the toughlove philosophy, with which many parents are acquainted. The twelve-step approach that the hospital integrates into its programs is familiar to the alcoholics, drug abusers, other addicts, and family members treated.

The unfamiliar and the familiar combine to provide Westside and Fairview professionals considerable authority in the interpretation and construction of domestic disorder. This is not one-sided in the sense that staff members in these organizations command all the resources for influencing those served. Of course, there are the linkages with community control agents used by Westside counselors to keep clients in attendance and, at Fairview, privileges on its adolescent services unit that may be withdrawn for misbehavior. But a more basic kind of bearing cuts across the variations in control, a bearing that is built into the prevailing discursive framework circumscribing the naming, sorting, and categorizing of family troubles in both settings. The unfamiliar not only is an encounter with the vocabulary of the family system or the democratic model of sentiments, as the case might be, but is an interpersonal engagement with the world of sickness, healing, and its treatment apparatus.

Whether individuals and families bring their troubled lives to Westside and Fairview on their own or are urged or required to do so by others, they encounter the settings and their respective understandings in a framework of pathological need. The young mother who feels betrayed by her alcoholic husband enters Fairview with an unsolved clinical problem, one for which she needs help. She is not sure whose problem it is exactly, but she does know that it frighteningly distresses her. Arriving at Fairview with her husband, the wife not only learns that he is sick, but that the entire domestic setting she hails from is sick. Her home is the scene of unrecognized or improperly expressed emotion, whose ill design figures in each member's troubles, including her own.

The framing tone of the young mother's encounter with Fairview differs from that for an approach to the police or her priest. When, several times, the mother did call the police to keep her husband from beating her during one of his drunken episodes, she sought physical restraint, not cure. The police dealt with a problem of community control and possible legal infraction. They hesitated to repeatedly intervene in her domestic turmoil, however, especially because it was unclear whether the husband actually was beating her. What could they do about the mere possibility? After several contacts, the police suggested that she might perhaps see a "specialist"—advice like that commonly mentioned by other Fairview and Westside family members as part of their preclinical experiences. Indeed, the young woman's priest, to whom she had turned before her husband's admission to Fairview, informed her that there was "just so much" he could do for her, that she needed professional help as much as prayer.

Like so many of her contemporaries, the young mother knew that one could get sick and need help in recovering even from experience, not just bodily lesions. Until she and her husband actually participated in Fairview's recovery program, she had not thought that she, as a mere family member, herself could be sick, nor that her home might be ill in its own right. The mother admitted that she contacted Fairview with apprehension, but it was not a skepticism about the existence of sickness in life, hers in particular, but worry about whether her husband could actually recover. A psychiatrist had noted that this was a normal response. Worry notwithstanding, the mother was ready to receive and learn a particular application of the language of sickness and recovery, for the sake of what she and others had come to know too well, namely, that life was "just not normal." With this attitude and others' encouragement, she engaged what specialists knew expertly, ready to give voice to her experience accordingly. The framing attitude prepared her for the veritable magic that Fairview staff, clients, and family members, similarly oriented, would "incite" each other and the mother to rationally elaborate (Foucault, 1980).

In this regard, we cannot simply speak of the power or influence that organizations, including Fairview and Westside, have over clients and their families. The awesome bearing which the familiar and unfamiliar bring to what the two settings do with domestic experiences is a diffuse control, prepared well ahead of as well as during participation in the settings. The total rationalization of experience that worried Weber not only is a manifold organizational imperative, but is a prevailing social desire, now enchantingly therapeutic. Contrary to Weber's view, there is always magic in the world, some new and some old, some sacred and some scientific.

Of course, there is individual variation in the familiarity and unfamiliarity. Some comes in the form of full-fledged personal skepticism concerning medicalization. My fieldwork showed this to be rare, articulated mainly in reference to particular life-styles. For example, a few men who had been required to seek hospitalization for drug abuse as a condition of employment were said to make a game, if not a mockery, of treatment. One man especially was overheard telling another patient that he had never considered himself to be sick, was not now sick, and never would be. He complained that it was his misfortune to have been caught using crack and been reported to his employer. He emphasized that his work performance had never suffered because he used drugs. The man thought of crack as a libation of choice, just as cocktails or beer suited others. According to him, there was nothing special about what Fairview did for drug users like himself; it was just another money-making scam. In his case, the familiar prepared him for what, upon hospitalization, he presumed to know only too well, except for a sprinkling of esoteric terms that were easily enough learned and expressed. Yet, as the man's equally reasoned lament about the *really* sick indicated, his was a skepticism about his own particular life-style and "choice" of habit, not personal sickness and domestic disorder in general.

There was another way that the familiar fed into the unfamiliar to produce skepticism. Chuck's mother, for one, had had extensive contact with treatment centers for her son's problems. Her occasional bursts of complaint in group indicated that what to many family members was engaging, for her was "the same old tune in new packaging." Her persistent domestic troubles with her son combined with her health problems to keep her seeking cure. Her skepticism was rooted in the fact that everything now seemed too familiar. There appeared to be no new treatment alternative. She had said all she could about herself. What more was there to tell her son? What more could he say to her? She had exhausted the analysis of their feelings. She had talked endlessly about her thoughts and domestic relations. Still, like the skeptical crack user, she was not prepared to doubt the existence of personal or interpersonal sickness in life or the possibility of healing.

Mainly, the familiar underwrote, rather than undermined, the unfamiliar in both settings. By their own admission, most families were deeply troubled, from drug abuse, alcoholism, domestic violence, and incorrigible behavior, among other problems. Family members were, or became, familiar enough with the idea of treatment for such problems to seek help. A considerable number had had some contact with other methods of treatment before their Westside or Fairview experience.

To staff's periodic chagrin in both settings, familiarity occasionally served to upstage efforts to present coherent programs of treatment. Westside consultant Al Borba, for one, was angered by some clients' attraction to the AA philosophy and the clients' infusion of AA language into the counseling process. Fairview therapist Dennis McDonald, for another, was clearly uncomfortable with family members who insisted that "a dose of good old-fashioned punishment" and ruling were called for in some cases. But, by and large, this was particularized, overridden by a shared desire to give and receive professional help.

FROM DOMESTIC PRIVACY TO PUBLIC CONCERN

There is a plethora of personal troubles in contemporary society, with experts and specialists ready to diagnose, cure, or contain the related behaviors, thoughts, and sentiments of both troubled and troublemakers (Emerson & Messinger, 1977). All manner of individual and interpersonal difficulties are subject to therapy, relegating problems of daily living to pathology. Initially, the emotionally disturbed child might be the trouble-making "kid" who persists in stirring up classmates in his elementary school. His referral to a multidisciplinary team of consultants produces a documented candidate for treatment and a recommendation of individual therapy or a referral to a treatment center (Buckholdt & Gubrium, 1979). A young man whose bizarre, uncontrolled actions frighten his neighbors comes into contact with the police. Figuring that the man has not broken the law, the police refer him to mental health professionals whose job it is to sort troublemakers from the pathologically disturbed (Holstein, 1984, 1988). The husband who begins to drink excessively, ignores his family, and becomes abusive to his wife, is perceived by the wife as under a great deal of pressure. The wife, like the young mother discussed earlier, initially hesitates to seek professional help, figuring that in time the drinking and the abuse will subside. She becomes increasingly anguished and, at others' urging, seeks counseling. An aging father with Alzheimer's disease progressively burdens his adult daughter with "36-hour" days of home care. The daughter turns to a support group for comfort (Gubrium, 1986). A broad spectrum of conduct brings into contact the troubled of all ages on the one side and the professionally concerned on the other.

In the process, a third facet typically is added, namely, the family or the home. The emotionally disturbed child's problem is traced to the dynamics of the household, to, say, the abiding tension between the mother and stepfather (see Whittaker, 1978). A young man's delinquency is said to be rooted in the "broken home" in which he grew up, with domestic disorder presumed to have significantly contributed to the man's instability (Emerson, 1969). As Laing and Esterson (1964) vividly describe in tracing schizophrenia to the "hidden" rituals of the household, the interactional minutiae of family life are linked to personal troubles. A mother and father's routine winking behind their daughter's back causes the daughter not to know what is genuine and what is artificial in life. The strain of an overburdened home care giver is related to a lack of support from other family members (Zarit, Orr, & Zarit, 1985).

Personal troubles bring domestic order within the purview of interpretive experts, transforming troubles and the related privacies of the home into public concerns. Although the family is routinely referenced as if it stood alone in society and some, like Skolnick (1983, p. 55), refer to it as "perhaps the most secret institution in American society," the contemporary home overlaps interpretively with the treatment organization.

Some decry the extent of the overlap. Lasch (1977) features the home as sanctuary, set against a hostile background of "experts." According to Lasch, the increasing invasion of the home and family by social or behavioral scholars and professionals is destroying the only remaining "haven in a heartless world." The home is the last bastion of formally unrationalized experience, a place where the gratuitous, the traditional, and the uncalculated provide sufficient reasons for being. Lasch's is a sense of moral outrage, ironically from the political left. What Lasch laments is the loss or passing of a certain design of daily living. His view is similar to Weber's in this regard, although Lasch's focus is more institutionally delimited.

But we live in a world and times in which the prevailing understanding of troubles is metaphorically therapeutic. This is not a unique organizational ideology nor a purely professional rhetoric. Against a background of widespread therapeutization, Westside House and Fairview Hospital do what is socially prevalent. They do what is done because it is widely taken for granted to be the right thing to do—heal domestic turmoil for the sake of the personally troubled.

Although Fairview and Westside have contrasting images of sickness and separate versions of treatment, they publicly scrutinize in order to heal. Some might say that Fairview's is a more authentic probe into experience because it centers therapeutic attention and builds its knowledge on feelings believed by many to be the foundation of experience. Yet, as I have documented in the substantive chapters of this book, the therapeutization of sentiments is as subject to interpretive rules and a particular language of experience as the therapeutization of authority. Both facilities systematically construct domestic disorder, however its essential quality is defined. Their differences diversify a socially prevalent framework, providing contrasting public designs for private orders in need of help.

With the manifold rationalization and therapeutization of disorder, the public family has arrived, even though some remain who look back nostalgically to an ostensible privacy with the goings on and troubles of the home matters supposed to be managed by family members and a limited number of unspecialized outsiders. Whether or not a time ever existed in which the family took traditional form and, indeed, was a secret institution is arguable (see Shorter, 1975; Tufte & Myerhoff, 1970); currently, family troubles are embedded in the philosophies, interests, and practices of many organizations outside the home. Troubles and domestic disorder are the stock-in-trade of professionals and experts, a situation unlikely to change overnight, let alone revert to an idealized past.

MAKING VISIBLE THE VOICING OF DISORDER

In this context, how do we answer the question of how experience is given voice? As our troubled young mother who feels betrayed by her alcoholic husband seeks help, she learns the broader dimensions of the problem. For better or worse, her home and family are implicated. Following a typical linkage of troubles with the home, the mother gives voice to personal experiences along domestic lines. She discovers how to view the organization of the sickness, framed by a locally pertinent image of family functioning. At Fairview, the young mother comes to understand that a configuration of individual feelings is at the heart of her problem, that there is less sense in forcing issues at home or remaining silent for the sake of the family than there is in openly and rationally sharing sentiments. At Westside, her counterpart realizes that her husband's problem and her own related troubles are not individual, but belong to the broader system of authority relations within which their respective lives are contained.

The answer to the question of how experience is given voice is tied to the social organization of voicing. From the variety of therapeutic experiences, it is evident that interpretations of domestic disorder have been diversely institutionalized. As Mary Douglas (1986) suggests in her book *How Institutions Think*, the domestically troubled give voice to the "thoughts" of the institutional domains in which troubles are presented. Because such domains are formally prevalent in contemporary life and their therapeutic languages enchantingly enticing, personal troubles are, accordingly, the pertinent troubles of modern living. Individually or collectively, as the young mother and others suffer and recover, they bemoan and rejoice over shared and organized understandings of what ails and cures them.

At the same time, arguing that the rationalization and therapeutization of domestic disorder is a social construction is a basis for an awareness that domestic sickness, wellness, and cure are inventions, "totalities" of our own making. Anything that is constructed can be deconstructed, that is, interpretively traced back from its end product, through its production, to its constituting circumstances and their agents. As in the substantive chapters of this book, the tracing back makes visible the active participation of all concerned, staff and family members included. All are incited to speak, but they inventively and diversely work at what they expect and hope to find and therapeutically address. In this regard, Westside is not just a treatment setting with a family systems approach, nor is Fairview merely an inpatient facility focused on interpersonal sentiments. They are public possibilities for the privately real. As sites for articulating domestic disorder surrounding troubles, they offer potential strategies for construing troubles. Other facilities provide additional sites, strategies, and possibilities.

The methodological implication of conceiving disorder as an invention of its interpretive settings is that there are concrete grounds for making visible the diverse ways of giving voice to domestic experience. Comparing Westside and Fairview indicates that the young betrayed mother, her alcoholic spouse, the misunderstood adolescent, the crack-abusing husband, and others have at least two existential options for constituting the domestic reality of their troubled lives. As Westside and Fairview develop their programs and alter their respective therapeutic understandings, participants in the programs expand or elaborate the interpretive realities of their experiences accordingly. Other facilities, as different from Westside and Fairview as the two are from each other, further ramify the possibilities. Silverman (1985) has suggested that methodology equally connotes policy, which in this case presents the option of altering the lived meaning of domestic disorder by changing its interpretive venue.

TEN

Language and Domestic Reality

Language is an integral part of the reality of the home. To cast a group of people in a particular place as a home is to convey a configuration of meanings. A home signifies a home base, a place where participants belong, in the sense that they feel personally attached to space and shelter. When street address is distinguished from home, "home" can denote a preferred identity, as in the remark "This is my address, but over there is my home." But, as Westsiders and Fairview staff frequently caution, "Home is not all it's cracked up to be," meaning that the reality of domestic life has its dark side. Although the ordinary language of home signals sanctuary and belonging, some homes are exceptional, not homelike, because "home" typically suggests otherwise. Casting a group of people as "just living together" further determines the household's reality. Although this may tell of location, even legal address, it warns against inferring interpersonal attachment, legal or sentimental; Westsiders and Fairview staff describe blood kin who "just live together," occupants who "come and go," "like strangers."

Language is more than just words or messages; it is practical. It is an integral feature of speakers' and listeners' actions. One who refers to a household as a home publicly conveys an attitude, a tendered disposition to be heard elaborating the depiction in forthcoming remarks about occupants. Having heard that a single mother, children, and the mother's live-in boyfriend make a "family," one expects to be told more about the group's filial responsibilities. Should it be noted that the children's family life is better than might be expected, given the absence of the father, a question might reasonably be raised about how the live-in boyfriend is a parent to the children. Although what is spoken might not actually follow these particular patterns, what is said nonetheless organizes short runs of communicative readiness and response. There is a shared disposal to communicatively embellish what is termed one thing or another until otherwise termed. The kind of father the live-in boyfriend presents is discussed, until, say, it is suggested and agreed that he is an exception to the fatherlike role such persons play in certain families.

REALITY WORK

The language of authority used to depict domestic disorder at Westside not only provides messages about the family life of particular clients, but also its image designates what is witnessed in videotaped presentations of family interaction in counseling sessions. In and about family members' talk and interaction, Westsiders witness the entity they call "the system." The language of basic domestic sentiments at Fairview Hospital features altogether different observations. From the talk and conversation of family members and patients in group, aftercare, parent effectiveness training, and other programs, staff members discern more or less sentimental entities they call the "democratic" or the "autocratic" family.

None of the entities is evident in a strictly perceptual sense. The system does not appear in black and white somewhere in the background or foreground of family members' videotaped interactions. What appears on tape are office settings with chairs and other furniture, and people, mostly family members, clients, a few significant others, and the staff counselor. Sound is mainly talk, some emotional expression, and ordinary background noise. Neither does the democratic or the autocratic family actually appear in the programs in which patients and family members participate at Fairview. Interacting with clients, Fairview staff see and hear individuals speak and express sentiments about their personal troubles and home lives. What is presented to staffers, families, and others in both facilities is, until something is made of it, merely sights and sounds. Even the seemingly obvious distinction between counselor and family member breaks down and blurs when the counselor gets sucked into the system.

Something meaningful has to be done before one can discern the system, the democratic family, the autocratic home, and other entities in the sights and sounds of treatment. As with William James's stream of consciousness, it is necessary to name, sort, and categorize sights and sounds for parts or wholes to appear as distinguishable objects. Before those concerned can proceed with the business of treatment and recovery, the objects of treatment must be constituted. Systems of authority have to be designated in one treatment setting just as sentimental order needs to be witnessed in the other setting.

Although extensive interpretive work affects the constitution of domestic reality, its principle entities are nonetheless taken for granted. At Westside House, if the system is unknown beforehand, it is assumed that clients and family members will, in due course, present domestic disorder during or following counseling sessions. What is not signaled in the precounseling process, such as while family members await the start of a session, takes shape during the session proper. Once the system meaningfully appears, it can be followed, evidenced in the continuous scrutiny of videotaped sights and sounds for the organization of family interaction. Even when the system is cognitively recalcitrant, not readily showing itself for what it is, it is understood that, in time and with some effort, it will appear in full dress. Similarly, at Fairview, it is assumed that if the basic sentimental order of the family is not immediately obvious, it will present in due course. It takes the savvy of a well-trained staff and cooperative clients to work up and point out the basic problem underlying family troubles.

What is done to constitute and reveal family disorder can be thought of as reality work. The idea is that domestic reality does not so much exist as a separate and distinct entity in its own right, independent of the sights and sounds of treatment, as it is produced in the very process of its designation. In this regard, Westsiders, Fairview staff, those treated, and their associates are

as much a tacit reality-producing enterprise as they are participants in formal treatment. At Westside, the tacit business is to constitute the system in order to get on with the primary therapeutic
function, namely, outpatient family counseling. At Fairview Hospital, the tacit business is to constitute the family's sentimental
order so as to officially engage in inpatient, family-oriented psychiatric treatment.

RULE USE

We can think of reality work and its tacit assumptions as a set of
constitutive rules about how concretely to use language: The life
world is a set of ways of putting language to work to give shape
and flow to experience (see Cicourel, 1970). In application to family
troubles, the rules reveal the related disorder of the household.
Domestic disorder is as much a product of cognitive attitude and
practical actions as it is a separate feature of the troubled home.

The first and most basic rule for witnessing domestic reality is
to presume the reality to be a feature of the home, not a product
of its constitutive work. It is taken for granted, in principle, that
the domestic disorder of the home exists within the household,
not within therapeutic philosophies or other frameworks for naming, interpreting, and treating troubles, nor in the naming, sorting, and categorizing process as such.

Westside staffers acknowledge that theirs is an official systems
approach to the family, underscoring the significance of authority
for effective functioning, but nonetheless assume that the approach
—any approach—is categorically distinct from what it represents.
Orienting to the facts and happenings of home life in a particular
way is not to create those facts and happenings, only to consider
or represent them. Even though new staff members sometimes
question the singularity of the approach and experienced staff
members occasionally disagree over how much to emphasize hierarchy in decision making, such questions and concerns refer to
matters of approach and emphasis, not the independent reality of
troubles and domestic disorder. Likewise, Fairview staff members are variously committed to treatment approaches such as the

twelve steps and toughlove, but they nonetheless take these and other approaches as applications to the domestic troubles that family members bring with them to the hospital for treatment, not as constituting the troubles. The rule applies equally to patients, clients, family members, and significant others.

The second rule for witnessing domestic reality as a feature of the home is to take account of context in concretely designating the home's separate and distinct order. Although it may be assumed across the board that family troubles are features of the home, not, for example, the therapeutic setting, the assumption does not by itself inform those concerned about the specific character of troubles and home life. Questions about the source, results, and consequences of, say, excessive drinking are not answered by simply keeping the reality of troubles in domestic focus. What is it about the home that effects its troubles? Why has family living come to be what it is? What are a family's prospects for the future, especially for recovery? Such concerns demand a substantive context, a basis for offering concrete answers beyond the understanding that family troubles are features of home life.

In contemporary life, it seems that the home itself provides little basis for answering such questions. Parents bring what to them are the clearly troubled lives of their children to Westside because they cannot make sense of the troubles on their own. As a distressed mother remarks, "I can't figure for the life of me what we're doing to have produced such awful kids." The mother's distress is real enough to her. She knows the facts and happenings of her home better than anyone—she claims to know them better than her husband—but she fails to discern overall meaning in her problem. She needs a context for interpreting what she knows too well, and turns to Westside. A depressed young woman who drinks excessively and soon realizes that she also loves too much, discovers at Fairview a basis for sorting through the morbid facts of her life. She has entertained a variety of self-treatment strategies but found them lacking. Although the strategies did provide a way of assigning meaning to her problems, in time she discovers that she needs professional help.

This is not to say that the home cannot be its own context or rule for substantive understanding. Conservative sentiment suggests that the home always has been and should continue to be so. But, because domestic troubles are prevalently thought of in terms of sickness, treatment, and recovery, family members voluntarily or involuntarily turn to treatment settings for answers, how to deal with troubles, and what to expect as a result. A therapeutic society virtually assures that.

In or out of the home, the rule of context offers a basis for action. Not only is meaning substantively assigned to domestic troubles, but knowing the meaning of the facts and happenings of home life provides grounds for doing something about the troubles. At Fairview, the young woman who drinks excessively and loves too much not only is provided a context for understanding what ails her, but also a mode of repair. She discovers that the basic reality of home life is substantively grounded in inappropriately expressed sentiment and that her way out is to establish a proper channel of expression. She learns how to self-disclose and communicate her feelings. At Westside House, her counterpart does not so much love too much as she discovers a sense of personal self-indulgence and inattention to overall family functioning. She confronts the need to get her sentiments under control for the sake of her husband and especially the children who turn to their parents for direction.

The third rule for witnessing domestic reality links contexts with the particulars of households and the individual lives of occupants. The rule actually is a configuration of practical linking rules, as the substantive chapters of this book have shown. At Westside House, the third rule comprises specific rules, such as the rule for observing domestic order in the seating or posture of family members. At Fairview, the third rule specifies the discovery of domestic sentiments in, for example, voice modulation. As with all rules, exceptions preserve the fundamental rule-like quality of principles.

The third rule is put into effect by means of what Garfinkel (1967) calls "practical reasoning." As practitioners of the reality of domestic life, staff, family members, consultants, and significant others set about naming, sorting, and categorizing troubles, prevalent images, and available terms of reference. In the process, additional, "ad hoc" rules are applied, further refining the circumstantial links between what is considered to be general and particular in matters under consideration. For example, the rule that concretely presents domestic disorder in seating arrangement is circumstantially specified as applicable only when family members have freely chosen where to sit or when there is enough seating available to permit a reasonable pattern of authority to appear. Practical reasoning puts forth the rule that it would not make much sense to trace domestic disorder in a seating arrangement determined by outsiders or in a room containing very few chairs most of which are occupied.

It is important to note that although I refer to rules and others speak of "rules of the game," the everyday level of awareness of such rules is gamelike only in the sense that the realities of everyday life are diversely "played out" in different domains (see Wittgenstein, 1953). The games of life in which various rules apply are not fully specified in rule books, nor are they wide-awake rhetorics or strategic encounters, although, in practice, they may appear to have that character (see Goffman, 1961, 1969; Gubrium, in press). Rather, the games are ordinary strategies for speaking and designating the objects and events of daily living, as the language of the system and the discourse of emotional democracy name, sort, and categorize their respective domestic realities. As Heritage (1984) quotes from Barnes (1982, p. 30), "proper usage is developed step by step, in processes involving successions of on-the-spot judgments. Every instance of use, or of proper use, of a concept must in the final analysis be accounted for separately, by reference to specific, local, contingent determinants." Still, context circumscribes experiential reality and, to that extent, there is a certain determination of meaning, especially as context is designated by formal organization.

This sense of rules contrasts with what Jacques Derrida (1977) and other deconstructionists (see Denzin, 1990) call a "continuous play of difference." Framed in terms of cultural studies and informed by deconstructionist thinking, Norman Denzin argues forcefully for the indeterminacy of meaning. Laying an image of literary deconstruction directly over everyday life, Denzin maintains that there are no determinate codes for assigning meaning to objects and events, or, in our case, troubles. There is only a "continuous play of difference," that is, a whirling constitution of experience drawn from the various perspectives and rhetorical angles of reality. The position underscores variation and diversity, but it ignores the social organization of meaning.

SUCCESSFUL THERAPY AND
REALITY CONSTRUCTION

In Durkheim's (1961) later work, especially his studies of the origins of religious life, he highlights the position that forms of order such as religion and morality are products of life's social conditions. As if to contain and locate the constitution of experience, Durkheim writes in the introduction to his book *The Elementary Forms of the Religious Life:*

> The general conclusion of the book which the reader has before him is that religion is something eminently social. Religious representations are collective representations which express collective realities; the rites are a manner of acting which take rise in the midst of the assembled groups and which are destined to excite, maintain or recreate certain mental states in these groups. (p. 22)

Shortly thereafter, in a discussion of how these collective representations are experienced, Durkheim writes that the "real question is to know how it comes that experience is not sufficient unto itself, but presupposes certain conditions which are exterior and prior to it" (p. 27). The general conclusion and the so-called real question seem to point us to a version of the social construction of reality (see Berger & Luckmann, 1966). As far as religion is concerned, Durkheim inverts the idea that "God constructs man in his own image" to "the gods are invented in accordance with human designs for living."

The position is applicable to domestic reality. As Durkheim might put it, domestic representations are collective representations that express collective realities. So it is that, as an assembled grouping, Westside House or Fairview Hospital ritually invents the form of domestic reality appropriate to its mission as a going concern. The articulated systems of authority witnessed at Westside are collectively representative of Westside's image of the fundamental reality of home life, just as the preferred democratic model of basic familial sentiments witnessed at Fairview is collectively representative of its understanding.

If domestic reality is a locally circumscribed collective representation, discursively concretized as the system in one instance and as the democratic model in the other, then, ultimately, successful therapy in each setting requires the construction of proper objects of therapeutic activity. As Foucault (1978) might describe it, what this means in practice is an institutionalized "incitement" to speak and hear domestic experience in certain terms. A common working language of authority makes it altogether natural for Westside House to incite descriptions of dysfunctional hierarchies and systemic chaos. The prevailing working vocabulary of domestic sentiments at Fairview bespeaks feelings out of control. All take up the discourse of domesticity as it is locally designed and, according to rules of collective representation, construct the disorder in need of treatment.

To be therapeutically successful is to design locally pertinent domestic illnesses as an interpretive condition of healing. This does not mean that illness is arbitrarily created out of nothing; something more concrete and practical is being argued. The social construction of domestic disorder is concrete in that the orientation of all concerned is to real, discernible family troubles, which clients, patients, and family members bring with them to the treatment settings. It is practical in that, in either setting, whatever is said, hypothesized, or asserted about family troubles is mundanely worked at, not conjured up: Successful therapy is as much an accomplishment as it is effective therapeutic application. Westside House not only attempts to restore hierarchy, but also it simultaneously constitutes the family troubles it aims to restore. Fairview not only more or less successfully heals troubled lives, but also it avails itself of the kind of reality therapeutically targeted. Neither the application nor the accomplishment is more real in practice, just different and yet equally necessary to the business at hand.

A POSTMODERN PERSPECTIVE?

For the greater part of our cultural history, reality has been considered a domain principally independent of language. In the vernacular, reality is said to be "out there," meaning that its ultimate existence does not depend on a particular point of view nor, in the final analysis, is reality out there because we are "over here" as it were. A basic problem of knowledge is how we, as human beings, know what this objective reality is. How do we come to find out what is there when, as subjects, we are over here looking onto, or over, the object of interest? In the matter of healing and domestic disorder, the initial question is how do we know the social disorganization of home life, followed by the question of what can be done about it.

The idea that reality is socially constructed, domestic disorder in particular, raises the issue of the status of reality in everyday life. Is reality merely a cognitive problem? The position I have laid out empirically in this book provides only a partially affirmative answer: Yes, domestic disorder is socially constructed, but its reality is a practical, cultural achievement. In the course of everyday life, family members and others encounter what they take to be troubles. They come to think about and speak of parts of their own or others' lives as troublesome. In their own ways, they indicate the source, condition, and consequences of the troubles. They report, agonize over, lament, worry about, grow angry toward, become violent with, cool down from, feel sorry for, more or less rationally address, and attempt to ignore what bothers them. For all practical purposes, theirs are "really" troubled lives. Not only do they describe and express the sentiments of their lives, but also they literally point to trouble's domestic happenings. They not only deeply feel trouble's personal consequences, but also indicate how their lives are affected. Together with those who treat them, all call upon the cultural apparatus at their disposal to make their point. Of course, they use the language of reality. A professional health care worker, annoyed that he is not getting what he believes is a true picture of the home, demands that an adolescent "get real" and "tell it like it is." Disgusted that her alcoholic husband, after two weeks in treatment, does not acknowledge the havoc he causes at home, a wife shouts that the husband still lives in a dream world and cannot face reality. A chronic runaway interrupts her parents in a counseling session, forcefully claiming that they do not know what they are talking about, that what really is going on at home would surprise everyone if they "only knew."

The cultural mechanics of authenticity also is called upon. Some weep about their troubles, which, when the weeping is taken to be genuine, conveys a sincerity that unemotional expression lacks. Some are expected to show clear evidence of what ails them. For example, the system that has become dysfunctional is denoted on videotape and thereby its observable reality taken to be demonstrated. Of course, there are exceptions, such as the rare person who is said never to show emotions but always can be expected to quietly tell the truth, or the person whose wildest fantasies are claimed to be truer than his or her actions. However idiosyncratic, these are exceptions to otherwise commonplace warrants for the real.

The real and its demonstration are part of the lives of both the troubled and those who treat them. Not only do they see, speak, and hear troubled lives in the basic terms of the real, they organize their activity and interactions accordingly. They seek the real and attempt to displace the unreal—unless, of course, the unreal becomes a project in its own right, as occurs in denial or delusion, among other ways of therapeutically cataloging the unreal.

In the last few decades, the idea of the real has been assiduously questioned. Indeed, the fact that the real is foundationally related to a cultural apparatus and referenced as an idea are indications of the significance of the concern. It is thought to be a modern notion that the real is principally beyond language; language represents, but does not construct the real. This gives rise to a "postmodern" view, in which the real stands categorically, if not ideologically (Poster, 1988), juxtaposed to the unreal and the otherwise, being neither more nor less authentic (see Lyotard, 1984). In the postmodern view, the leading question is not what is real, but how reality is sensed as ultimately distinguishable from the unreal or the otherwise. The focus is on communication or the organization of signs.

This brings us to Westside House and Fairview Hospital. Although I have taken the approach that domestic disorder is constructed and have shown details of its social organization, the effort stems from the understanding that the reality of family troubles is a most fundamental notion to all concerned. Domestic reality is a serious and concrete project, one whose lives depend on it, as it were. In taking the relation between language and domestic reality as a project, I place the lives and homes undergoing treatment at Westside and Fairview in the twilight between the modern and postmodern. As a practical activity, in the context of one setting or the other, domestic disorder comes alive, is witnessed, communicated, and subjected to appropriate treatment. A comparison of settings shows how much bearing culture has on the activity—how naming, sorting, and categorization feature the appropriate realities of immediate concern, and how the local organization of it all discursively secures what is desired for treatment. There is much that is downright philosophical about the activity, but also much that is not, mundanely resting on the practical relation between language and reality. If domestic reality is to be considered a project, it is one undertaken in concrete time and space, within the ordinary borders of what is locally practiced, as all concerned take account of lives out of control.

Doing the Fieldwork

The fieldwork on which this book is based had two sources. One was a growing interest in family and domestic order as they interpretively related to other organizations. The interest suggested that I gain access to a setting that targeted the family as a focal concern. A history of research in treatment and care facilities directed me toward the likes of Westside House and Fairview Hospital. The second source was my doctoral student Maude Rittman's suggestion that she might be able to secure entry to a treatment facility that would provide material for a dissertation on the social construction of illness. Rittman was a psychiatric nurse by training, combined that with graduate work in sociology, and had professional connections with a number of facilities we both considered appropriate sites for the kind of study we had in mind. We struck a deal that directly launched the project. If she succeeded in securing permission to do fieldwork in a treatment facility, I would train her in participant observation.

GETTING STARTED

Securing permission to do research in formal organizations, especially treatment settings, is rather complicated, going well beyond establishing rapport with gatekeepers and participants.

Proposals must be written, in a language accessible to laypersons and professionals of diverse persuasion, appropriate to the immediate circumstances of a particular setting. Legal papers for obtaining informed consent must be drawn up, approved, and signed. Seemingly endless meetings with administrators, working professionals, clients, and families are required to explain the purpose and method of the study. And, needless to say, various organizational committees and interest groups bring their own schedules, preferences, and requirements into play.

After what seemed like months of preparation, Westside House agreed to participate in the study. Rittman reminded me that Westsiders had been most enthusiastic about the proposed research and now, as we both initially had guessed they might, they came through. We immediately set about the traditional start-up tasks of participant observation: acquainting ourselves with the daily rhythms of the setting; spending time with each staff member in order to get a sense of his or her work routine; finding our bearings in and around records, treatment schedules, and organizational apparatus; and figuring how we would fit into it all.

To our surprise, in short order, Fairview also welcomed us to its facility. We had assessed the initial response from the hospital as rather cool and had guessed that we would never gain access. Having started the process of securing permission, however, we had perfunctorily but competently gone through all the steps required. We now found ourselves with two field sites to manage. This was going to be a new experience. I had conducted several field studies of treatment facilities, but never simultaneous comparative research. My comparisons had been limited to ethnographic materials collected in different projects. Here was an opportunity to build a comparative component directly into the fieldwork, to expressly do comparative ethnography.

DEFINING THE PROJECT

As we proceeded to figure out how two field sites would be integrated into a project focused on the social construction of domestic disorder, we simultaneously spent considerable time at the two facilities getting our bearings. Increasingly, we began to have a sense of "how the institutions think," as Douglas (1986) puts it. Following Fairview's surprise welcome, we initially had decided it would be just another field site for observing the social construction process. But as we moved along in both facilities, it became apparent that, although both treated families in the process of curing persons, they contrasted in what they understood to be the basic reality of home life.

This was not completely a matter of discovery. I had been arguing for a number of years and set out in a book entitled *Analyzing Field Reality* (Gubrium, 1988a) that interpretation in everyday life is not just an "artful" process, to use Garfinkel's (1967) colorful term. Interpretation was circumscribed by conditions of understanding. If patients, clients, staff members, consultants, and others work at constituting domestic disorder in the process of treating what they believe to be the source of family troubles, the effort is organizationally embedded. Although organizational embeddedness, of course, administratively conditions the process of interpretation, more important for the connotation of "domestic disorder" are contrasting organizational images that mediate interpretation.

Taking advantage of good fortune, we defined our research as a comparative study of the social construction of domestic disorder. It was to be a kind of field experiment, with similar family troubles observed as presented in different interpretive contexts to produce contrasting senses of the personal and interpersonal facts of troubled domestic lives.

MANAGING THE OBSERVATION

We managed the observation as an apprenticeship. Rittman had had course work with me and was familiar with the theoretical framework we were bringing to the data, but she lacked skill in concretely connecting the framework with the empirical world. As far as possible, it was important, at first, that we be present together in the particular site being observed. This would provide the opportunity to talk theory, as it were, about matters both of us were observing. It offered a concrete basis for suggesting that particular courses of interaction and forms of talk represented some feature of the constitution of disorder. In turn, it made it possible to cross-check, in our separate observations of the same events, the way field occurrences spoke to our developing ideas and sense of the whole.

Although to some extent the observations were "grounded" in the manner of Glaser and Strauss (1967), the observation was always more concertedly theoretical and focused on discourse. Our view of what we were observing was not as naturalistic. Our aim was not as much to reconstruct the social world of participants in the facilities as it was to make visible how participants constituted the natural domestic worlds they beheld or were troubled by.

We eventually divided the labor. This proved to be especially helpful because the therapeutic schedules both within and between the two facilities frequently coincided. For example, Wednesday evening was a period of extensive family programming at Fairview, with different family and patient groups meeting at the same time in the units observed. We rotated weekly between the meetings. At Westside House, we did not have the opportunity to actually participate in counseling sessions, but we were permitted to watch live soup and review as many videotaped counseling sessions as we wished. We were free to participate in group soup. Both of us spent considerable time talking with the individual counselors and informally interacting with them during breaks in their work schedules. At Fairview Hospital, we participated in all group activities involving treatment on the ADU and ASU, from aftercare to parent effectiveness training and toughlove. We did not observe individual counseling sessions with patients. As Rittman developed her own research interests, she concentrated on select programming. My own research activities proceeded likewise.

The greatest share of the data are in the form of field notes taken during or after observation. Most group sessions in both facilities permitted some writing of field notes during proceedings. Staff members themselves often would take notes and, in that respect, our own note taking did not stand out. Staff and family members expressed concern on a few occasions, but it dissipated when we showed them that our notes were simply handwritten transcriptions. Mainly, we sat at the edge of proceedings, managing to be part of the background of ongoing talk and interaction. To the extent possible, it was our policy to record what was actually said in the settings, to and by whom, in the form of a script. When talk focused on the fine details of a point, we recorded "elaborates." Our aim was not to attempt to take down a tapelike facsimile of the proceedings, which would have been unrealistic for note taking, but to capture the substantive thrust of talk and interaction, focusing on the social construction process. Videotapings, of course, eased the note-taking task considerably, making possible later review of what was said. Some field notes were reconstructions of casual conversations with individual patients, staff, and family members.

Other data were documentary. Select case materials were made available to us in both facilities, on the assumption that they were to be treated as privileged and confidential. We also had access to a variety of educational materials, including videotapes, handbooks, and guides for patients and families.

In presenting scripts of talk, interaction, and documentary materials in this book, I have fictionalized the names of all persons and places. In several instances, in order to further secure anonymity, the gender of those observed has been changed or different pseudonyms used for the same person. In general, places have not been identified by name.

DEALING WITH OURSELVES

Research participation in everyday life is, at best, far from purely objective observation. Of course, one attempts to record talk and interaction in field notes as neutrally as possible, faithfully setting down what is said and done, in which manner, and in what context. But the participant observer also brings his or her own personal attitudes and sentiments to the task. Although these do not necessarily intrude into research materials, they are matters to contend with in dealing with oneself in the field.

The central personal hazard of fieldwork might be called the mirror effect, or seeing one's own experience in others. (See Jeffrey Sluka's [1989] field study of the Irish Republican Army for a riveting account of another kind of personal hazard.) I experienced the mirror effect many times in the course of 20 years of participant observation in care and treatment settings. I may have informally named it while doing fieldwork in the seventies in a residential treatment center for emotionally disturbed children (Buckholdt & Gubrium, 1979). I was studying the ways in which institutional conditions enter into the development of case materials. The study was planned as a deep organizational probe into the social processes entailed. In deep probes, one gets very close to those studied, listening to and observing them at work, play, and rest, in anger and in joy.

At the time, my twin daughters were 4 years old. My wife, who had her own career, and I felt that the first few years raising the girls had been difficult. There were time commitments that we grudgingly worked around and work schedules were constantly being juggled. Outsiders told us that we managed beautifully and that the girls were gems. But we were not convinced; we felt the girls were problems.

The mirror effect came in the process of doing participant observation at the center, as I compared my own children, the daily difficulties they presented, and my responses to them, with the disturbed children's familial experiences. Before the study actually got under way, I had been prepared to observe and listen to emotionally disturbed children, framed by an image of behavior one would expect to reveal "disturbance." My observations were in many ways confirmed. Here were admitted con artists, bizarre activities, withdrawn youngsters, wildly excitable kids, loners, and the overdependent, among a range of characters. But here, too, were personal characteristics that any collection of children might have.

The amazing thing was that when I put the characteristics in context, in the concrete circumstances in which they were realized, from the so-called bizarre to the ordinary, they seemed so reasonable. I kept thinking to myself, "Now that's the way Linnie and Erika [my daughters] would respond," or "That's the way they behaved in a similar situation." The originally strange and bizarre became the familiar and explainable. Were my daughters emotionally disturbed? No. Were the center's children really normal? No. The mirror effect—my seeing my daughters in the center's children—occurred when I limited my perceptions to their re-spective characters, ignoring the social constructionist fact that disturbance and normality, among other characteristics, are as much features of circumstance and interpersonal definition as they are traits of individuals. The mirror effect led me to see what similar kinds of individuals my daughters and the center's chil-dren were; the social constructionist fact sobered me in a way this and other treatment organizations could not accept, because they dealt with clients and illnesses, not social constructions.

The mirror effect took hold many times because the concept of the individual in our kind of culture is so basic to the organization of person perception, my own included. At Westside House and Fairview Hospital, I again imagined my daughters or their friends, now all high school students. I saw parents like myself agonize about, worry over, and become angry with their children, who, in turn, could either care deeply about their parents' reactions to their problems or not "give a fuck," as some of the children bluntly put it.

I vividly recall sharing bouts of anger with Rittman about what some of these teenagers were doing to their parents and what the parents, in turn, were doing to sons, daughters, and stepchildren. I put myself in their places and rehearsed their attitudes and feelings, amazing myself at how exasperated or unnerved I could be. I remember listening to teenaged boys and girls talk and whine at length in aftercare about the "awful ways" their parents treated them and feeling that they were being completely self-indulgent, as I occasionally believed my own daughters sometimes were. I heard parents complaining about the gross misconduct of their children and thought how difficult it must be for them (thinking as a parent of course). At Westside and Fairview, I witnessed talk of, and emotional responses to, many behaviors and reactions that shocked me at the time—and, equally shocking, thought that my own life could, but for the grace of God, be the same.

One might suppose that the experienced field-worker gets into the habit of contextualizing differences and thereby can put the mirror effect into social perspective, but the field is never just a re-search setting. It is as engrossing as any set of real-life occasions. It persists in being an encounter with others at both the research and personal levels and enduringly presents its ironies to the observer. Put in social perspective, the mirror effect in this project showed troubled families, with the help of those who treat them, desperately trying to get to the reality of their problems, as local understandings and a therapeutic culture entered into their attempts to construct the very thing they aimed to heal. Yet, social perspective is a very difficult attitude to maintain in the immediate face of dire life events and has a way of being lost—a continuing hazard.

References

Alcoholics Anonymous World Services. (1952). *Twelve steps and twelve traditions.* New York: Alcoholics Anonymous World Services.

Alcoholics Anonymous World Services. (1976). *Alcoholics anonymous: The story of how many thousands of men and women have recovered from alcoholism.* New York: Alcoholics Anonymous World Services. (Originally published 1939)

Barnes, B. (1982). *T. S. Kuhn and social science.* London: Macmillan.

Bendix, R. (1960). *Max Weber: An intellectual portrait.* New York: Doubleday.

Berger, P. L., & Kellner, H. (1970). Marriage and the construction of reality. In H. P. Dreitzel (Ed.), *Recent sociology* (No. 2, pp. 50-72). New York: Macmillan.

Berger, P. L., & Luckmann, T. (1966). *The social construction of reality.* New York: Doubleday.

Bernardes, J. (1987). "Doing things with words": Sociology and "family policy" debates. *Sociological Review, 35,* 679-702.

Buckholdt, D. R., & Gubrium, J. F. (1979). *Caretakers: Treating emotionally disturbed children.* Beverly Hills, CA: Sage.

Burgess, E. W. (1926). The family as a unity of interacting personalities. *The Family, 7,* 3-9.

Cicourel, A. (1970). Basic and normative rules for the negotiation of status and role. In H. P. Dreitzel (Ed.), *Recent Sociology* (No. 2, pp. 4-45). New York: Macmillan.

Denzin, N. K. (1990). Reading cultural texts: Comment on Griswold. *American Journal of Sociology, 95,* 1577-1580.

Derrida, J. (1977). *Of grammatology.* Baltimore, MD: Johns Hopkins University Press.

deShazer, S. (1980). Brief family therapy: A metaphorical task. *Journal of Marital and Family Therapy, 6,* 471-476.

deShazer, S., & Berg, I. K. (1988). Constructing solutions. *Family Therapy Networker, 12,* 42-43.

Dingwall, R., Eekelaar, J., & Murray, T. (1983). *The protection of children: State intervention and family life.* Oxford, UK: Blackwell.

Dinkmeyer, D., & McKay, G. D. (1983). *STEP/Teen*. Circle Pines, MN: American Guidance Service.

Douglas, M. (1986). *How institutions think*. Syracuse, NY: Syracuse University Press.

Durkheim, É. (1951). *Suicide*. New York: Free Press. (Original work published 1897)

Durkheim, É. (1961). *The elementary forms of the religious life*. New York: Free Press. (Original work published 1912)

Durkheim, É. (1964a). *The division of labor in society*. New York: Free Press. (Original work published 1893)

Durkheim, É. (1964b). *The rules of the sociological method*. New York: Free Press. (Original work published 1895)

Emerson, R. M. (1969). *Judging delinquents*. Chicago: Aldine.

Emerson, R. M., & Messinger, S. L. (1977). The micro-politics of trouble. *Social Problems, 25*, 121-135.

Efran, J. S., Lukens, R. J., & Lukens, M. (1988). Constructivism: What's in it for you? *Family Therapy Networker, 12*, 27-35.

Family Therapy Networker. (1988). *12* (5).

Foucault, M. (1978). *The history of sexuality* (Vol. 1). New York: Random House.

Foucault, M. (1980). *Power/knowledge*. (C. Gordon, Ed.). New York: Pantheon.

Garfinkel, H. (1967). *Studies in ethnomethodology*. Englewood Cliffs, NJ: Prentice-Hall.

Gerth, H., & Mills, C. W. (Eds.). (1946). *From Max Weber: Essays in sociology*. New York: Oxford University Press.

Glaser, B. G., & Strauss, A. L. (1967). *The discovery of grounded theory*. Chicago: Aldine.

Goffman, E. (1961). *Encounters: Two studies in the sociology of interaction*. Indianapolis: Bobbs-Merrill.

Goffman, E. (1969). *Strategic interaction*. Philadelphia: University of Pennsylvania Press.

Goffman, E. (1974). *Frame analysis*. New York: Harper & Row.

Gubrium, J. F. (1986). *Oldtimers and Alzheimer's: The descriptive organization of senility*. Greenwich, CT: JAI Press.

Gubrium, J. F. (1987). Organizational embeddedness and family life. In T. Brubaker (Ed.), *Aging, health, and family: Long-term care* (pp. 23-41). Newbury Park, CA: Sage.

Gubrium, J. F. (1988a). *Analyzing field reality*. Newbury Park, CA: Sage.

Gubrium, J. F. (1988b). Incommunicables and poetic documentation in the Alzheimer's disease experience. *Semiotica, 72*, 235-253.

Gubrium, J. F. (in press). For a cautious naturalism. In J. A. Holstein & G. Miller (Eds.), *Perspectives on social problems* (Vol. 4B). Greenwich, CT: JAI Press.

Gubrium, J. F., & Holstein, J. A. (1987). The private image: Experiential location and method in family studies. *Journal of Marriage and the Family, 49*, 773-786.

Gubrium, J. F., & Holstein, J. A. (1990). *What is family?* Mountain View, CA: Mayfield.

Haley, J. (1976). *Problem-solving therapy*. New York: Harper & Row.

Heritage, J. 1984. *Garfinkel and ethnomethodology*. Cambridge, UK: Polity Press.

Hess, R. D., & Handel, G. (1959). *Family worlds*. Chicago: University of Chicago Press.

Hoffman, L. (1988). A constructivist position for family therapy. *Irish Journal of Psychology, 9*.

Holstein, J. A. (1984). The placement of insanity: Assessments of grave disability and involuntary commitment decisions. *Urban Life, 13,* 35-62.

Holstein, J. A. (1988). Studying family usage: Family image and discourse in mental hospitalization decisions. *Journal of Contemporary Ethnography, 17,* 261-284.

James, W. (1890). *Principles of psychology.* New York: Henry Holt.

Jameson, F. (1972). *The prison-house of language.* Princeton, NJ: Princeton University Press.

Kuhn, T. (1962). *The structure of scientific revolutions.* Chicago: University of Chicago Press.

Kurtz, E. (1979). *Not-god: A history of alcoholics anonymous.* Center City, MN: Hazelden.

Laing, R. D., & Esterson, A. (1964). *Sanity, madness and the family.* Baltimore, MD: Penguin.

Lasch, C. (1977). *Haven in a heartless world.* New York: Basic Books.

Levi-Strauss, C. (1962). *The savage mind.* London: Weidenfeld and Nicholson.

Lyotard, J.-F. (1984). *The postmodern condition: A report on knowledge.* Minneapolis: University of Minnesota Press.

Mayer, J. P. (1943). *Max Weber and German politics.* London: Faber and Faber.

Pollner, M. (1987). *Mundane reason.* New York: Cambridge University Press.

Poster, M. (Ed.). (1988). *Jean Baudrillard: Selected writings.* Stanford, CA: Stanford University Press.

Reiss, D. (1981). *The family's construction of reality.* Cambridge, MA: Harvard University Press.

Said, E. W. (1978). *Orientalism.* New York: Random House.

Saussure, F. de. (1966). *Course in general linguistics.* New York: McGraw-Hill.

Shorter, E. (1975). *The making of the modern family.* New York: Basic Books.

Silverman, D. (1970). *The theory of organizations.* New York: Basic Books.

Silverman, D. (1985). *Qualitative methodology and sociology.* Aldershot, UK: Gower.

Silverman, D., & Bloor, M. (1990). Patient-centered medicine: Some sociological observations on its constitution, penetration, and cultural assonance. *Advances in Medical Sociology, 1,* 3-25.

Simmel, G. (1950). *The sociology of Georg Simmel.* New York: Free Press.

Simon, F. B., Stierlin, H., & Wynne, L. C. (1985). *The language of family therapy: A systematic vocabulary and sourcebook.* New York: Family Process Press.

Skolnick, A. S. (1983). *The intimate environment.* Boston: Little, Brown.

Sluka, J. A. (1989). *Hearts and minds, water and fish: Support for the IRA and the INRA in a Northern Irish ghetto.* Greenwich, CT: JAI Press.

Sudnow, D. (Ed.). (1972). *Studies in social interaction.* New York: Free Press.

Torgovnick, M. (1990). *Gone primitive: Savage intellects, modern lives.* Chicago: University of Chicago Press.

Tufte, V., & Myerhoff, B. (Eds.). (1970). *Changing images of the family.* New Haven, CT: Yale University Press.

Turner, B. S. (1990). Periodization and politics in the postmodern. In B. S. Turner (Ed.), *Theories of modernity and postmodernity* (pp. 1-13). Newbury Park, CA: Sage.

Wagner, H. R. (1970). Introduction. In H. R. Wagner (Ed.), *Alfred Schutz: Phenomenology and social relations* (pp. 1-50). Chicago: University of Chicago Press.

Watzlawick, P. (1984). *The invented reality: How do we know what we believe we know?* New York: Norton.

Weakland, J. H., Fisch, R., Watzlawick, P., & Bodin, A. M. (1974). Brief therapy: Focused problem resolution. *Family Process, 13,* 141-68.

Whittaker, J. K. (1978). The changing character of residential child care: An ecological perspective. *Social Service Review, 52*, 21-36.

Wiley, N. F. (1985). Marriage and the construction of reality: Then and now. In G. Handel (Ed.), *The psychosocial interior of the family* (pp. 21-32). New York: Aldine.

Wittgenstein, L. (1953). *Philosophical investigations.* London: Basil Blackwell.

York, P., & York, D. (1983). *Toughlove: A self-help manual for kids.* Doylestown, PA: Toughlove.

York, P., York, D., & Wachtel, T. (1983). *Toughlove.* New York: Bantam Books.

Zarit, S. H., Orr, N. K., & Zarit, J. M. (1985). *The hidden victims of Alzheimer's disease: Families under stress.* New York: New York University Press.

Index

About the Author

Jaber F. Gubrium is Professor in the Department of Sociology at the University of Florida. He has conducted research on the social organization of care in diverse treatment settings, from nursing homes and physical rehabilitation to counseling centers and family therapy. His continuing fieldwork on the organizational embeddedness of social forms serves as a basis for the formulation of an interpretive comparative ethnography. Professor Gubrium is the editor of *Journal of Aging Studies* and author of *Living and Dying at Murray Manor* (1975), *Oldtimers and Alzheimer's* (1986), *Analyzing Field Reality* (1988), and *The Mosaic of Care* (1991). He recently coauthored the book *What is Family?* (1990), which, with a focus on discourse, presents a social constructionist approach to domestic order.